Gender, Crime, & Justice

Gender, Crime, & Justice

Exploring the Dynamics

Andrew Wilczak

LYNNE
RIENNER
PUBLISHERS

BOULDER
LONDON

Published in the United States of America in 2017 by
Lynne Rienner Publishers, Inc.
1800 30th Street, Boulder, Colorado 80301
www.rienner.com

and in the United Kingdom by
Lynne Rienner Publishers, Inc.
3 Henrietta Street, Covent Garden, London WC2E 8LU

Library of Congress Cataloging-in-Publication Data
Names: Wilczak, Andrew, 1980– author.
Title: Gender, crime, and justice : exploring the dynamics / Andrew
Wilczak, PhD, Wilkes University.
Description: Boulder, Colorado : Lynne Rienner Publishers, Inc., [2017] |
  Includes bibliographical references and index.
Identifiers: LCCN 2017005756 | ISBN 9781626376595 (hardcover : alk.
  paper) | ISBN 9781626376601 (pbk. : alk. paper)
Subjects: LCSH: Female offenders. | Criminal justice, Administration of. |
  Feminist criminology.
Classification: LCC HV6046 .W55 2017 | DDC 364.3/7—dc23
LC record available at https://lccn.loc.gov/2017005756

British Cataloguing in Publication Data
A Cataloguing in Publication record for this book
is available from the British Library.

Printed and bound in the United States of America

 The paper used in this publication meets the requirements
of the American National Standard for Permanence of
Paper for Printed Library Materials Z39.48-1992.

5 4 3 2 1

For Charlie

Contents

    What Makes Juvenile Delinquency Unique? 77
    Summer Vacation and the
        Social Consequences of Puberty 80
    Another Brick in the Wall 84
    Transgender Adolescents and Gender Fluidity 86
    The Nightmare of High School 88
    "You're All Growed Up" 95
    Timing of Transitions 99
    Prison as a Life Course Transition 101
    Crime Among the Elderly 103

5   Gangs and Drug Violence   105

    Where Did This Come From? A Brief History of
        Gangs in the United States 106
    Modern Gangs: Violence and Community Service 108
    Girl Gangs 114
    Drug Dealing and Drug Use 119
    Rural Gangs 120
    Gang Membership as a Life Transition 122
    Getting Out of the Game 123

6   Relationship Violence   129

    The Role of Power and Control 132
    Child Abuse and Molestation 136
    Stalking and Cyberstalking 141
    Family Violence 143
    Relationship/Acquaintance Rape 148
    Violence in Same-Sex Relationships 151

7   Sexual Violence   153

    The Realities of Rape 155
    Stranger Rape 158
    Sexual Assault on Campuses 159
    Rape in Government Institutions:
        Prisons and the Military 161
    Violence in Sex Work 165
    Child Pornography 178
    Human Trafficking and the International Sex Trade 180
    Sex Slavery? Not in My Backyard 182

Preface

This book is centered on gender—not on women and femininity, not on men and masculinity, but on gender. I treat gender as a spectrum of behaviors, while also using the familiar framework of male and female that many instructors and students are used to, in a way that helps us to better understand both criminal perpetration and criminal justice in the lives of people who are involved in our system of social control.

Unavoidably, I write from the perspective of a white, cisgender, upper-middle-class man. I am privileged. I understand that what is presented here is not the full picture, and my interpretations may have been inadvertently biased by my own social standing.

It takes a village to raise an author, and I am no exception. At Lynne Rienner Publishers, I would like to thank Andrew Berzanskis for having faith in me at the beginning of this project and Alexander Holzman for helping me to see it through to the end. I am grateful to the anonymous reviewers for their extremely valuable insights. Thank you also to Lynne Rienner and everyone else at Lynne Rienner Publishers for all of the work that went into creating this book.

Thanks go to my colleagues at Wilkes University for their assistance along the way; without you, this project would never have gotten off the ground. I owe a tremendous debt of gratitude to a number of friends, colleagues, and students who helped me through this project in more ways than they realize: Woodly Augustin, Jason L. Blair, Scott Blair, Catherine Conte, Andrew Doran, Adam Griffin, Sean Grundy, Alex Harrington, Tyheed Jackson, Kristy Krivickas, Matt Loveland, Heidi Lyons, Bill Parsons, Carlos Rivera, Torrey Shimp, Pete Smith, Dani Soto, Jennifer Taylor, Grace Valenzano, Santana Velez, Breea Willingham, and Lecinda Yevchak.

I would like to especially thank my parents, Dan and Kathy Wilczak, who now hold in their hands the result of years of patience with and belief in me. I hope that this book will find a place of prominence in their collection.

I owe a towering and infinite amount of thanks and love to my wife, Jenny, who has given me so much support during this project, especially when I doubted myself, and who is surely holding a copy of this book in my face right now and reminding me that she told me that I'd be able to finish it. Jenny, you were right.

1

Studying Crime and Gender: Why Does It Matter?

Does gender matter? In 1816, Ann Carson was considered the most notorious woman in the state of Pennsylvania. By the end of the year, she had endured two sensational criminal trials that dominated the news in New England—and under circumstances we would deem nothing short of miraculous today, she was acquitted both times. In the first trial, Carson stood accused as an accessory to murder in the death of her husband; John Carson had been shot in the face at point-blank range by Richard Smith, a man also claiming to be her husband. John Carson, a sailor and an alcoholic, had left Ann and their children to fend for themselves in Philadelphia while he was employed on a ship. Upon hearing a rumor that he had died in Russia, Ann remarried, setting the stage for this battle between the two would-be husbands. Though Ann Carson was acquitted of the accessory charge, Richard Smith was convicted of murder and sentenced to death. This ultimately led to Ann Carson's second trial for conspiracy, as she immediately hatched a plan to break into the prison where Smith was being held and free him. When that plan proved too risky, she moved on to a new scheme: kidnapping Pennsylvania governor Simon Snyder (or one of his children) and forcing him to pardon Smith. While she was in prison awaiting trial, Richard Smith was hanged, leaving behind an angry letter damning her. Again, despite an overwhelming amount of evidence pointing to her role in this unbelievable plan to kidnap the governor, Ann Carson was found not guilty. The jury acquitted not because it believed her innocent, but rather because acknowledging her guilt would force society to deal with the reality that women like Ann Carson—smart, capable, and brave enough to carry out a crime of this magnitude—existed (Branson 2008). Ann Carson was saved by the bias against her gender.

The story of Ann Carson, while fascinating, may strike some as outdated—obviously, none of us were alive to follow along as the Carson trials played out, and much has changed in our society since then. Perhaps this story does nothing more than remind us of a time long since forgotten. Does gender still matter?

Daniel Holtzclaw had a good life. He was the star linebacker on his high school football team, and then at the collegiate level, he played three seasons at Eastern Michigan University. He won several awards and came close to a career in the National Football League. He was not drafted, however, and his opportunities to express power and dominance—two masculine traits—seemed to have ended with his football career. Using his degree in criminal justice, Holtzclaw got a job as a police officer in Oklahoma City, near his hometown of Enid, Oklahoma. Apparently Holtzclaw's need to express his dominance had found a new outlet, as in the approximately six years since the conclusion of his playing career, he had learned that he could satisfy his craving for violence and control in another arena. Beginning in June 2014, Holtzclaw began using his position of power in the community to terrorize women. Over a period of six months, he targeted black women from Oklahoma City's poorest neighborhoods, becoming a serial rapist whose his victims ranged in age from seventeen to fifty-seven years old. Holtzclaw specifically targeted women with criminal backgrounds, thinking that their status, in addition to their poverty and his trusted position in the community, would immunize him against any retaliation (McLaughlin, Sidner, and Martinez 2016). Who would take the word of a poor black woman with a criminal record over that of a white police officer in good standing?

It turns out that plenty of people would.

In January 2016, a jury convicted Daniel Holtzclaw of eighteen out of a possible thirty-six charges, including four counts of first-degree rape. As the guilty verdicts were announced to the court, the once-mighty titan of the gridiron began crying, rocking back and forth in his seat as his world crumbled down around him. A man who had thought he could use his position of power in the community to prey upon some of its most powerless members, people he was responsible for serving and protecting, was sentenced to 263 years in prison for his crimes. Does gender still matter?

A sentence of 263 years certainly seems incredibly punitive, and perhaps the trial of Daniel Holtzclaw will go down in history as an aberration in our society. Consider the case of Brock Turner, a swimmer at Stanford University. Like Holtzclaw, Turner showed a great deal of talent for his sport of choice and had moved across the country to begin his college career. Whereas Holtzclaw dreamed of playing football professionally, Turner was an Olympic hopeful who aspired to attend medical school (M. Miller 2016). In January 2015, Turner was charged with one count of attempted rape, two counts of felony sexual assault, and two counts of rape after two exchange students found him assaulting a young woman (referred to in the trial and in this text as Emily Doe) behind a dumpster. His trial began in March 2016 and highlighted the role of drinking on college campuses and how alcohol consumption—or overconsumption, in this case—makes determining consent difficult. Some rallied against Turner, setting him up as a symbol of all violent, entitled student-athletes in the United States. Others defended him, suggesting that the prosecution was bowing to outside pressure and that there was no reason to ruin Turner's life over a misunderstanding. The judge apparently agreed with Turner's supporters. After his conviction, Turner received a mere six months in jail, with three years of probation and a mandate to register as a sex offender upon release. Of those six months, Turner served only three. Though Turner's punishment bordered on laughable, the most important aspect of this case was Emily Doe's victim-impact statement, which was released to the public. Beyond calling attention to how her life had been affected since Turner victimized her, Doe also had much to say about the unfair treatment she received during the trial; Turner's well-being was considered at every turn, whereas hers was not. This letter draws attention not only to the many problems victims of sexual violence deal with but also the ways gender can frame the discussion of a crime in both the court of law and the court of public opinion. In part, she says,

> Lastly you said, I want to show people that one night of drinking can ruin a life.
>
> A life, one life, yours, you forgot about mine. Let me rephrase for you, I want to show people that one night of drinking can ruin two lives. You and me. You are the cause, I am the effect. You have dragged me through this hell with you, dipped me back into that night again and again. You knocked down both our towers, I collapsed at the same time you did. If you think I was spared, came out unscathed, that today I ride off into sunset, while you suffer the greatest blow, you are mistaken. Nobody wins. We have all been devastated, we have all been trying to find some meaning in all of this suffering. Your damage was concrete: stripped of titles, degrees, enrollment. My damage was internal, unseen, I carry it with me. You took away my worth, my privacy, my energy, my time, my safety, my intimacy, my confidence, my own voice, until today.
>
> See one thing we have in common is that we were both unable to get up in the morning. I am no stranger to suffering. You made me a victim. In newspapers my name was "unconscious intoxicated woman," ten syllables, and nothing more than that. For a while, I believed that that was all I was. I had to force myself to relearn my real name, my identity. To relearn that this is not all that I am. That I am not just a drunk victim at a frat party found behind a dumpster, while you are the All-American swimmer at a top university, innocent until proven guilty, with so much at stake. I am a human being who has been irreversibly hurt, my life was put on hold for over a year, waiting to figure out if I was worth something. (K. Baker 2016)

Does gender still matter? Emily Doe would say so.

The relationships between gender and crime, and between gender and criminal justice, matter for the plain and simple reason that not everyone comes to crime or experiences the criminal justice system the same way. The longer version of that answer is much more complicated, requiring us to think about why people commit crime, the various factors that influence their behavior, their view of themselves as people, and their outlook on life. We also have to remember that the men and women serving in the justice system are too often treated as a homogenous group—the so-called thin blue line. Throughout this book, we'll examine many of the different ways that men and women experience crime and justice differently, as well as the many different ways that masculinity and femininity both shape and influence how people experience these things.

Furthering our understanding of the nuanced relationship between gender, crime, and justice matters for many reasons. I don't want to just repeat the cliché that we live in an increasingly diverse society, because in fact the United States has always been extremely diverse—we're just now starting to appreciate the wide range of experiences around us. We're diverse not only in the types of people who populate the United States but also in the types of ideas we have about how the world does and should work, what the biggest problems facing our society are, and how best to solve them. While this diversity is appreciated and even encouraged—the United States is supposed to be a melting pot of people, culture, and ideas, after all—we also require a certain degree of conformity from our citizens. We can equate conformity with predictability, and so while we yearn for new and different ideas, everything has to occur within a setting comfortable to everyone. We want our new ideas presented to us in bits and pieces. We don't really like surprises or disruption. That's one of the things that makes people so fascinating to study.

Kai Erikson (1962) suggests that deviant behavior emerges as a natural by-product of a society that demands both diversity and conformity. Simply put, being deviant means you are violating some social norm, or rule to live by. Norms can be written or unwritten, formal or informal. Violating a norm carries with it some kind of sanction or penalty, which can range in severity from the cold shoulder or a side-eye glare to life in prison or capital punishment—and everything in between. Crime is the violation of a norm so revered by society that the state must officially and formally punish the act in some way. In terms of gender, then, we can ask, how might the lenses of femininity and masculinity alter the experience of crime and justice? Are there differences in how we conform? Do we have different perceptions and experiences of conformity? Does the pushback against our deviant behavior—or even the types of deviancy people care about—differ? What about the concept of conformity itself—are there gender differences in terms of the norms society expects people to conform to?

In talking about crime, a number of questions come to mind, the most basic being, Why does it happen? We all know about the possible punishments for breaking the law, but every day people from all walks of life choose to violate the law in some way. Why? Do all men and women do it? Are there things that tend to happen more to one gender or the other?

I want to make one last point before we start talking about the larger themes of this text. In a book centered on any element of social structure (e.g., gender, race/ethnicity, social class), the assumption within the discipline is that the discussion will be entirely about the differences that exist within a particular group. However, there are undoubtedly instances in which any difference that exists is trivial, minor, or maybe even nonexistent. I don't want to slam the door on the idea of experiences that do not substantially vary by gender. Prison, for example, is an awful experience in general. Being a victim is, overall, horrible, regardless of gender. To have an accurate and complete understanding of the role of gender in crime and justice, we need to acknowledge similarities as well as differences.

When it comes to criminal behavior, many tend to label criminals as fundamentally bad, evil, or crazy people who commit crimes because they were just born wrong. In reality, someone who has committed a crime often doesn't differ a whole lot from someone who has not. Many times, it's just an issue of whether he or she was caught, had the opportunity, or was in the wrong place at the wrong time. Our ultimate purpose in studying crime is to find ways to make our society a better place for everyone. By "everyone" I mean that we're also trying to improve the situations of people in prison and people who are out committing crime and haven't been caught yet, because they're also important. Part of doing this well is challenging ourselves to have empathy for the people we're studying and to recognize that many people, if things had gone differently, could have found themselves in prison today.

On the gender side of the coin, some of you might have some stereotypes and misconceptions that I would like to get out in the open right now. This book looks at the relationship between gender—an element of social structure—and crime and justice. It will not look exclusively at the reasons why only women or only men commit crime; it is not going to look at how only women or only men experience the criminal justice system. We're going to look at how gender plays a part in everyone's life.

Now, taking this approach requires that we understand there is a fundamental difference between *sex* and *gender*. Sex is purely biological; gender is a much more fluid concept. Sure, there is a division between masculinity and femininity, but gender is more of a spectrum than an either/or proposition. Everyone has some masculine and feminine traits. But there is no natural or "right" way to be masculine or feminine—to be male or female. Gender is performative. This means that no behaviors associated with gender are inherently biological; for example, many boys are socialized to be involved with sports and be highly competitive, but there is no instinctive biological drive to play football hard-wired into our DNA. However, much of the research on this subject conflates the two terms and thinks about gender as a dichotomy: you are either male or female; all males are the same, and all females are the same. We know today that this isn't true; nor is the two-sex dichotomy true in nature (there are three sexes: male, female, and intersex). It is true that gender is much more complex than sex, is connected to and created by our history and our culture, and is a part of our sociological rather than our biological structure (Daly and Chesney-Lind 1988).

Because so much research in the past has treated gender as a dichotomy, in our discussions throughout this book on the various

ways gender relates to crime and the criminal justice system, we
will sometimes be forced to utilize this false dichotomy. However,
it does pose an interesting question for us to think about throughout
the book: Based on everything that we talk about in the pages to
come, how would thinking about gender as a continuum, ranging
from being completely and totally masculine to being completely
and totally feminine, change our discussion? In other words, how
does being more masculine or more feminine (or somewhere in
between) change how we might think about why people commit
crime and how they experience the criminal justice system?

There is also the issue of the role and experience of women in
both the perpetration of crime and the experience of justice. As
we'll see, much of the research on crime and justice does not
include women—and so this book aims to make the lives and
experiences of women a central part of the conversation, something not done for a long time (Daly and Chesney-Lind 1988).

The History of Crime and Gender

From a criminological standpoint, why should we care about gender? How are gender and crime related? It's incredibly hard to
talk about crime seriously without recognizing the multiple ways
that gender shapes behavior. In reality criminological research
often confuses the terms *sex* and *gender*. Many theories of crime
excluded gender (as well as biological sex) when they were first
developed, and thus we can only speculate about how gender, as a
continuum of behaviors, can influence criminality. Due to the
assumption that so many people conform to strict gender roles
(whether they agree with them or not), researchers have measured
biological sex and called it gender.

One would think that the law should apply equally to everyone in society. It is supposed to be objective—justice is justice
and should not be open to interpretation. Bad behavior is bad
behavior. Historically, however, that hasn't been the case. In fact,
we could say that the opposite is true. Because of an imbalance
in the political realm—politicians being almost entirely men and

women not even having the right to vote until 1920—the idea that the law was applied equally to all persons is rather naive. In reality, the legal system was used not only to dispense justice to actual criminals but also as a tool of oppression designed to maintain a very strict system of gender roles. The legal system operated to maintain a very narrow version of "femininity," often punishing girls and women for acts that boys and men would rarely be arrested for, such as smoking, truancy, or curfew violations. By policing the behavior of girls in this way, the system worked to oppress women by dictating what was and was not acceptable feminine conduct. The "boys will be boys" philosophy remained embedded in both the criminal and civil law.

As time progressed and the criminal justice system became more sophisticated, so did both the ways that we theorized about crime and the lengths to which women and their behavior were excluded from the conversation. As we'll discuss, many of the resulting theories of crime and delinquency completely excluded women. Discrimination isn't always malicious. In this case theorists may have been operating under the assumption that female behavior is exactly the same as male behavior—which is problematic, as I'm sure you can think of all kinds of ways that men and women behave differently—or perhaps they just didn't care about women.

The oppression of women became somewhat more sophisticated over time. Discrimination can work in nefarious ways, finding creative means to keep people in their "place." It can even sometimes come from within. Over the course of modern American history, we've seen multiple attempts to police the behavior of women and girls in political, legal, and cultural ways. A differential application of the law has punished girls more for deviating from expected gender roles and less for actual criminal behavior. That's an unfortunate reality of the justice system that doesn't really get talked about a lot: we think it's set up only to punish people who are breaking the law and will treat everyone equally, but that is not always how it works.

With everything we will discuss throughout this book, try to keep the following question in mind: Was it always like this? The answer is more frustrating than you might think. In many ways, yes, things have always been like this. There has always been an imbalance, and there has always been injustice. That isn't anything new. However, in many other ways, the answer is no, as much has changed in a relatively short time. That's what makes this such a challenging and fascinating topic: in many ways, nothing's any better now than it was a hundred years ago; in others, because of new ideas that have been introduced and accepted in bits and pieces, it's an entirely different world.

Theories of Crime

One of the most basic questions a criminologist can ask is, Why does crime happen? In the first section of this book, we'll explore different theoretical explanations for why crime occurs. The answer to that question is much more sophisticated than simply saying all criminals are evil people. In fact, most criminals are not evil, and their reasons for offending are quite complex. As we examine the different theoretical perspectives on how and why crime happens, we'll also examine gender differences in each of the major theoretical areas. Each theory we'll talk about identifies a specific process argued to be the most significant cause of crime — and in our discussion of that argument, we'll talk about whether that process is as important for girls and women as it is for boys and men. For example, one of the biggest theoretical explanations of crime is social bond theory (Hirschi 1969), which holds that people with a strong bond to pro-social institutions, especially the family, are less likely to become involved in any kind of criminal behavior because doing so would upset the people in that institution. In thinking about gender, we could ask whether these social bonds have the same meaning for women as for men, based on everything we know about differences in how men and women value relationships. If we think about this in terms of adolescents, we could ask whether boys and girls view their parents the same way. We could even ask whether there are differences in how boys and girls do or do not become bonded to their families (or any other social institution). In doing so, we're not trying to discredit this theory of crime or any other; we're looking for ways to improve it and make it more nuanced.

In the discussion of theory, we'll also spend some time talking about the idea of feminism, where it came from, and how it intersects with criminology. For so long, people have just assumed that the experiences and perceptions of men and women completely overlap, and have developed theories that make sweeping generalizations based on this assumption that there really is no difference in male and female behavior, which we know is just not true. Thanks to feminism and feminist criminologists, we've learned so much more about how men and women come to crime and about some types of crime that may be unique to women, which previous generations of social scientists didn't take seriously. We'll talk about the different waves of feminism, starting with the suffrage movement in the late nineteenth and early twentieth centuries. Feminism has evolved over time, transforming from a perspective concerned with the legal equality of women, to one that identifies key differences in the lived experiences of women and men, such as the role of victimization in female behavior (Chesney-Lind 1989) and the role of strict adherence to masculinity in male behavior (Messerschmidt 1993), to one that focuses on problems experienced by both women and men, like prison violence or violence against people who are transgender.

Throughout the discussion of theory, we will think about how any given theory may work differently for men and women. These differences can be major, like those mentioned above, or minor. For instance, minor differences may relate to how said theory works: Do women and men have the same values or do they experience things with the same intensity as each other?

The Context of Crime

After going into all of the major theoretical explanations of criminal behavior and talking about the different ways gender matters there, we'll spend some time talking about different contexts in which crime occurs. Context refers to the time, place, or other circumstances that shape why the crime happened, how everyone involved perceives it, and what unique aspect of that context could necessitate an equally unique response. We'll be spending much of our time here talking about two different factors: age and location.

Age presents a massive contextual issue when we're talking about gender and crime, because it forces us to recognize all the different ways that adolescents differ from adults: they have different perspectives on life, respond to stress differently, differ biologically, and have all sorts of nonadult problems. Just think about what your own life was like when you were fourteen and how much you've changed since then—you likely feel like a completely different person now. For all these reasons, it just doesn't make a lot of sense to treat adolescent behavior the same way we treat adult behavior. Not only does imposing adult penalties not make a lot of sense, but some make the moral argument that children can be saved. The Child Savers Movement majorly influenced the development of the juvenile justice system in the United States today.

Age also presents an interesting contextual challenge because it forces us to look at criminal behavior over the long term. We know that most offenses are committed by people in their late teens and early twenties, after which the rate of offending decreases over time (i.e., Farrington 1986). Many theories of crime stop at investigating why people commit crimes. Obviously, not all offenders are caught by the police and punished—so it stands to reason that an awful lot of people who have gotten into crime one day got out of it for some reason or another, right? These people have found their own way back into the world of pro-social behavior without spending a day behind bars or paying a dime in court costs. Maybe if we could find a way to replicate that ability across society, crime would go down. Also, if we're going to be thinking about different ways that boys and girls become involved in crime, we can't just assume that all criminals get out of that world for the same reasons. Maybe there are differences in how men and women stop offending too. We can think about this in terms of people's different life trajectories and different transitions (Sampson and Laub 1992, 1993; Elder 1994), which can have a tremendous effect on self-concept and behavior and can push people away from crime. These transitions include getting married, finding employment, and having children; why they cause people to desist from criminal behavior, however, is unclear.

In addition to age, we'll also be talking about location, in terms not of specific neighborhoods (which we will address in our theory chapter) but of crime in urban areas. Specifically, we will talk about widespread drug use and drug dealing as well as gang violence. A great deal of work has been done on life in cities since the birth of American sociology (i.e., Park 1926), because the population explosion in urban centers across the country was one factor that gave rise to that discipline in the United States in the first place. Never before had so many people lived in such a concentrated area, and for sociologists like Robert Park, it was important to get out there and learn as much as possible about how people would react to living on top of each other—almost literally in some cases.

Since then, we've been acutely aware of all the problems of city life and how it transforms people, and we've learned a lot about problems with crime seemingly concentrated in these areas. News stories on gang violence, drug dealers, or both in cities across the country are commonplace. Some cities have even been nicknamed to reflect the amount of violence in their communities (i.e., Baltimore, Maryland, depicted as Bodymore, Murdaland, in HBO's series *The Wire*). And despite a wide variety of social classes in cities, the media have focused almost exclusively on crimes committed in predominantly poor, nonwhite communities and ignored what's happening in wealthier, whiter areas, giving some the inaccurate perception that the behaviors of those living in those more affluent communities are as pure as new-fallen snow.

Gang violence and drug dealing were historically associated with urban areas, while the suburbs were thought to be safe havens from those problems. This resulted in a substantial amount of research into gangs and drugs in urban centers. However, more recent research has begun to focus on how these historically urban problems have begun to manifest in rural and suburban areas, which gives us an opportunity to talk about gender differences in people's experience of their surroundings. There's also a lot to talk about here in terms of the city and immigration to the United States, because gang violence and drug dealing are tied up in the history of both in many ways. After all, there were no drug corners when the United States was "discovered"; Plymouth Rock didn't get tagged by local gangs as Crip or Blood territory. So where did these social ills come from? How did we let them happen? We can even extend that question beyond drugs and gangs. Where did all the people in these cities come from? Where did the government come from? Where did the police come from? If we can answer these questions, then we can trace the development of these issues from their origins to today and, in doing so, identify some (painfully obvious, as it turns out) solutions.

As we will focus on gender throughout this text, you can ask yourself now how it factors into the types of urban crime we will be talking about. Are there differences in how boys and girls come to gang life? Are girls even involved in gangs? If so, how? What does gang membership mean to them? What about drug use— does that come about the same way for girls as it does boys? This is an excellent thought experiment as we get ready to examine all the ways that gender matters: Based on what you know about why people use drugs, and what you already know about men and women, can you think of different reasons why men and women might turn to substance use? Is everyone seeking the same thrill? Is everyone hurting in the same way? Probably not.

Gang violence and drug use are certainly not the only types of urban crime. New York City, Chicago, Cleveland, Miami, Los Angeles, and Las Vegas all have a long history with organized crime dating back to the early twentieth century, as the first Irish and Italian gangs assimilated into society and became more sophisticated in their operations. Vice crimes like gambling and prostitution were the scourge of law enforcement in the first half of the twentieth century, and men like Mickey Cohen delighted in taunting the police nationally. Besides that, sexual violence, intimate partner violence, juvenile delinquency, corporate crime—all things discussed in later chapters—also happen in urban, suburban, and rural areas in varying ways, as we'll see.

Gender-Based Violence

Having discussed context, we'll move onto our discussions of gender-based violence. There are a couple of different approaches to this topic. First, we will spend some time looking at intimate partner violence (IPV) and the different ways people can be abused in the context of a relationship, be it marriage, dating, or even a new acquaintance. The point is, some sort of (potential) romance is in the air. Talking about IPV is incredibly important, no matter how uncomfortable these discussions might be.

It is also important to talk about violence that can occur in familial relationships, where there isn't any kind of romantic love present. Obviously, an abusive husband can also be an abusive father. This violence isn't always only physical—sexual and emotional violence is just as important to talk about with regard to IPV. Intimate partner violence, one of the most common types of violence in society, was once culturally acceptable and legitimized by the government. In the grand scheme of things, it hasn't been that long since the government (and by extension the police) started taking IPV seriously.

Beyond intimate and family relationships, there are many opportunities for gender-based violence to occur in sexual relationships. It's difficult sometimes to think about rape and sexual assault in the context of IPV, but these things do happen in those relationships—contrary to what some might have you believe is appropriate behavior. But there is much of importance to discuss regarding sexual violence outside the family context. We're also going to talk about the larger concept of sex work and think about ways that violence can and does occur in the lives of the men and women who have chosen (or, more likely, been pushed into) this specific line of work.

The Criminal Justice System

In the last section of the book, we'll focus more on the justice side of the equation and less on crime. As I'm sure you know, the criminal justice system is divided into three very basic parts: the police, who look for criminals; the courts, which determine whether someone has committed a crime; and the prisons, which hold those convicted for a prescribed period.

The criminal justice system is fascinating in terms of gender in that work that focuses on the perception of criminals—the millions of men and women processed through the system each year—gets a lot of attention. We talk frequently about their experiences with the police, and the types of justice they receive in court. Rightfully so, of course—the criminal justice system is supposed to serve us, the people, and so research into how the system does or does not live up to that expectation is righteous. That said, we very rarely think about the criminal justice system in terms of the people responsible for acting as its agents. We rarely talk about the people caught up in the system at any level—from those people housed in maximum-security prisons to those on probation or parole. This is an incredible injustice to them and in some ways exemplifies how positive stereotypes can hurt people. Ask yourself, why don't more people think about the lives of people in the system? Is it because so many people hold the police in high esteem and applaud them for their bravery? Do we not want to be accused of drawing unnecessary criticism to people who are out there every day keeping us safe? Or do we just not really care all that much?

After the police come the courts, which hand down what many might consider proper justice. Here, we'll talk about the different ways that the courts view women and men as they go through the justice system. It might come as a surprise, but despite the old cliché that "justice is blind," in reality, it has a good idea of who stands before it and makes all sorts of decisions based on stereotypes before the accused has opened his or her mouth. This is a chance for us to think about the social power of stereotypes, which entail so much more than some of the phobias or isms harbored by individuals. In other words, it's one thing for an ordinary citizen to have ideas about what men and women are like; it's something else altogether when a judge is making decisions about a person's behavior based on gender stereotypes.

This is another opportunity to talk about some of the gender similarities I mentioned earlier. For everyone, going to prison is very difficult. This makes sense: prison isn't supposed to be fun. Some prison experiences are common to both men and women, regardless of age. Think about the assumptions you might have about what goes on behind those walls, and multiply them a hundred times over: drug use and addiction, gang violence, sexual violence, and so on. That this similarity exists probably either frustrates or pleases you, depending on your feelings about the criminal justice system.

While we will discuss each of the justice system's three parts, we'll also spend considerable time looking at a stage during which alleged offenders often slip through the cracks: the pretrial phase. Not everyone arrested and charged with a crime gets released on bail; many people remain incarcerated prior to trial. The pretrial phase tends to vary quite drastically in terms of not only gender but race and age — assuming that the defendant makes it to that point. For instance, the tragic death of Sandra Bland — a black woman detained following a problematic traffic stop, who died in her cell days later under questionable circumstances — is a grim reminder that justice is not always served.

In reality the vast majority of people currently in jail or prison will return to their communities. In the course of a given year, approximately 650,000 people will leave the prison system and return home ("Prisoners and Prisoner Reentry" n.d.). The concept of prisoner reentry is a growing concern in the United States because prisons do so little to improve (or correct) offenders' behavior. If you think about criminology and sociology in terms of how to apply these concepts to the real world, prepare yourself to enter a maddening realm of blocked opportunity after blocked opportunity after blocked opportunity. In many ways, because men and women are treated similarly once convicted (though there are differences in the severity of those convictions and the treatment they receive inside), they reenter society facing the same barriers constructed by their incarceration. That is to say, both meet the same restrictions on their post-release behavior. However, because of the immense complexity of gender as a social institution, differing factors either prevent ex-convicts from successfully returning to society or actually help them make this transition smoother. This means that gender expectations interact with barriers to reentry to create unique challenges based on a person's femininity or masculinity. As we'll see, expectations within the family dynamic (i.e., for emotional relationships, for one's identity as family provider, for what it means to be a mom or dad) can severely hinder a person's ability to successfully reenter society after incarceration. Furthermore, prisoners' goals may also differ. Obviously they have to try to pick up the pieces of the lives they left behind and move forward. The path won't be the same for every ex-convict, because femininity and masculinity offer different avenues into society and create different barriers for successful reintegration. Most, if not all, offenders return to the same situation they were in when they committed the crime that got them arrested. They're probably going back to the same neighborhood, the same family, and the same group of friends. But even though so much is the same, as we'll see, everything may have changed—including the way the ex-convicts themselves see their place in the world.

Obviously, we will spend a great deal of time pulling apart many of the ways in which gender matters in issues of crime and justice, how it manifests in criminal behavior, and how men and women experience the criminal justice system differently, both as offenders and as agents of justice. That said, gender is not the only element of social structure that influences criminal behavior or the criminal justice system. It's important that we acknowledge this, because we live in the real world, and the real world is so much more complex than most people want to believe. Yes, gender is extraordinarily important and often overlooked in matters of crime and justice. But it's not the only thing that matters. The different ways gender affects and is affected by other elements of social structure is called *intersectionality*. If we are going to truly understand how gender affects us, we also have to recognize that the experience of gender varies across racial, ethnic, and socio-economic lines.

So what else should we be focusing on besides gender? The two major elements of social structure that come up in discussions of crime and justice are socioeconomic status and race/ethnicity, so we'll spend some time talking about how gender interacts with class and race in regard to crime. For instance, we'll talk about masculinity all throughout this book and the multitude of ways that strict conformity to it might not be the healthiest decision that some men could make. However, we cannot and should not assume that masculinity manifests itself the same way for men in the upper class as it does for men in poverty; we cannot and should not assume it has the same effects for white men as it does for men of color either.

We'll also revisit the role that age plays and explore the impact of time. Our social history helps us understand why things are the way they are today. Gender has undergone very significant changes over the course of human history, and a conversation about gender, crime, and justice in the early twenty-first century differs vastly from the one we would have had in the early twentieth century. It's important to acknowledge a number of incredibly important changes to the concept of gender as a facet of social structure over the past forty years.

In addition to talking about how race/ethnicity and socioeconomic status interact with gender in different ways, it's also important to discuss intersectionality in terms of some of the ways people experience crime. We will talk here about a few different aspects of crime—especially violence, both in terms of being a victim and an offender. A major theme of this book is that there isn't only one way to experience the world; in fact, people perceive events in their lives in all sorts of different ways. This is especially important when it comes to violence, because it represents the most primal type of crime and has devastating consequences that can span generations. You might think that violence is violence and that we could not possibly disagree about that. In truth, as we'll find out, people can and do view violent behavior differently—depending on who's the perpetrator, who's the victim, and what those individuals look like. In short, intersectionality helps us better understand the wide variety of ways in which people experience the world, so that any proposed solution to help make the world a better place resists the sort of one-size-fits-all approach of past programs.

Taking an intersectional approach allows us to shine a light into all the corners of criminology where gender matters but, for whatever reason, hasn't gotten the mainstream attention it deserves. We'll have an opportunity to talk about gender and drugs in the suburbs, about drug use among suburban women, and about domestic violence in rural areas. We'll explore gender differences in the experience of a criminal justice professional. Finally, we'll explore the different challenges incarcerated people face when they return to their homes and communities.

2

The Critical Perspective

Beginning at the end of the nineteenth century and coming to a head in the early twentieth, the women's suffrage movement generated a historic shift in the balance of power in the United States when it won women the legal right to vote. As with all such momentous changes, some people were steadfastly against it. For instance, here is the opening shot in an argument against giving women the right to vote, prepared in 1911 by J. B. Sanford, chairman of the Democratic Caucus:

> The mother's influence is needed in the home. She can do little good by gadding the streets and neglecting her children. Let her teach her daughters that modesty, patience, and gentleness are the charms of a woman. Let her teach her sons that an honest conscience is every man's first political law; that no splendor can rob him nor no force justify the surrender of simplest right of a free and independent citizen. The mothers of this country can shape the destinies of the nation by keeping their places and attending to those duties that God Almighty intended for them. The kindly, gentle influence of the mother in the home and the dignified influence of the teacher in the school will far outweigh all the influence of all the mannish female politicians on earth. (Sanford 1911)

Despite this plea to stop "gadding about" and remain in their station, women did gain the right to vote and did gain entry into politics.

We flash ahead to life in the United States some thirty years later. In World War II, the United States saw a major shift in gender roles related to the workforce, which in turn might have had broader repercussions for the treatment of gender societally. The exodus of so many men to enlist in the military created a sudden, immediate, and extremely urgent need for new workers to support the war effort, and much of this burden fell on the American women who stayed behind. While this dramatic shift was obviously necessary in hindsight, getting people to accept it was not easy. To help, the iconic image of "Rosie the Riveter," created by Norman Rockwell encouraged women to leave the home and enter the workforce—and convinced their husbands and other disapproving family members that it was OK for them to do so. As a result of much ultimately successful effort, many women entered the workforce for the very first time.

Following the war, as the nation transitioned to peacetime and the soldiers came home, expecting to resume their normal, civilian lives, many women who had made a significant contribution to the war effort were unceremoniously fired and told to return to the domestic sphere. And just as propaganda was used to motivate them to work, it also helped push them out of the workforce and into their homes in the newly created suburbs, where they would live in the lap of luxury, surrounded by modern technology, which would make their lives so much easier. While this campaign was somewhat successful in restoring the image of the work force to its prewar dynamic (most women were fired anyway, whether they accepted it or not), there was really no going back, and the next stage in the larger equal rights movement had begun. "Rosie the Riveter" went from a character on a wartime motivational poster to a symbol of one of the most misunderstood and demonized theoretical and social movements in modern American history: feminism. The United States entered its period of global dominance while struggling to understand the new reality that forty years of social and political change had brought about: we were a global power internationally while unsure of how our own domestic future was going to play out.

Before discussing many of the theories of crime and how they relate to gender, it's important to talk first about the role of feminism in criminology. *Feminism* is possibly one of the most misunderstood terms in our society today, associated with so many negative stereotypes that many people don't really understand what it stands for. We begin by discussing the origin of feminism in terms of another wildly misunderstood (at least, by the general public) sociological perspective: Marxism.

Marx and Crime

Karl Marx is, to many people, a sort of boogeyman. He famously predicted the fall of capitalism at the hands of a global workers' rebellion, which would transform the world into a socialist paradise, where the tyranny of greed and selfishness would give way to true equality. His work helped set into motion revolutions throughout Asia and Central and South America, altering the course of human history in no small way. In fact, we are still dealing with the ramifications of Marx's work in the political realm today, and it appears that this will remain a global issue for some time. Because of this, as well as the fascist regimes his work helped to inspire, many people vilify Marx. This is perfectly understandable, and I have no intention of discussing any of the supposed communist revolutions that have happened in world history. There is no point in revisiting those conflicts and all the bloodshed that resulted. Instead, I draw attention to Marx not to focus on the political consequences of his work but rather to revisit the original ideas that garnered him such attention and discuss how they relate to criminal behavior.

When reading and discussing Marx, it's vital to remember that he, too, was shaped by the context in which he lived. He was influenced by the world around him, just like anyone else. We can't look at his ideas through the lens of what they inspired or without recognizing that our lives in the early twenty-first century

are very, very different from Marx's experience. Marx, along with
Friedrich Engels, studied society during a period of history when
industry was growing at an unprecedented rate and capitalism was
running virtually unchained across Europe and the United States.
Laborers lived in absolute poverty and desolation, in ghettos in
the truest form, at the absolute mercy of the industrialists who
paid them virtually nothing for their labor. This stark imbalance of
power led Marx to conclude that one day the workers of the world
would unite and overthrow the economic system. In a strange
irony, people at the bottom of the economic ladder seemed to support the system that did not benefit them in any conceivable way.
The most significant message in Marx's work is that the economic
system that defines a society is the single most powerful force
guiding human behavior in that society.

What does this have to do with crime and gender? As originally situated, Marxism considered criminals a drain on society,
another barrier to the advent of a communist revolution. Marx
believed that the criminal class, or lumpenproletariat, comprised a
category of people unlikely to develop any kind of class con-
sciousness, or sense of self as part of a larger community, where
the struggle of the individual is the struggle of the entire group.
However, after Marx's death, the view of Marxism as a school of
thought vis-à-vis the criminal element in society changed drastically. Criminals were no longer barriers to the revolution; instead,
some came to see them as the true revolutionaries.

The field of critical criminology is grounded primarily in
Marxist principals. Rather than focusing on criminals as a fac-
tion of society that impedes progress, critical criminologists
view society's criminal element as a symptom of much larger
systemic problems and, like I just mentioned, as potentially able
to bring about the types of widespread social and economic
change Marx predicted. While most criminological research
focuses on topics that involve violence, property crime, drug
use, and so on, the critical perspective argues that these are all
endemic to life in a capitalistic society. Therefore, rather than
theorize about why someone might get involved in a gang or rob
a bank or what have you, critical criminologists argue that we
should focus entirely on the people in society who benefit the

most from the system. Specifically, they believe we should focus on the crimes of the rich and powerful and devote our time to understanding how capitalism perpetuates oppressive systems that keep the poor in poverty and minorities under control. Critical criminologists, in other words, argue that our time is better spent looking at crimes committed by the government and by major corporations rather than more ordinary or typical criminal behavior.

Many consider Richard Quinney the godfather of critical criminology. Quinney began publishing on the subject in the 1970s and morphed over time from what many would consider a hardline Marxist criminologist into someone who saw justice in more spiritual terms than anything else. For instance, in his *Class, State, and Crime*, Quinney (1977) argues that the entire criminal justice system exists not to enforce the law and to serve and protect the people but rather to oppress them. He saw the law as a tool wielded by people in power to perpetuate the status quo and maintain their position in society, a perspective that differs 100 percent from what most of you have been taught about crime, the law, and the criminal justice system. Later, he moved toward a more spiritual approach to crime and justice, specifically in the area of peacemaking criminology, which emphasized ending suffering and finding nonviolent ways to address issues of crime in the community. Quinney's *Providence: The Reconstruction of Social and Moral Order* (1980) is as much a religious text as it is a book on criminological theory.

What do Marxism and critical criminology have to do with gender and crime? Feminism developed as part of Marxism and grew out of our understanding of how systems of oppression work in society. While Marxism focused more on oppressive conditions perpetuated by economic institutions in terms of poverty (in the United States it was also grounded in the civil rights movement and the understanding that structural racism was very much still a problem tied very closely to issues of poverty and economic oppression), early feminism was our first effort to understand oppression in terms of gender and sexuality and to examine how the lives of women in reality differed greatly from what men claimed they were like.

Crime and Early Feminism

While feminism was developing into what we think of it today during the civil rights movement, it didn't immediately find its way into criminological thinking and theorizing. It took a little while. By the beginning of the 1970s, however, two competing ideas about the relationship between gender and crime had helped set the foundation for how many people think about these issues today. These ideas stemmed from a realization that existing theories of crime assumed men and women were affected similarly (if not completely identically) by the social forces around us that motivate crime; in other words, the relationships between ourselves and our families, friends, neighborhoods, and so forth, were presumed to work the same for both sexes and for everyone across the spectrum of gender (Heidensohn 1968; Bertrand 1969; Daly and Chesney-Lind 1988).

Granted, these modern notions of gender and sexual fluidity were not really talked about then, making it easier to think about the world in simplistic terms of "men" and "women," but we'll discuss that more in a bit. The recognition of this massive hole in our understanding of criminal behavior launched many criminologists on a quest to reimagine the discipline, in a way—initiating a painful transition away from thinking about competing theoretical perspectives and toward thinking in terms of differing social structural positions. Why do you think people assumed that these earlier theories could explain male and female behavior equally, anyway? A common explanation is that because the vast majority of criminologists were men, they developed theories from a male perspective that were therefore more likely to explain male behavior. That's why it's important to think about whom you're getting your ideas from, because the social structural positions people occupy in the world influence their perspective.

Recognition of the lack of scientific explanations of crime dedicated to female criminality stems from what people refer to as second-wave feminism, the branch that I was talking about when I introduced feminism as a relative of Marxism—the feminism of the civil rights movement in the 1960s. Research on female criminality was not completely nonexistent. Cesare Lombroso published the definitive study on women in crime in 1893, focusing on the relationship between criminality and evolution (as did his previous work, which focused on crime among men). With an approach rooted in Charles Darwin's theory of evolution, Lombroso—who believed that women were naturally inferior to men—concluded that while crime among men was due to their not having evolved to the same level as the rest of society, criminal women were actually much craftier and more cunning than noncriminal women (Lombroso and Ferrero 1893 [2004]).

The label "second-wave feminism" implies that a feminism of some sort came before it. The origin of first-wave feminism is hard to pin down, but I can tell you definitively what it was about: legal and political equality. We can think of first-wave feminism in the United States as the suffrage movement, with women fighting to gain the right not only to vote in political elections but also to run for elected office. (Did you know that there was a lot of controversy among the suffragettes about how they should go about fighting for the right to vote? For more on the history of the suffrage movement, see Box 2.1.) When the Nineteenth Amendment to the US Constitution was ratified in 1920, the first-wave of feminism arguably came to an end because it had accomplished its mission. But legal equality for women did not, as we know, truly extend to all women. The United States remained (and remains today) a very segregated society, and the rise of Jim Crow in the South all but cut black women out of the picture. Other laws targeted other nonwhite minorities (drug laws provide one constant example; we can also look at Japanese internment camps during World War II as another).

Basically, the complete lack of racial equality (or, maybe a better way to put it, the existence of almost absolute racial inequality), coupled with a counterculture that embraced Marx's work, helped spark second-wave feminism. In terms of criminological research and criminological theory, the focus was on how the existing theories could or could not explain the behavior of women. In addition to this generalizability problem, early feminist criminologists also had to deal with the gender-ratio problem,

Box 2.1 Conflict in the Women's Suffrage Movement

The quest among the suffragettes in the late 1800s and early 1900s is often glossed over as a uniform political movement to give women the right to vote. We treat these women as a homogenous group that worked as a well-oiled machine. The movement was anything but that.

First, there existed the American Equal Rights Association (AERA), whose mission was the extension of equal rights to all Americans, regardless of sex, race, or ethnic background. The AERA was especially interested in extending voting rights to all. However, a major schism occurred surrounding the Fifteenth Amendment, which extended the right to vote to newly freed black men in America. The constituents of the AERA could not come to terms on whether to support the amendment, and they split in half following their annual meeting in 1869. There now existed two major organizations fighting for women's suffrage: the National Woman Suffrage Association (NWSA), founded in 1869 and led by Susan B. Anthony and Elizabeth Cady Stanton, and the American Women's Suffrage Association (AWSA), founded by Lucy Stone, Julia Ward Howe, and Henry Blackwell, also in 1869.

The AWSA and NWSA differed in their support of the Fifteenth Amendment. The NWSA was strongly against it, because it did not extend voting rights to everyone in the United States and instead only extended male suffrage, giving black men the right to vote. A year before the founding of the NWSA, Elizabeth Cady Stanton gave a speech titled "The Destructive Male," which concluded with the following passage:

> With violence and disturbance in the natural world, we see a constant effort to maintain an equilibrium of forces. Nature, like a loving mother, is ever trying to keep land and sea, mountain and valley, each in its place, to hush the angry winds and waves, balance the extremes of heat and cold, of rain and drought, that peace, harmony, and beauty may reign supreme. There is a striking analogy between matter and mind, and the present disorganization of society warns us that in the

dethronement of woman we have let loose the elements of violence and ruin that she only has the power to curb. If the civilization of the age calls for an extension of the suffrage, surely a government of the most virtuous educated men and women would better represent the whole and protect the interests of all than could the representation of either sex alone. ("Elizabeth Cady Stanton" 1868).

Conversely, the AWSA favored the Fifteenth Amendment and feared that it would not survive the legislative process if altered to extend the right to vote to everyone. In their mind, it represented a fair compromise and people shouldn't get greedy and jeopardize it.

This split lasted for over twenty years, until it became obvious that the groups would never succeed in their quest for women's suffrage without coming together. They united under Anna Howard Shaw (1847–1919), leader of the newly formed National American Woman Suffrage Association (NAWSA). Shaw was another major figure in the twentieth century Progressive movement, not only giving speeches on suffrage but also preaching temperance (meaning she was against alcohol and would have favored Prohibition, had she lived to see it). Eventually, Shaw stepped down from the NAWSA because she disapproved of how militant the group was becoming—the very militancy that had divided the original group in the first place.

which is the reality that boys and men commit crime at a much higher rate than girls and women. This ratio persists, and some theorists are still working on it. What about you? What do you think could possibly explain that difference in behavior, besides just saying that boys will be boys?

Several new theories on the relationship between gender and crime arose. First, let's talk about the liberation hypothesis, developed by Freda Adler. In *Sisters in Crime* Adler (1975) wrote about the apparent rise in the number of women committing crimes, and she argued that female criminality could be linked to the success of the women's liberation movement. She argued that the rise in

female criminality was correlated with the number of women who
were experiencing newfound independence—not only the formal
legal independence established in the first wave of feminism but
the more social and cultural freedom to work, marry, make parenting decisions, and so on. Essentially, Adler argued that the
women's liberation movement had given women the right to be
masculine and behave in more masculine ways. She believed that
the independence afforded women, specifically the freedom to
take part in masculinity, had made them more likely to commit
crimes. This is a very controversial idea because, if it is true, then
the logical solution to stopping women from committing crime is
to turn back the clock and go back to a society that is more
oppressive of them. That hardly seems like a civilized approach to
me, though. Besides, the liberation hypothesis doesn't really hold
much water anymore. We know that things like poverty and drug
use are much more powerful explanations for female criminality
than women's liberation (i.e., Kruttschnitt 1996).

Instead of thinking about gender and crime in terms of women
trying to be more like men, others began looking at experiences
unique to men and women that could create conditions favorable
to committing crimes. In other words, these criminologists wanted
to know what things women experienced, and men didn't, that
could lead them to crime, and vice versa. This required criminologists then, as it does today, to rethink how we utilize the concept
of gender. As Daly and Chesney-Lind (1988, 504) write,

1. Gender is not a natural fact but a complex social, historical,
   and cultural product; it is related to, but not simply derived
   from, biological sex difference and reproductive capacities.
2. Gender and gender relations order social life and social institutions in fundamental ways.
3. Gender relations and constructs of masculinity and femininity are not symmetrical but are based on an organizing principle of men's superiority and social and political-economic
   dominance over women.
4. Systems of knowledge reflect men's views of the natural and
   social world; the production of knowledge is gendered.

5. Women should be at the center of intellectual inquiry, not
   peripheral, invisible, or appendages to men.

Daly and Chesney-Lind argue, in other words, that we cannot
and should not treat sex and gender as two words to describe the
same thing; they are mutually exclusive. Sex is biological, while
gender is social. Gender roles and other types of gendered behavior are all socially constructed, meaning that they are not natural,
biological, or otherwise inevitable. There's nothing "natural"
about hairstyles, about fashion, about hobbies, about careers—
none are things that boys and girls, women and men, are just
"supposed" to do. None of them are behaviors that people feel
naturally and inevitably compelled to perform. They just exist,
and we put positive or negative value on them and act accordingly. The idea that something is inherently masculine or feminine
is false—everything is socially constructed.

I also want to draw your attention to Daly and Chesney-Lind's
final point, which says that women should be central to intellectual inquiry rather than pushed off to the side. This is another way
of saying that the lives of women were not taken into serious consideration in the development of all the theories of crime we will
cover in the next chapter. It also means that women working in
the field were not taken seriously and their ideas weren't included
in the conversation (this is putting it lightly, to say the least).
Things have gotten better in terms of the centrality of women in
the development of criminological theories since 1988, but let's
talk about how we got there first.

Following Daly and Chesney-Lind's (1988) article, two separate lines of inquiry developed on the relationship between gender
and criminality: one focused on the lives of women, and one looked
at the lives of men. This isn't to say that Daly and Chesney-Lind's
argument on the difference between sex and gender itself launched
this movement, but it was a flashpoint. Chesney-Lind (1989) followed up on this work with a critique of the theoretical explanations of juvenile delinquency, arguing that the existing ideas failed
not only to take the experiences of girls into consideration but
also to recognize that the criminal justice system mistreated girls

in terms of the relationship between their lives and their motivations to offend. This neglect of girls' behavior is not some minor oversight; Chesney-Lind points to Albert Cohen and Travis Hirschi, who say, for all intents and purposes, that girls are not present in their research. The foundations of criminological thought quite literally ignored female behavior. In her 1989 piece, Chesney-Lind points out gender differences in delinquency in terms of the types of behaviors boys and girls are arrested for, with girls much more likely than boys—25.3 to 8.3 percent, respectively, in 1986—to be arrested for status offenses (i.e., skipping school, curfew violations, underage drinking). If we take official arrest records as gospel, then this would indicate that girls commit way more status offenses than boys—that something about being a girl makes them more likely than boys to run away or skip school. All these wild and out-of-control girls make life awful for everyone, right? Nope. In fact, the opposite is true; self-report data—an anonymous survey of the population asking whether they had engaged in a litany of behaviors—shows that girls were overrepresented in the arrest records, which basically means that more girls were being arrested than should have been. The behavior of the police skewed the reality of the situation; they seem to have been letting more boys go and arresting more girls for the same behavior.

Chesney-Lind (1989) uses this discrepancy and the lack of any theoretical explanation for it as an example of how lacking the existing theories of crime and delinquency really are. Further, she states that this is largely due to the way the criminal justice system, and in this specific case the juvenile justice system, developed, particularly the early-twentieth-century Child Savers Movement. Existing sexism is part of the problem, but the way it manifests in the system clearly causes this theoretical discrepancy. The Child Savers Movement is largely credited with creating the juvenile justice system, at least in terms of forcing society to recognize that adolescent behavior and adolescence in general are quite different from adult criminality and adulthood overall. The Child Savers' basic idea was that criminal or otherwise deviant behavior exhibited by young people could still be corrected, whereas adults doing the same thing were beyond hope. In other words, young people still had enough life left ahead of them that it was possible to correct their behavior now so that they did not become full-fledged criminals later in life, while it was too late for an adult in that same situation. They were literally trying to save kids from themselves and set them (back) on the right path.

The problem with the Child Savers Movement, according to Chesney-Lind (1989), was that it (1) became a hammer to force girls into traditional gender roles, treating those whose behavior was unladylike as delinquent, while simultaneously calling on domestic roles associated with women as a means of correcting this behavior, and (2) led academics to romanticize images of the working-class male delinquent, the "romantic rogue male challenging a rigid and unequal class structure" (Chesney-Lind 1989, 17), with the result that research on not only female behavior but also middle-class delinquency was completely ignored. Existing criminologists were just more interested in the behaviors of working-class boys, and nothing more.

How, then, does she see female delinquency? Without trying to develop a fully feminist explanation of delinquent behavior (remember, this piece is just part of the beginning of criminology's exploration of gender, so a full-blown explanation of it right out of the box is a lot to ask for), Chesney-Lind (1989) points to the role of the family in the onset and management of delinquent behavior. First, she notes that parents refer girls, more than boys, to the courts—meaning that many times, mom and dad are policing gender roles on their own and using the criminal justice system as a tool to wedge their daughter into a specific type of behavior. Second, girls are much more likely to experience abuse in the home, especially sexual abuse, which could then cause them to run away. This is a clear gender difference in the motivation for particular status offenses, but it does not stop there. Once they have escaped the immediate threat of sexual violence in the home, these newly emancipated girls often turn to delinquency, including theft and prostitution, as a way to survive on the street—and yet they were not completely into the idea of "being" bad. In fact, Chesney-Lind argues that they resent being labeled delinquent. This appears to contrast with male behavior on the street, where a man's delinquency and subsequent delinquent label would likely not only be completely embraced, but actively centered in the guy's identity.

This difference in victimization patterns is important. To be clear, boys in general experience significantly more violent victimization overall than girls, and girls are not alone in experiencing sexual violence. However, gender dictates the context of girls' victimization as well as their reactions to it (Chesney-Lind 1989). Girls are more likely to be victims of sexual abuse within the family because fathers in strongly patriarchal families view their daughters as their own sexual property (Finkelhor 1982; Chesney-Lind 1989). Living in a strongly patriarchal society, girls who experience this victimization are oftentimes coerced into staying in their homes (giving their abuser easier access to them) and have their claims of abuse ignored by the authorities (and see the authorities manipulated by their abuser) (Chesney-Lind 1989). Thus, their only option is to run away—and as their parents use the criminal justice system to try to bring them home, a system that is supposed to protect them puts them in harm's way. And those girls who evade their parents and the authorities take on the lives of "escaped convicts . . . forced onto the streets" (Chesney-Lind 1989: 24). They resort to delinquent behavior because they cannot go to school or take a legitimate job, both of which will exponentially increase their risk of capture. Further still, because our society has sexualized young girls, they find themselves having to treat their sexuality as a resource for survival, a situation few young men on the street find themselves in.

In short, in her discussion of how patriarchal society has shaped the criminal justice system into something that is (or was) actively working against girls, and how sexual victimization is a driving force behind female delinquency, Chesney-Lind (1989) isn't saying that victimization is the cause of girl's delinquency or that the flawed criminal justice system is the biggest issue facing women. Rather, she points out two concrete ways in which the experiences of girls differ completely from those of boys. The question then becomes, if girls (and women) experience the criminal justice system differently than boys, do they experience other social institutions differently? And if the experience of and reaction to sexual abuse is different for girls than for boys, what other experiences wholly unique to women could explain their criminality in ways that don't apply to men?

This now brings us face to face with Messerschmidt (1993), the other major contributor to early discussions of gender and crime, with his examination of the connection between masculinity and crime. Messerschmidt argued that existing theories in criminology and feminism were lacking because they failed to fully embrace intersectionality and too often put one dimension of race, class, or gender at the center of their work, ignoring the complex interplay among all three. Keeping that in mind, Messerschmidt argued that the idea of hegemonic masculinity is central to the relationship between gender and crime. When we think about gender and how people behave in masculine and feminine ways, it's important to remember that there are multiple ways to "be" masculine or feminine—an idea we will explore further. In any event, in the scope of types of masculinities, the idea is that the character traits associated with being a "real" man—being strong, being aggressive, not being emotional, being tough—constitute the most dominant type of masculinity. Messerschmidt means this type of masculinity when talking about hegemonic masculinity. According to Messerschmidt, it drives criminality for men and manifests in many, many different ways. As we'll see multiple times throughout this book, men's over- or hyperconformity to this form of masculinity sparks violence, be it on the street, in the workplace, or in a relationship. Buying into the idea of being a "real man" too strongly does not tend to have very good outcomes.

In Messerschmidt's view, we cannot and should not talk about the relationship between gender and crime without also talking about the roles that social class and race play as well. This focus on the interplay between gender, race, and social class is called intersectionality, and we will touch on it at the conclusion of the book. Suffice it to say, not only does masculinity take on a number of different forms, but hegemonic masculinity manifests itself in different ways depending on the larger social structural context.

So, now we have discussed the second wave of feminism and the beginning of feminist criminology. What is the shape of things today?

Modern Feminism

Adler's, Chesney-Lind's, and Messerschmidt's groundbreaking work was part of the end of second-wave feminism in the United States. Women's advancements in a number of areas throughout society shifted feminism's focus (in criminology and elsewhere) to the idea that women and men have different experiences that lead to different types of behavior. What some people refer to as the "sex wars"—the inability of feminist thinkers to agree on how to treat female sexuality, including debates surrounding prostitution, pornography, same-sex dating and marriage—really ended this wave of feminism, however. As we'll see momentarily, these debates are still happening today.

It might seem strange that people get so intensely angry about the issue of human sexuality, but you have to remember that historically, especially in the United States, we've been very afraid of sex. American culture is extremely prudish. That we find sex icky and confusing gives rise to ridiculous scenes like a woman being chastised for breastfeeding in front of a Victoria's Secret. We want sexual tension but still find the human body gross and refuse to view or discuss perfectly normal and natural physical functions. Get it?

And discussion of sex and sexuality among women has generally been taboo. American society doesn't permit women to be sexual beings. They receive sex rather than being active participants. So at a time when women's equality and our understanding of the social role of gender were growing by leaps and bounds, human sexuality presented a serious challenge—female sexuality, as an academic topic, was in many ways an undiscovered country. This is problematic for criminology because sexuality entails a lot of potential for violence and substance abuse. It hasn't always been this way: as we'll see in Chapter 7, when we talk about sexual violence and sex work, at one point in American history prostitution was a thriving industry that operated completely out in the open without shame. The Progressive movement in the late nineteenth century reshaped American attitudes toward prostitution and pushed it almost completely underground, where it remains today.

Two basic schools of thought surround the subject of sex work. On one hand, some feminists argue that prostitution and pornography are inherently antiwoman and operate as tools men use to continue to oppress women. In this view, not only do these types of sex work allow and encourage men to objectify women, but the demand for sex work—the existence of the market itself—leads, for instance, to the abduction and trafficking of women and children as sex slaves. This perspective argues that no woman willingly chooses sex work. Furthermore, this group of feminists strongly objects to sexual practices like BDSM (the abbreviation encompasses multiple terms—"bondage," "discipline," "dominance," "submission," and "sadomasochism") as a type of sexual deviance, because the violent imagery not only can physically and mentally harm women but also further demeans them in general.

The second school of thought holds that the sex-work taboo is an artifact of our society's puritanical heritage and that there is nothing wrong with engaging in it (obviously excluding instances in which people are forced into it against their will). This perspective takes a "sex-positive" approach to sex work, attempting to normalize human sexuality rather than shame people for engaging in a perfectly natural behavior. The sex-positive approach argues for establishing more safeguards for people involved in the sex-work industry (including prostitution and pornography), if not the complete legalization of prostitution. While the sex-positive message certainly has some value, in reality many women and children are forced into sex work.

In terms of criminology, following the initial push to think about crime in terms of experiences unique to men and women, work on gender focused in large part on gender differences in the major theoretical perspectives. We will talk about that more in the next chapter, when we review those ideas. I want to clarify here, however, that that's not all that happened. Over time—and I don't

really want to link this to one wave or era of feminism—our understanding of crime shifted. Our romantic relationship to male juvenile gang members, the rogues that Chesney-Lind (1989) talked
about, ended. The discipline's focus broadened, and research on sex
work and sexuality became more prominent. Our understanding of
sexual violence and intimate partner violence grew by leaps and
bounds, and our overall willingness to recognize masculinity for
what it is significantly improved.

Later in this book we will talk about sexual violence and intimate partner violence in much more detail, but I want to take this
opportunity to talk about a type of behavior, now recognized as
criminal, that, had it not been for the victories of feminist criminology, we might not have taken seriously otherwise. As romantic
relationships develop—as two people become a couple—certain
things have to happen. To be blunt, at least according to some traditional social norms in the United States, guys have to have some
kind of game, right? They need some kind of charm or swagger to
hide all the fear and insecurity. Now, not all guys agree on what constitutes charm or romance. Some guys think having a good game
involves being extremely aggressive or making grand romantic ges-
tures that, in practice, are pretty creepy.

Once upon a time, a guy who, for example, frequently showed
up unannounced at a woman's workplace, or always asked to be
seated in her section of a restaurant, or left gifts for her on her
windshield or front porch, or called incessantly, wasn't considered
sketchy or creepy; he was persistent. Friends and family often
told a woman experiencing those behaviors to give in and
reward him for his persistence. Today, we recognize such conduct as problematic and label it as either harassment or stalking.
It might sound like no big deal, but stalking can develop into a
dangerously unhealthy obsession and potentially lead to serious
physical violence. It's a crime that we must take seriously, and
without a substantially increased focus on gender in criminological research, we would still largely deem this type of behavior
acceptable.

Modern feminism helped bring about this new perspective on
relationship and sexual violence and the propriety of different

relationship strategies. This isn't its only contribution, of course. This entire wave drew attention to situations unique to women and behaviors problematic to them that otherwise never would have been addressed because men generally don't have to worry about them. Let's go over a couple other examples.

Modern feminism revealed behaviors that are by and large more common among women than men. These behaviors may not be criminal but are certainly deviant. Take compulsive shopping, for example. We can think of being a so-called shopaholic, or having a shopping addiction, as another form of over- or hyperconformity: women who engage in this behavior are overconforming to classic visions of what they are supposed to be like. Now, everyone shops, but men and women are socialized to think about it differently. For women, shopping is a hobby; men see it as a chore (C. Campbell 2000).

Being a shopaholic can encompass a number of different types of behavior. For some, it actually involves compulsive purchasing; for others, it involves just being drawn to shopping spots and spending time there (like in the movie *Mallrats*). Some people spend hours browsing without buying anything; some go on incredible spending sprees without giving any thought to whether they need their purchases, will use them, or can even afford them (C. Campbell 2000). This type of addiction would not have become part of our collective understanding without a concerted effort to better understand the lives of women and some of the challenges they face.

Eating disorders have also evolved into a much more serious issue because of modern feminism. As with shopping, men and women both eat, obviously, but their approaches to food are different. Men are expected to eat whatever they want, whenever they want; they are not supposed to think about "dieting." To say that the opposite holds true for women is putting it nicely. Women face enormous societal pressure to strive for a level of physical perfection rarely achieved without the aid of plastic surgery. Our relationship to food often connects to how we see our bodies and our selves, and something as simple as feeding ourselves can shape our larger identity. Hsu (1989) concludes that eating disorders are more common among women simply because women are more likely to try to control their weight. Martz, Handley, and Eisler (1995) link eating disorders to high stress related to feminine gender roles and specifically to body image. A 2002 report summarizes the causes of eating disorders best and demonstrates that they reflect far more than a desire to lose weight. Polivy and Herman (2002) point to a multitude of factors contributing to eating disorders: media, family influences, peer influences, low self-esteem, and body dissatisfaction all fuel them.

This gets really interesting when we refocus questions about eating and body dissatisfaction on boys. Young men tend to express displeasure with their bodies because they're not getting as big as they wish, especially when they first hit puberty. Because feminism also includes breaking down some of the walls around hegemonic masculinity, we're now seeing evidence of similar dysfunctional eating behaviors in adolescent boys and adult men—especially if we view these behaviors as part of a spectrum and not an either/or condition (Muise, Stein, and Arbess 2003).

Again, I highlight this research on compulsive shopping and eating disorders to point out other ways that the feminist movement in general has helped improve our understanding of the world around us. Modern feminism, however, is not the be all and end all of the movement. Like so many other perspectives, feminism has evolved and changed over time.

Postmodern Feminism

This leads us to third-wave, or postmodern, feminism. Though the sex wars haven't ended, feminism has evolved into a social perspective that focuses on all gendered experiences for people from all racial, ethnic, or socioeconomic backgrounds. This means that, yes, feminism in the twenty-first century is concerned with issues related to men, crime, and the criminal justice system. It also thinks of gender as performative and no longer views masculinity and femininity as polar opposites, allowing us to see some of the more nuanced and subtle ways in which gender affects behavior.

For instance, later in this book we will look at sexual violence in terms of both male and female victims. If it wasn't for feminist criminology, not only would we ignore this topic completely, but we'd likely do male victims of sexual violence an even greater disservice than we already do. As we'll see, all victims of sexual violence experience incredible fear in coming forward, disclosing what has happened to them, and naming their accusers, but this fear manifests differently for men and women. Male victims of sexual violence must cope with the physical and emotional pain, as well as the stigma, of their victimization, and they must also overcome the notion that men just aren't supposed to be victimized in this way. Some men see being a victim of sexual violence as feminizing, making male victims substantially more unwilling to come forward.

Beyond focusing on all the challenges of sexual violence, feminist criminology is perhaps solely responsible for drawing attention to sexual violence in prisons. Prison rape happens in both men's and women's prisons and in adult and juvenile facilities, perpetrated by both other inmates and prison staff. Yet very few people in the mainstream care. Many treat this massive human rights violation as a joke, and only because of the work of feminist criminologists does anyone really care or talk about it as a serious issue today. Only very recently did President Barack Obama order a review of violence in prisons—that's how fresh this issue is in terms of its importance to the government.

If you think about it, feminism and feminist criminology have enabled us to talk about men and male behavior much differently than ever before. Chesney-Lind's (1989) point about old theorists' romanticizing male delinquency is relevant to this discussion. Not only did this approach highlight male behavior at the expense of attention to female delinquency, but it also revealed a bias even among academics supposedly studying behavior objectively: a bias that only certain types of men committed crime as heroic rebellion against an unjust system, which ultimately rewarded that form of masculinity.

Third-wave feminism has also recognized that race and class differences need not only be acknowledged but explored more fully. I would argue that this is especially relevant in the lives of young black girls, whom, as Jody Miller (2008) argues in the preface to *Getting Played*, we have completely turned our backs on. Put differently, second-wave feminism, shaped by our larger culture of white supremacy, did not concern itself with the lives of women of color—it was not intersectional. Miller talks about the "code of the street," a concept developed by Elijah Anderson (1999), which we will cover later in the book, when we talk about street crime. Anderson argues that violence in the inner city results from a lack of economic opportunities, generating an inability to develop prestige within the community, and so violence (and a quest for respect) replaced the traditional middle-class idea of success. This violence runs the spectrum, from fighting with rival gangs, to brawling in schools, to using violence against women to demonstrate manhood (for instance, Miller opens with a discussion of gang rape as an exhibition of masculinity). In communities where the code of the street is the dominant culture, it's still practiced by a minority of residents, but because it's so unpredictable and dangerous, the majority of the people living in these neighborhoods will adhere to it if need be. Miller (2008) argues that this adherence to the street code and willingness to let it dominate leads to an unspoken acceptance of violence against women, which—in this particular form, in this particular context—becomes an entirely unique experience for black women. Does this mean that no other women experience violence in their communities, on their campuses, or in their relationships? Absolutely not. To suggest that would be ridiculous. This does mean that the context of violence differs for black women; their experience differs because their worldview and life experiences differ.

As with other waves of feminism, not everyone is comfortable with the idea offered by third-wave feminists. This comes with the territory when you're talking about theories, but because of what feminism is fighting for, the resistance to it seems especially high, not only from people who might identify as antifeminist but oftentimes from within feminism itself.

SWERFs and TERFs

It might seem odd to think about emerging issues in a chapter that's been all about a theoretical perspective, but here we are. Theories aren't just born, never to change; they're revised and manipulated and massaged and challenged and reshaped over and over, generation after generation. That's why we've been talking about the different waves of feminism, a theory and philosophy that changed to meet the needs of the disciplines it serves and the world we live in.

Today, feminism is being challenged in terms of who falls under the umbrella of "feminist" and who deserves the advocacy of the larger feminist community. Some feminist circles have specifically identified two groups as questionable: sex workers and transwomen. People who believe the scope of feminism should include sex workers and transwomen have labelled their opponents SWERFs (sex-worker-exclusionary radical feminists) and TERFs (trans-exclusionary radical feminists).

For the purpose of this book, I am taking the side that both groups deserve fair treatment. That said, how do you think feminism might justify excluding one or both groups from its advocacy? Let's look at the concept of being trans. You may have heard this term in the news lately, or maybe it's come up in your introduction-to-sociology class. Maybe you have heard it used in reference to someone who is a transsexual, which is kind of related, but not exactly. A simple way to think about the difference between being transgender and transsexual is that the former refers to the mind, while the latter refers to the body. Someone who undergoes surgery and begins taking hormones to physically transition from being biologically male to biologically female (or vice versa) is transsexual. Our biological sex is assigned to us at birth, and that's what transsexuals are changing. American society treats biological sex as a dichotomy: you're either male or female, end of story. (In reality, there's a third sex—called intersex—but our society doesn't really accept this category. Most people born intersex receive plastic surgery as infants to make them female.)

Gender, unlike sex, is a much more fluid concept. Masculinity and femininity lie along a spectrum rather than being an either/or proposition. Everyone has some combination of masculine and feminine traits. There is no natural or "right" way to be male or female. This is where the idea of being transgender comes in. People who are transgender do not identify with the gender assigned to them at birth.

So, what does any of this have to do with feminism? According to some feminist thinkers—so-called TERFs—transwomen are not "real" women; they're men pretending to be women. Therefore their lives and experiences do not fall under the larger umbrella of feminism. This view is especially problematic from a criminological perspective, as violence toward the trans community is a legitimate concern. It claimed the lives of at least fourteen people in 2014 and almost twice that in 2015 ("Addressing Anti-transgender Violence" n.d.). This is clearly a hate crime, and downplaying or ignoring the experiences of these women (and men) based on the idea that they are fake is, in my view, appalling.

Presumably, the internal battle between SWERFs, TERFs, and third-wave feminists will resolve itself somehow, and feminism as a perspective will continue to evolve in ways that we can only try to predict. It is important that we continue to focus on the life experiences of all people, regardless of their gender identity or presentation. There's no turning back now, as our culture becomes more willing, in some ways, to embrace gender fluidity. That isn't to say we're at a point where the majority of people are accepting of this—for instance, a planned worldwide conversation between strictly heterosexual men advocating for the legitimacy of rape was recently shut down, so there is a pushback against the idea of accepting gender equality (Duffy 2016).

Gender- and Sexuality-Based Hate Crimes

Since we've been talking about feminist criminology as an entity that has shed light on a number of topics previously overlooked or, in some cases, intentionally ignored, I want to take a moment to discuss a couple of other concepts that I think feminist criminology deserves some, if not all, of the credit for bringing to light. Let's talk about violence in same-sex relationships and violence toward the LGBT community. This story begins with the murder on October 12, 1998, of Matthew Shepard, a student at the University of Wyoming who was robbed, beaten, tortured, and left to die by a pair of men. Shepard's death gained national attention and sparked a call for hate-crime legislation that would add another level of punishment for crimes motivated by offenders' prejudices—in this case, Shepard was gay, and prosecutors argued that is why he was targeted.

Nearly twenty years after Shepard's death, things have improved, somewhat. Our understanding of same-sex relationships is growing every year, and the taboo against being LGBT appears to be diminishing rapidly. More and more, we seem to be moving toward a point where someone's coming out as gay or lesbian is no longer newsworthy. Unfortunately, we're not there yet. From an academic perspective, research on virtually anything related to the LGBT community has been off-limits for quite some time. So, while feminist criminology helped shed light on domestic violence and sexual assault as legitimate criminal problems rooted in society, not biology, violence in same-sex relationships has not gained a lot of traction within the discipline.

This also means that crimes committed against members of the LGBT community have been treated wrongly. The seriousness of this violence was downplayed, and we've been seeing people try to perform some pretty spectacular mental gymnastics to keep hegemonic masculinity in place. Consider, for example, the "gay panic" or "trans panic" murder defense, wherein defendant(s) claim to have been pushed to a state of temporary insanity (this defense was used to explain the murder of Matthew Shepard). Obviously (I hope) you know that a hate crime is a crime committed against someone because of his or her sexual orientation, gender identity, or membership in a particular racial, ethnic, or religious group. We will explore this in much more depth later in this book.

It is also important to note that just because there now exists a legal category called hate crime, hate crimes didn't just stop happening. Take, for instance, the case of Islan Nettles, a twenty-one-year-old black trans woman from Harlem. On August 17, 2013, a group of men assaulted Nettles near her home, ironically, near a police station. The men had been following Nettles, shouting homophobic slurs at her. Attacked and beaten mercilessly, she slipped into a coma, dying days later. It appeared to be an open-and-shut case when the police arrested twenty-year-old Paris Wilson for the attack; later, another man came forward and also confessed to the attack, claiming responsibility for Nettle's death. This confession only muddies the water for the police, making it more difficult to determine who is truly at fault for this young woman's death (McCormack 2015).

We can also credit feminism, at least in part, for really pushing us toward understanding the diversity of experiences in American society. The intersectional perspective has helped the #BlackLivesMatter movement not only gain but maintain momentum, forcing our society to finally recognize the consequences of the extreme racial divide that exists in our country. Many people inside and outside the academy, myself most definitely included, have had to revisit their stances on many issues and rethink how they approach the world, from writing about crime to interacting with students and people in the community. It's also caused some people to double down and further entrench themselves in hatred.

There isn't really any way to know if or when we'll see the inner turmoil between feminism and the SWERFs and TERFs resolved, or if feminism as an idea will fracture again. I don't know what comes next after looking at gender inclusively, bringing an intersectional perspective to the forefront. I know that, obviously, these trends pose a massive challenge to the status quo and will upset a lot of people. I don't think hurt feelings will do anything to stop these ideas, though. It may seem like a weak conclusion, but the best I can tell you is to wait and see—unless you have some better idea of what's going to come next.

3

A Refresher on Theories of Crime

The critical perspective on gender and crime is only one of many, many theoretical explanations for why crime persists in our society despite our best efforts to contain it. Remember, the key here is to be open-minded; not all criminals are evil, crazy people. When we no longer accept madness as the only reason why crime occurs, the possible explanations that take its place are almost limitless.

This chapter doesn't aim to convince you that one theoretical perspective is superior to another or to present an exhaustive list of every variation of every theory. I would encourage you to learn more about the intricacies of the different theories presented here, especially if you find yourself particularly interested in their ideas about why crime occurs. Instead of giving you a complete rundown of the various theoretical perspectives, I will present the four largest, the processes each identifies as the most significant predictor of crime, and how the mechanisms identified by each vary by gender.

First, though, the purpose of these theories warrants discussion. Remember, criminology is an empirical discipline that studies crime scientifically: we aren't simply stating opinions about why we think crime happens without seeking evidence to support our views; we aren't asking for the opinions of people on the street about why they think crime might exist. Instead, we are searching for scientific explanations for why crime happens through rigorous empirical research. Now, because theory is science and not purely opinion, many people tune out of the discussion—it invokes memorizing complex equations and laws, which might not be the most appealing thing in the world for some students (we'll save that for your quantitative analysis classes). Here we will talk about ideas that you've probably been exposed to elsewhere, just in a different context. That's right you've been theorizing about behavior all this time, without realizing it! Look at you.

As we go through each of the major theoretical perspectives, try to keep this question in mind: Do the processes identified by each of these theories work the same for boys and girls, or are they more applicable to one or the other? This question is much more difficult to answer than some might think, because, as discussed in Chapter 1, gender is now commonly understood as a continuum, not a dichotomy. The relation of gender, as a spectrum of traits, to criminality is a relatively new area of inquiry. For the purposes of this book, we will talk about existing criminological theories in terms of their application to male or female behavior, with an understanding that this might not cover all possible definitions of masculinity or femininity. How the spectrum of gender applies to the major theories of crime is a fascinating question for another time.

Learning and Control

The first major theoretical perspectives we'll talk about center on the concept of *socialization*, the process by which we learn our place in the world. Through socialization we learn what's considered proper clothing to wear to school and how to behave in public; we learn that what's considered appropriate behavior around Grandma differs a lot from what's appropriate when we're with our closest friends. Socialization happens from the moment we're conceived (What kinds of clothes should the baby wear? What color should the nursery be? What should its name be?) and continues through the rest of our lives as we learn about ourselves and discover how and where we fit into the world.

One aspect of the socialization process is learning right from wrong, which is where our discussion of criminological theories comes in. We can think of this in terms of how the people in our lives—our friends and family—influence our behaviors throughout life. More than that, this dimension of criminological theory calls our attention to one of the most basic questions about human nature: Are people born naturally good or bad? A couple of major theoretical ideas deal with this process of how we're socialized into pro- or antisocial behavior.

Social bond theory (Hirschi 1969), also referred to as social control theory, posits that people are born bad and socialized to be good over time. Many types of criminal behavior speak to our most basic, animalistic impulses: crime can be fun, it can be immensely satisfying, it can fulfill an immediate need, and so on. Hirschi argues that pro-social forces in our lives can steer us away from these impulses and prevent us from engaging in criminal behavior. Hirschi names four key elements of a social bond: attachment, commitment, involvement, and belief. Note that Hirschi only applies these to pro-social institutions. You can think of *attachment* as the emotional bond you have to a pro-social institution—in terms of committing crime, the idea that being caught would make mom sad could be enough to stop anyone in his or her tracks. Another dimension of the social bond is the level of *commitment* to a pro-social institution, or whether a person has something to lose if he or she gets in trouble. To continue the previous example, maybe your bad behavior will upset mom so much that she will throw you out of the house and cut you off from your family, which, if you value those relationships, would obviously be a bad thing. The third dimension of control is *involvement* with pro-social institutions; this speaks to the amount of time spent doing things related to them. This could mean game night with your family, church softball leagues, student government—any use of your time geared toward decidedly pro-social rather than antisocial goals. Simply put, the more time you spend on pro-social activities, the less time you have for antisocial behavior. Finally, our *belief* in pro-social values can determine whether criminal (or otherwise deviant) behavior appeals to us. People who go to school may be involved in a pro-social activity, but if they do not value education, then they might feel comfortable cheating on a test or plagiarizing a paper.

In considering sources of social control, think about things in your life that you would risk losing—or people you might seriously upset—if you broke the law. If you don't want to jeopardize certain opportunities or relationships, then they are a source of social control. Therefore, social control can extend well beyond our relationships with our parents. For adolescents, relationships with friends and romantic partners can be sources of social control. Involvement in athletics, clubs, or other organizations can be a source of social control. Even school, believe it or not, can be a source of social control. This idea doesn't only apply to children and adolescents, either, as we will see when we discuss the life course perspective.

Our relationships with our parents can influence us in a different way. Gottfredson and Hirschi (1990) argue in *A General Theory of Crime* that all behavior, including crime, stems from the amount of self-control or impulse control we have, which in turn depends on whether and how our parents disciplined us when we broke the rules. Specifically, our parents (or caregivers) need to (1) recognize deviant or delinquent behavior when it occurs, (2) punish that behavior, and (3) punish it consistently. In other words, caregivers who fail to monitor a child's behavior will probably never teach him or her right from wrong, much less why delayed gratification is a necessary part of life. Other caregivers might recognize deviant or delinquent behavior but not punish it. Maybe they themselves engage in similar behavior or rationalize it as normal (boys will be boys!). Parents and caregivers who do punish their children for bad behavior must do so consistently— they must always punish it, and the severity of the punishment has to make sense relative to the severity of the misbehavior. In other words, a parent who only sometimes punishes truancy or breaking curfew isn't helping the child; a parent who responds to relatively minor offenses in extremely harsh ways while simultaneously administering little or no punishment for more serious offenses also does more harm than good.

Gottfredson and Hirschi garnered a lot of criticism for the idea that this dimension of our lives dictates and actually predicts all future behavior—and that, for each and every one of us, our level of self-control is set by age seven. The idea that individual criminality has been etched in stone, for all intents and purposes, by such a young age was a major point of contention. Subsequent research has demonstrated that while important in understanding how and why crime happens, self-control isn't the only factor; nor is it necessarily stable across one's life (Burt, Simons, and Simons 2006; Na and Paternoster 2012). That said, while not as concrete as Gottfredson and Hirschi imagined, and perhaps not the single most important factor in determining whether someone will engage in criminal (or deviant or risky) behavior, self-control is still an important factor to consider.

Now, what, if any, gender differences exist with regard to how social control and self-control might prevent criminal behavior? The answer seems pretty straightforward. First, in their research on adolescents, Booth, Farrell, and Varano (2008) found that parental attachment had no relationship to female delinquency, but strong parental attachment could inhibit serious delinquency in boys. This isn't to say that it doesn't matter in general whether girls have a strong emotional bond to their parents; it just doesn't matter in preventing serious delinquency, defined as gang membership, frequent physical fighting, and carrying a weapon, all of which are dimensions of violence. In other words, a strong emotional attachment to their parents can make boys less likely to be violent. De Li and Mackenzie (2003) found that, among adult offenders, social bonds inhibited future offending for men but facilitated offending among women. This finding is not to be taken lightly, especially because it's so confusing. Having good relationships can make women more likely to commit crime? How? Why? De Li and Mackenzie offer a number of possible explanations. Perhaps these women are being pulled into criminal offending because of a romantic relationship; maybe their partner is offending and they feel offending themselves will help build and maintain the relationship; or perhaps the partner is forcing them to commit crime. De Li and Mackenzie also note that the types of

intimate partners available to women with a criminal background
are limited, because society is less forgiving of female than of
male criminals; so women with a criminal history don't really have
access to the same pool of romantic partners as other women. De
Li and Mackenzie further argue that other sources of social control, like work or school, might actually serve as criminal opportunities for some women (e.g., you can't embezzle if you don't
have a job; you can't sell drugs in school if you aren't in school),
especially those who never really got a foot into either of those
worlds in the past. While perhaps this is the case for some
women, it feels like an awfully cynical conclusion to me and definitely something that should be looked into further. It is worth
noting that De Li and Mackenzie exclusively looked at people on
probation, which raises a cause-and-effect issue, since we don't
really know what these individuals' relationships were like prior
to prison—we don't know how their incarceration affected the
quality of their relationships. However, this isn't to say their
research is without merit; as we'll see later in this book, the quality of a person's postprison relationships is vitally important to
whether he or she will offend again.

What about self-control? This is trickier to parse because it has
different dimensions: risk taking, impulsivity, selfishness, and so
on. On one hand, DeLisi et al. (2010) found that among a sample
of institutionalized youths, self-control was a greater predictor of
misconduct within the institution among males than among
females. LaGrange and Silverman (1999) found evidence that the
relationship between the various components of self-control and
delinquency did vary by gender, such that generally speaking, self-
control was a greater predictor of delinquency among boys than
among girls. Yet, different dimensions of self-control (i.e., an
attraction to risk-taking behaviors versus impulsivity) could
explain delinquency among girls and boys differently, making it
difficult to conclude that low self-control is a stronger predictor
overall for boys.

Social and self-control theorists take the basic approach that
everyone is born with an innate desire to commit crime and that
we learn how to conform. Social learning theory takes the oppo-

site approach, arguing that everyone is born inherently good and learns bad behavior over time. Edwin Sutherland first developed this perspective in 1947, when he proposed his theory of differential association. Sutherland wanted to examine how basically good people transform over time into criminals. Like social control and self-control proponents, he argued that behavior is learned—but rather than focusing on parental relationships, he theorized that criminal behavior stems from our relationships with our friends. Sutherland argued that the more people you knew with an excess of criminal definitions—that is, a worldview that favors breaking the rules more often than following them—the likelier you were to become a criminal. He outlined nine key points in how this process works, concluding that by submerging yourself in a delinquent or otherwise deviant peer group, you would learn the motivations for engaging in these behaviors— why they are good, cool, acceptable, justifiable, and so on—as well as the technical skills required to participate in certain acts (i.e., how to hotwire a car, how to make crack cocaine).

The problem with Sutherland's original hypothesis is that it views people as passive, as if we absorb our peers' perspectives through osmosis. We know that learning is much more complicated than that. If you put down this book right now and enrolled in an upper-level class on theoretical physics, you wouldn't necessarily become the next Stephen Hawking just by sitting in on the lectures (although, you never know!). Burgess and Akers (1966) first revisited Sutherland's original work and emphasized the importance not only of differential association but also of differential reinforcement, the idea that deviant peers can pass along the knowledge that some rules aren't always enforced. Laws on the books aren't always taken seriously or rigorously enforced, and kids learn who will be all bark and no bite when it comes to making sure they follow the rules to the letter. The gradual decriminalization of marijuana is a good example of this: while smoking marijuana recreationally is still illegal in the majority of the country as of this writing, police officers in some cities aren't going to throw the book at someone for possessing a small amount of marijuana for personal use (note that this wasn't always the case, and some people are serving a lot of prison time for possessing a small amount of marijuana). The final aspect of social learning theory is imitation: it's still up to the individual to take the step to replicate a friend's delinquent behavior. In other words, putting a kid into a larger group of adolescents who are delinquent in some way doesn't automatically ensure that the kid will also become delinquent—he or she must admire and respect the people committing these delinquent acts as well. When kids see delinquents as role models, they themselves are more likely to become delinquent.

The ideas developed by Gottfredson and Hirschi, Sutherland, and Burgess and Akers are all core to criminological theory, especially to understanding how our relationships with the people around us can influence our behavior. That said, research has shed much light on the complex ways kids interact with each other and the world around them. How do kids respond to bad behavior among their peers? What about kids who don't fit in? Do seemingly pro-social institutions and activities actually reinforce delinquent behaviors? We'll explore these questions further in Chapter 4, when we discuss juvenile delinquency in more detail.

How do the mechanisms here differ by gender? Do any theories not apply to male or female behavior? Conversely, do any theories uniquely explain masculine or feminine reactions to potentially criminogenic stimuli? The answer is yes and no. Rather than wondering whether one theory or another is completely inapplicable to one gender, we should ask ourselves if the various processes identified by these theories work the same for women and men. Isn't that the same question? Not quite. Think about it like this: Is there a gender difference in how we relate to our friends and family? Do men and women experience the same kinds of stress and cope with it similarly? Do we age the same? Allowing for slight differences means that these theories, overall, may still be valid. There's no sense in throwing the baby out with the bathwater.

We'll start by revisiting learning theories and asking whether girls and boys interact with their friends in the same way. Remember, social learning and control perspectives view crime as something that we're socialized into or away from. Heimer and De

Coster (1999) do an excellent job of comparing the mechanisms in social control and self-control with differential association and the different ways relationships can affect criminal behavior in boys and girls. They find that, at least with regard to violent delinquency, criminal definitions affect girls less because they are less likely to be exposed to delinquent peers (although girls exposed to definitions favorable to violence are influenced by them). Girls are more likely to be influenced by emotional familial bonds than boys, who respond more to discipline. Furthermore, gender socialization plays a key part in this, especially in terms of traditional or stereotypical gender roles—for many girls, the idea of being violent runs so counter to the idea of femininity that engaging in violence is practically unthinkable. Boys, on the other hand, are taught from a young age that part of masculinity is an ability, perhaps even a willingness, to be violent if necessary. In this sense, boys learn violence more readily.

When thinking about the ways that peers can affect behavior during adolescence, the original versions of differential association (Sutherland 1947) and social learning theory (Burgess and Akers 1966) treated one's peer group as a homogenous block of people—everyone was basically the same. But we know that it's more complex than that, and treating teen friendship groups as uniform does them a disservice. Haynie et al. (2005) broaden the social learning concept to look at the ways that intimate partners can influence delinquent behavior. They find that romantic partners can have a separate and distinct influence on delinquency above and beyond the effect of having delinquent friends. Furthermore, they also find that romantic partners have a greater influence on minor delinquency (truancy, smoking cigarettes, drinking, skipping school, and fighting) in girls than in boys—in other words, at least in terms of less serious behavior, girls are more likely than boys to be influenced by whom they're dating.

In fact, the relationship between delinquency—especially violent delinquency—peer groups, and gender is incredibly problematic during adolescence, especially for males. The context in which misbehavior occurs can also be confusing. At worst, some males are rewarded for it; at best, it is simply overlooked, but not necessarily frowned upon, because of who they are. This can happen in a couple of ways.

Athletics is often overlooked as a source of antisocial behavior. Many youths who attend school are only interested in playing sports throughout the school year—academics might not come up on their radar as even remotely important. Because our culture values athleticism over intelligence, there has been an ongoing concern that schools will go to great lengths to bolster student-athletes' dismal grades and pass them along to make their teams as competitive as possible (for an example of this at the collegiate level, see the ongoing scandal at the University of North Carolina, which fraudulently passed several thousand students but is, as of this writing, not at risk of losing its accreditation). No one wants to acknowledge this elephant in the room, despite evidence that student-athletes are at a disadvantage academically (Maloney and McCormick 1993) or at least face unique problems that hinder academic achievement (Crosnoe 2002).

Furthermore, because sports in general are so popular, people tend to go out of their way to justify continued participation in them, even when presented with evidence that doing so might not be worthwhile: sports (allegedly) build character, tenacity, leadership skills, and so on. Are all the outcomes positive, though? Kreager (2007a) focuses on the relationship between sports and the likelihood of adolescent violence. He argues that while participation in sports may very well instill these positive qualities in young people, to be successful athletically one must also develop a number of potentially less desirable character traits, including aggression and a tendency to intimidate. While perhaps contributing to success on the field, these traits might not translate well into other dimensions of life. In other words, the constant ferocity and physicality required to be a successful power forward or defensive lineman do not make one a good student, boyfriend, employee, and so on.

Kreager (2007a) finds that the relationship between sports and violence depends on the type of sport—with students involved with football or wrestling more likely to get into fights than students involved with noncontact sports like baseball or tennis.

Moreover, he also finds that students with friends on the football team are more likely to get into fights than students not connected to the team socially. This could indicate that participation in aggressive or violent sports generally and involvement in violent delinquency could be learned behaviors, in keeping with differential association and social learning theory. That makes sense. However, this conclusion could also reflect what's called a selection effect. Does football makes kids violent? Or are violent kids attracted to football? If the former, then it would seem reasonable—albeit costly and unpopular—for schools to abandon their football programs outright. However, if football itself isn't causing the problem, but rather acting as a staging area for potentially violent youths to come together and bond, then disbanding the football program might only force these kids to find some other avenue for violence—perhaps the lack of practice and games would lead them to get into more fights.

When talking about sports, it's easy to get up on a soapbox and rant and rave about how obviously bad they are for any number of reasons. This attitude comes from an adult perspective, which has the benefit of hindsight. But we aren't talking about adults. When trying to explain juvenile behavior (as we'll see in Chapter 4), you can't think about things the way an adult would. You have to try to put yourself in the position of the kids involved. When we do this, violence can make a lot of sense.

Stress and Culture

Another possible explanation for how and why crime occurs in terms of the external forces acting on us has to do not with the quality of our relationships, but rather with the messages we receive from the people we value about what's important in life. These messages, together with how we're treated in general by those around us, can have a seriously negative influence on our behavior.

This line of thinking began with Émile Durkheim's (1897 [1979]) concept of *anomie*. Have you ever found yourself in a situation where you didn't feel like you belonged? Have you ever experienced a substantial amount of emotional distress because you felt so out of step with the world around you? Have you felt like you just didn't fit in and didn't know how to follow the rules? Then you've experienced some degree of anomie.

Though Durkheim was writing about the experience of norm-lessness in late nineteenth-century Europe, his idea is certainly applicable to life in the United States. Robert Merton's (1938) strain theory is a prime example of the application of anomie to American society. Merton argued that willingness to adopt the work ethic associated with belief in the American dream was related to the propensity to commit crime. Specifically, Merton identified five different modes of adaptation to the American dream and its demands on individual behavior: conformity, ritual-ism, innovation, retreatism, and rebellion. This typology, or set of categories, depends on two things: (1) whether a person agrees with goals generally agreed on throughout society (i.e., striving for material wealth), and (2) whether a person buys into the cul-turally agreed-on means of accomplishing these goals (i.e., years of education and dedicated labor). Conformists accept both the goals and the means of accomplishing them. Ritualists reject the goals but accept the means—in other words, they're comfortable in the middle of the pack, have no real desire to work hard to earn promotion, won't put in the extra effort on a project, and so on. They're content with being average. Most people fall into one of these two categories.

Where do criminals fit into this typology? They fall into the remaining three categories, though that doesn't mean everyone in these groups is by definition a criminal. For instance, innovators, the third group, believe in culturally valued goals but not the means of achieving them. This doesn't mean they're antisocial; rather, they're the ones who are going to take risks to develop new ideas and technology. Bill Gates is a prime example of an innovator, and he is hardly a master criminal. However, some innovators do commit crimes. People who sell drugs, for example, might be trying to make money faster than they would in a con-ventional job; the same could be said for prostitutes. Some white-collar or corporate criminals may also be innovators; some of the biggest white-collar cases in recent history have involved people who found innovative, yet illegal, ways to make money.

Retreatists, the fourth group in the typology, reject both the cultural goals and the means to achieve them. They give up, in other words. Think of someone who drops out of school to live on the streets rather than deal with the harsh reality of final exams, for example. Retreatists run away from the system and refuse to play the game. This by itself doesn't make them criminals, but when you fully reject the rules of society, chances are you will end up committing some crime. There are laws that punish people who retreat, in a way rendering their very existence criminal. For example, several major US cities have effectively criminalized homelessness, making it illegal for the homeless to sleep in public spaces. Some have gone so far as to install concrete spikes on sidewalks in places that would provide attractive temporary shelters. Note that by no means does this criminalization apply to all retreatists—someone who chooses to inhabit a cabin in the woods, living off the land and off the grid, isn't committing any crime (assuming that person owns the land, pays for any public utilities used, etc.).

Most criminals, however, fall into the category of rebels. Like retreatists, they reject the culturally valued goals and means. But whereas retreatists stop there and effectively drift through life, rebels substitute a new set of goals and means; they change the rules of the game altogether. Achieving the American dream through hard work holds no appeal. This rejection of the American dream stems beyond the notion of hard work for material gain, too—this encompasses other aspects of the dream, like the idea that anyone has the freedom to accomplish these things. People who rebel against the system can include members of political groups whose actions get them arrested—for instance, people who are arrested during the course of protesting would be considered rebellious. Some gang members might also be considered rebels, depending on the context of their behavior and relationship with the surrounding community. Some could also be thought of as innovators, depending on those same factors. Slotting individuals and groups into one of Merton's categories can be tricky, but that's OK. The true purpose is to define different ideal categories that exhaust all possible modes of adaptation.

Elijah Anderson (1999) revisited the idea of cultural norms and values related to the possibility of leading a successful life in the United States in *Code of the Street*. Anderson's study examined how violence in inner-city Philadelphia persisted, despite numerous legislative attempts to eliminate it, and how members of the community perceived violent behavior. Anderson's findings triggered a new line of research based on his code-of-the-street hypothesis: that violence persists in many urban areas because of a lack of economic opportunity (which exists for a number of reasons, including, but not limited to, an economic shift away from manufacturing jobs and the systemic racism that pervades society). The inability to achieve typical middle-class goals, Anderson argues, has led some within these communities to reject the existing rules of the system altogether and replace them with their own. The ideal of respect has replaced quintessential middle-class goals like a salaried job and a house with a white picket fence and two-car garage. Respect, Anderson argues, is an incredibly rare and precious commodity, and those who have it must remain constantly vigilant against those who might rise up and challenge them. This is why violence persists despite constant policing and harsh punishments—one has to be willing to become violent, extremely so if need be, to gain or maintain respect. It's an unwinnable game that many people continue to play for (a perceived) lack of access to any other legitimate form of success.

Importantly, Anderson (1999) and others who have done similar work (i.e., Goffman 2014) do not label everyone living in an impoverished nonwhite community as having gone mad looking for respect. His theory applies only to a small percentage of residents. In fact, most people living in disadvantaged neighborhoods are decent, hardworking, law-abiding citizens. Unfortunately, violence in our society is incredibly corrosive, and even the nonviolent residents of these communities must be hypersensitive to their surroundings and willing to defend themselves, lest they become targets (Anderson 1999).

If this street code exists as a means of protecting oneself from violence—on the theory that no one will mess with someone with a reputation for going off at the slightest perceived threat—then shouldn't this idea of respect create a sort of stratification system, or some other way of limiting the amount of violence that occurs? Based on Anderson's idea that the code would protect people from the violence around them, Stewart, Schreck, and Simons (2006) looked at a sample of 720 African American youths from 259 neighborhoods to assess how adopting the code of the street affected the likelihood of their being victimized sometime in the future. They found that in reality the opposite held: youths who adopted the code of the street and made violence and respect a core part of their lives were at a much greater risk of future victimization than those adolescents who chose not to participate. This may or may not surprise you, but the best strategy to avoid violence, regardless of who you are or where you live, is to not engage in it.

Anderson's work on the code of the street and subsequent research into everyday life in disadvantaged areas took place alongside another line of inquiry into the role of anomie in our lives. Robert Agnew (1992), drawing on the work of Merton and Durkheim before him, developed the general strain theory (GST), which builds on prior research on strain and crime by acknowledging that there is more to life than just work and money. Struggling to attain a certain lifestyle is stressful and obviously relates directly to attaining culturally valued goals. But not all sources of stress in life relate directly to money. Agnew originally proposed that stress could result from three different mechanisms: failure to achieve positively valued goals, the (threatened) introduction of negatively valued stimuli, and the (threatened) removal of positively valued stimuli; think of losing a best friend or needing to quit a club you love but can't fit into your schedule. Again, this stress could certainly relate directly or indirectly to the cultural goals Merton (1938) identified in his conceptualization of strain, but again, Agnew recognized that stress can come from other sources as well. Children whose parents are divorcing may experience a tremendous spike in stress, for example, that doesn't necessarily relate to any economic issues. On the flip side, being with an abusive parent or a partner is obviously stressful. When that person comes home from work, the sound of ice cubes hitting the bottom of a glass can trigger serious stress. Even teenage melodrama—Who said what about who? When? What! No! I can't believe she said that!—is a source of stress for the participants involved and has nothing to do with money.

Agnew (2001) later amended GST to further clarify different ways that stressful experiences could trigger criminal behavior. He argues that there are two types of strain: objective and subjective. Objective strain is almost universally viewed as stressful. For instance, no one wants to go hungry or experience a serious physical assault. Subjective strain is stressful to the people impacted but may be viewed as positive or neutral by others. For example, a divorce may be stressful for the couple involved, but perhaps the wife's family is relieved to be rid of a good-for-nothing son-in-law who won't shut up about the textbook he's writing. Watching your favorite team lose a championship might be a heartbreaking experience that you feel you can only remedy by publicly setting fire to your couch, but someone who doesn't "get" sports isn't going to view this loss as worth committing arson over. Agnew also argues that four characteristics of a stressful experience could lead to criminal behavior: the person(s) involved (1) see the stressor as unjust, (2) perceive it as high in magnitude (extremely stressful), (3) associate it with low social control, and (4) find some incentive to engage in crime as a means of directly reducing or eliminating that stressor.

Agnew (2001) argues that an experience will be seen as unjust if it provokes a negative emotional response that is conducive to criminal coping, such as anger, and violates some culturally agreed on norm. For instance, falling victim to a crime could provoke anger and be viewed as unfair. Similarly, students in an introductory criminology class might view as unfair a requirement to write a seventy-page research paper for a course of that level and feel quite angry about it. In trying to determine what factors might make one stressor seem higher in magnitude than another, Agnew suggests we look at its duration, frequency, recency, and centrality (how much it effects our lives). Someone who is constantly victimized and severely injured after each encounter might perceive his or her victimization as higher in magnitude than someone who gets into a playground slapping fight. Unexpectedly losing a job that is key to your identity is much more difficult to deal with than being laid off from a job you're ambivalent about; it could also create a sense of reduced social control and encourage criminal coping. Loss of a home or job could force someone to engage in crime to make ends meet, and the feeling that they have little left to lose gives them little reason to remain on the right side of the law.

Agnew (2002) further builds on GST by introducing the idea of vicarious strain, as well as expanding on a previous discussion of anticipated (threatened) strain (Agnew 1992). We'll focus on vicarious strain here. This idea posits that experiences that don't directly affect you but still cause distress to people close to you can lead to some involvement in crime. Agnew argues that this especially applies to violent victimization: if someone close to you is victimized, you might feel compelled to strike back at his or her attacker(s) because your loved one is angry and wants revenge. This vicarious victimization could also create anticipated strain, depending on the motivation for the attack: it could instill in kids a fear that their minority status (for instance) is all the justification someone needs to hurt them, which could in turn lead them to skip school to avoid potential harm.

We should also think about how the processes outlined by GST relate to gender (Agnew 1992). Remember, Agnew argues that stress leads to criminal or otherwise deviant behavior, but not all stressors are the same—they vary in magnitude, duration, and so on. When we add gender into the discussion, two hopefully obvious questions should immediately come to mind. First, do men and women cope with stress the same way? Second, do men and women experience the same types of stress?

We should think in terms not of whether men or women handle stress better, necessarily, but of how they experience it. Broidy and Agnew (1997) discuss research (i.e., Mirowsky and Ross 1995) on women and men's emotional reactions to stressful conditions.

While it might seem anecdotally obvious that men get angrier than women, research actually shows that everyone has basically the same chance of becoming angry when facing stress. The difference, Broidy and Agnew argue, has to do with the emotions that accompany anger: for women, these are depression, guilt, and anxiety; for men, it's moral outrage (A. Campbell 1993; Broidy and Agnew 1997).

Neighborhoods

So far, we've talked about how the people in our lives can influence us directly or indirectly, pushing us toward or pulling us away from criminal behavior. Criminological theories haven't focused only on how the people in our lives can affect us, however. The places where we live also play a major part in shaping us and can substantially influence criminality.

The idea that the places where we live can influence our behavior is a bedrock of sociological research, dating back to work done at the University of Chicago in the early part of the twentieth century. The Chicago School founded urban sociology in the United States. For the purposes of understanding the relationship between neighborhoods or cities and crime, we turn to the work of Robert Park and Ernest Burgess (1924). They studied the geography of Chicago, with a specific focus on what the different sections of the city were like and where crime was happening. They found that crime clustered in parts of Chicago they classified as zones of transition, located between the growing industrial areas and the working-class residential areas; they applied the "transition" tag because the growing industrial areas would eventually subsume the working-class residential areas, pushing the residents further away from the city center. Because the zones would inevitably be swallowed up, they provided obvious staging areas for crime, because the current occupants no longer had a reason to care about what happened there, and the future tenants would be tearing everything down and starting over from scratch.

It is important to remember what was happening in the United States at the beginning of the twentieth century and how cities of that era compare to cities of today. Park and Burgess and other early social ecologists and urban sociologists were making their observations during a time of unprecedented growth—it is easy to look at their diagrams of concentric circles and imagine them pulsing outward, growing larger and larger as the city grows and expands. However, the late twentieth century saw the end of this rapid growth for many US cities, rendering the idea of zones of transition virtually irrelevant: if crime is a characteristic of growth, what happens when cities stop growing?

Today, we don't think about cities in terms of population growth and its effect on crime; rather we look at how where you live can influence individual criminality. We will explore this in much more detail in Chapter 5, but I do want to touch on it briefly here. Social disorganization theory (Shaw and McKay 1942, 1969) looks at crime in terms of neighborhoods characteristics instead of individual behaviors. What is it about some neighborhoods that makes them more likely to have more crime than others? According to the theory, neighborhoods with a high degree of residential turnover (meaning people aren't living there for a long time) and a high degree of racial/ethnic diversity—which historically hasn't engendered a lot of trust among people—have bigger problems with crime. Really it boils down to the barriers that these factors raise. In terms of population turnover, if you're not going to be living in the same place for a long time, you're not going to care about what's happening in your community. In terms of race and ethnicity, we've always used those as excuses to hate each other and wage war against each other; neighborhoods with a high level of ethnic diversity are more likely to be hotbeds of conflict. When both factors are present, crime is more likely to develop because no one is invested enough in the community to stop it.

Because we will be exploring gender and crime as they relate to neighborhoods more thoroughly in Chapter 5, I want to hold off on that discussion here. Instead, I want you to think about what specific aspects of a neighborhood could act as either protective or risk factors for crime, and how men and women, or boys and girls, might approach them differently. For instance, Bjerregaard and Smith (1993) found that gang involvement related to risk for substance abuse and future delinquency among both boys and girls; however, not doing well in school was a bigger issue for females than males. Why do you think that is? What else could be going on in our neighborhoods?

The Life Course Perspective

The life course perspective, one of the most recent developments in criminological theory, takes a wildly different approach to studying crime than all of the theoretical perspectives that preceded it. Rather than identifying some social or psychological factor as the single most dominant explanation of criminal behavior, it holds that all previously identified theoretical perspectives have some merit. The life course perspective recognizes that none of the processes identified by prior theorists exist in a bubble: our friends and families can play some role, the neighborhood we live in can affect our peer groups, the stressors our families experience when we're young can take their toll, and so on. Trying to prove that one or another is the dominant factor in criminal behavior is, in the minds of life course theorists, a fool's errand. Further, in their view, all previous theories have ignored one of the most basic aspects of life, the one thing that invariably affects all of us: time.

While other theoretical perspectives focus entirely on what causes crime, the life course perspective calls attention not only to the many reasons why people offend but also to those factors that keep them offending and those that cause them to desist. Because the life course perspective makes no real argument about what causes crime—other than the fact that time is incredibly important—this section focuses entirely on the multitude of ways that time can affect our lives.

Glen Elder Jr. (1994) developed the basis for the life course perspective. He lists four key components to this method of thinking about how time affects us: (1) lives in historical times, (2) the timing of lives, (3) linked lives, and (4) human agency. As Elder puts it, the life course is constrained by the historical era in which we live: the time in which we live limits our life choices and chances. Put simply, think about what your grandparents' or great-grandparents' lives were like and the choices that they made. Some of the basics might be similar—fighting in wars, fighting to build a life for themselves—but much will be different. Your grandmother might not have had the opportunity to go to college, and if she did, her choices of major were probably quite limited—if she even graduated. Maybe your grandfather began his career as soon as he finished high school. Even the commonalities across generations are different in their own way. The way wars are fought, for example, has drastically changed during recent American history, and so while the thread of war can tie past generations together, the methods of fighting—and their impact on civilian life—differ substantially. And think of the cultural differences—Grandma never had a Twitter beef with anyone when she was growing up (though it is entirely possible that she's having one now); Grandpa never had to worry about someone turning a picture of him passed out into a meme (again, possible now). This isn't to say that previous generations had it any better or worse; life was just different. The period in which we live largely dictates the shape our lives.

The timing of lives refers to the sequence of events in our lives. We experience a series of generally expected accomplishments or transitions: graduating from high school and possibly college, getting married, having a kid or two, and hopefully one day retiring. Many of these transitions accompany especially significant ages: sixteen, eighteen, twenty-one, thirty, and so on. Elder (1994) makes the key point that the timing of these transitions can have immense importance. For instance, according to the Pew Research Center (Cohn et al. 2011), the median age at first marriage is 26.5 years for women and 28.7 years for men. This means that someone who gets married for the first time at, say, twenty years old, experiences this transition much earlier than most people. Someone who gets married for the first time at forty is making this transition later than normal and may experience some stigma for it, likely in the form of awkward jokes about how much the family paid the new spouse to finally take him or her off their hands. This type of awful dad joking might seem harmless, but it's still stigmatizing nonetheless.

The concept of linked lives simply means that we are all connected—that the decisions we make affect not only us, but the people around us, for better or worse. A person's choice of career, for example, has a direct effect on the quality of life of their immediate family, should they marry and have children. In this scenario, the parent may begin abusing alcohol as a way to cope with the stress of their work, but their alcohol abuse is also going to have an effect on their partner and child. We can expand this beyond the family dynamic into other potential relationships, and start thinking about the ways in which our behavior affects the lives of our friends, our coworkers, and our neighbors. In short, the concept of linked lives reminds us that our actions do not take place in a vacuum.

Finally, human agency refers to the idea that, despite all the external and internal forces acting on us and pushing us in different and oftentimes contradictory directions—family expectations for school, religious expectations for morality, friends' expectations for socializing, internal motivations, and societal barriers constructed around race, gender, and sexuality—we all have within us some ability to fight against these currents and change our station in life.

The concepts developed by Elder laid the groundwork for a life course approach to sociological research, but how can we apply this perspective to the study of crime? In truth, addition of the life course perspective has been one of the most significant developments in criminological research in the past twenty years or more. The role of time is incredible; it allows us to look at theoretical mechanisms over the long term, to identify different types of offenders, and to think in a completely new way about offending. Whereas prior theoretical work often demanded that people choose a side, the life course perspective recognizes that all theoretical viewpoints are valid in their own right. Any of the theories discussed up to this point can be considered in terms of time: How do your relationships with your peers change over time?

How does social control manifest itself in your life over time? How do we see ourselves differently as we grow up? And so on. Furthermore, by examining time and the aging process as an undeniable and inevitable part of life, this perspective has helped us reframe criminality: instead of thinking about how and/or why people become involved in crime, ask how and why they remain involved and what causes those people who stop offending to do so.

Life course criminology is rapidly growing as a subset of criminology, and I can't possibly highlight all the advancements in the field in this text. Instead, I want to highlight a few core ideas that uniquely show what the life course perspective is all about. First, the work of Sampson and Laub (1992, 1993, 1997; Laub and Sampson 1993) develops the idea that change matters throughout our lives and that we shouldn't think of our lives as collections of individual experiences. Sampson and Laub argue that change is a vital component of life. Essentially, this relates to a very basic philosophical question: Can people change over time? Proponents of stability of behavior say no, that character traits related to criminality like aggression (Huesmann et al. 1984) or impulse control (Gottfredson and Hirschi 1990) are established at a very young age and remain constant. Age, they argue, is irrelevant (Gottfredson and Hirschi 1986); it should be viewed as a natural process that affects everyone equally and is not worth studying. Adulthood is not important, in their view.

Sampson and Laub obviously disagree. They argue that understanding criminality necessitates an understanding of people across the entirety of their lives, not just a focus on a very limited period in which certain traits become fully established. Take, for example, the concept of desistance, which refers to the transition from being a criminal to not being a criminal, or from being involved in crime to no longer being involved in crime. Desistance may be about a change in a person's state of mind or opportunity to commit crime. The criminal justice system only notices so many people's criminal behavior; not everyone who commits a crime in a given year is arrested, prosecuted, and convicted. As such, it stands to reason that a great many people manage to go their entire lives without experiencing significant interference from the criminal justice system and can offend however they choose (for the purposes of this example, we'll treat all types of crime equally, though obviously extreme cases, like murder, don't apply as well as other, less serious crimes). If these offenders aren't caught by the system, what else could possibly cause them to desist? Sampson and Laub (1992) argue that the driving force behind desistance is a change experienced by the offender; in other words, something has happened to motivate desistance. Otherwise they would still be offending, wouldn't they? Laub and Sampson (1992, 1993) argue that these changes are events that steer the individual toward a more pro-social lifestyle. Things like stable employment or marriage give these people a stake in the pro-social world and a reason to behave that they wouldn't have otherwise had. This is called age-graded social control. The motivation for their behavior is identical to the elements of social control theory first stated by Hirschi (1969), only now, rather than something pushed onto young people as a means of preventing them from offending, social control is viewed as a way to bring antisocial persons back into the mainstream. With this argument Sampson and Laub recognize that although the ideas behind social control theory are good, as is the idea of imposing or creating these bonds for children and adolescents, sometimes you have to let people come around to an idea on their own. Plenty of people with a bad relationship with parents or siblings might be soured on the idea (and value) of a family later in life. Plenty of people who had bad experiences with school might not be bonded to or believe in the value of hard work. Being rebellious and defiant is a part of adolescent culture in the United States—and no amount of pleading, begging, negotiating, screaming, or crying will get teenagers to behave the way you think they should. Look at your classmates—we all know there's a kid in here who wouldn't read for class if paid to. The point is, for these individuals, the idea of pro-social bonds might not take in childhood, and they have come around to it on their own. In fact, the strongest predictor of desistance is marriage (Sampson, Laub, and Wimer 2006).

While there is agreement among researchers that marriage is a major cause of desistance, the mechanics behind this transition are up for debate. It could simply be age-graded social control. To be clear, this idea suggests that people desist from crime to avoid losing a spouse—just as social control theory as originally stated could be thought of as the "mom's mad/sad" theory of crime, the idea being that a significant other's anger or shame is the driving force here.

But what else happens when a person gets married, assuming that it's a good marriage? Warr (1998) shows that a good marriage brings with it a change in how we spend our time and with whom. Single life might have involved nights out with the guys and exposure to and involvement in all kinds of bad ideas. A good marriage changes that. Spending more time with a spouse means spending less time with those people in our lives who might lead us astray. You may have seen this in your own lives, too, as you or your friends have entered into serious intimate relationships. Slowly but surely, your friends are becoming other couples. And that's fine.

The arguments by Laub and Sampson (1993) and Warr (1998) view the individual getting married as a fairly passive participant in this transition, like they just woke up one day and they were married. Remember, though, that Elder (1994) argued that human agency was a key component of the life course. From a marriage standpoint, this suggests that change brought on by marriage could really be a function of the individual. For example, Giordano, Cernkovich, and Rudolph (2002) examine Warr's (1998) research on changes in friendship networks and argue that while marriage can reduce time spent with delinquent peers, it isn't an absolute guarantee that these forces will disappear from a person's life. To prevent delinquent peers from influencing future behavior, they argue, the individual has to be motivated to change. How, then, does this happen? They argue that adulthood brings with it a number of cognitive changes that reduce the likelihood of committing crime—a self-perception as less easily influenced by friends, less concerned with looking tough in the eyes of peers, or less concerned with being thought of as cool—which also increase the likelihood of desistance. Are these transitions as important as marriage? No, but they still play a part, and our transitions into other adult roles could help spur our own cognitive shift.

Not only do our perceptions of ourselves change as we age, directly or indirectly due to adult transitions, but our emotions change as well. The emotions associated with a good marriage could also explain why this specific transition drives the desistance process. Giordano, Schroeder, and Cernkovich (2007) demonstrate that the positive emotions associated with a good marriage can cause someone to cease offending. They argue that these emotions replace any positive (or negative) emotions associated with criminal activities; in other words, the negative emotions driving criminal behavior, or the positive emotions gained from engaging in it, give way to a greater level of happiness that comes with marital bliss.

Giordano et al. (2002) are also concerned with whether the traditional measures of desistance apply to both men and women, as the concept of social control appears to apply more accurately to male than to female behavior. In fact, in their research, the idea of marriage and employment leading to desistance didn't really play out the way that the theory suggested it would. From the interviews conducted with people over the course of their project, they conclude that marriage might not have the same meaning for people today as it did for the people in the data used to develop the idea of age-graded social control. In fact, many of the men and women in their study were worse off, in general, than the men in the original Sampson and Laub (1992) work, suggesting a generational shift in how the desistance process works.

Giordano et al. (2002) do show a considerable amount of overlap between the lives of the men and women in their study. They report the same problems and types of changes, with differences emerging in the catalysts for change and how their identities transform. Giordano et al. found that women tended to identify their children as their reason for changing and to focus on their religious identities overall, whereas men cited prison as a reason for changing their behavior and focused more on the overall family man identity. Both are significant social psychological changes that can be very difficult, and both are obviously geared toward bettering the life of the individual, but the path to righteousness varies.

While the relationship between age-graded transitions and criminal behavior has yielded a fruitful area of research, I want to emphasize again the term *age-graded*. This is important because, especially with marriage, the parties involved should be emotionally and psychologically ready. The major transitions identified by Sampson and Laub—marriage, stable employment, and military service—also typically entail a significant amount of prep time. In all cases though, the question is whether or not the person is prepared to make the transition, and that readiness almost always depends on age. That said, the early exit hypothesis provides another way to think about crime over the life course. This approach demonstrates how victimization during adolescence can cause premature entry into adulthood with the assumption of adult roles that one is not psychologically or financially (or both) ready for. For instance, Hagan and Foster (2001) show that violence in intimate relationships during adolescence increases the likelihood of a teen's running away, dropping out of school, developing depression, and having suicidal thoughts. Haynie et al. (2009) find that not only does direct exposure to violence increase the risk of these transitions, but so can indirect exposure to violence (i.e., witnessing victimization). Kuhl, Warner, and Wilczak (2012) also show that youths who experience serious violence are at greater risk of early marriage or cohabitation. Considering the number of youths who engage in violence every year (not to mention the presumably much higher number who are victimized but don't come forward, especially in intimate partner relationships), the importance of reducing violence among adolescents becomes that much more serious.

But what about those victimized youths who do transition into adulthood earlier than they should? What happens next? We can think of this as a sort of downward spiral, in which this premature transition severely limits the individual's ability to succeed in other areas of life—obviously, the chances of finding a career that pays six figures are diminished considerably if you've dropped out of high school—and requires adjusted expectations for the future and new definitions of success. In a society obsessed with materialism and material wealth, accepting the reality that they will never have all the shiny toys advertised on TV is tough for some people. We're taught that we're failures if we can't purchase all the nice products on the market, and no one likes to think of him- or herself as a failure. That can then lead to depression, substance use and abuse, and maybe even suicide (Hagan and Foster 2001).

As I mentioned at the beginning of this chapter, there are a lot of ways we can attempt to explain criminal behavior, and the theories discussed here are by no means the only ideas out there. We can be socialized into both pro- and antisocial behavior through our interactions with our family and friends; we can find ourselves pushed into crime by the culture of our neighborhood, or we can turn to crime as the solution for some stress in our life. Crime can be situational. Crime can also just be a phase in someone's life. In any event, the explanation for why crime happens is multifaceted.

4

From Juvenile Delinquency
to Adult Crime

Throughout his life, Mickey Cohen was the embodiment of masculinity. You might say he overconformed to the masculine ideal. He was the kind of guy who couldn't help but find himself in some sort of trouble. Born Meyer Harris Cohen in September 1913 in Brooklyn, he developed a reputation for a fiery temper and a criminal propensity at a young age. His criminal career began during Prohibition, when he worked as a delivery boy for his older brother's illegal gin mill. As a teenager, Cohen developed a fascination with boxing, participating in a number of illegal fights. Like so many young men, he thought the rules simply did not apply to him. This disregard for authority, propensity for violence, and enterprising persona would make Cohen a natural for the world of organized crime. He later found himself essentially apprenticing for Al Capone in Chicago before moving to Los Angeles, joining up with Bugsy Siegel, and eventually replacing him (after Siegel was gunned down in the front living room of his home), becoming the face of organized crime on the West Coast. After a couple stints in Alcatraz for tax evasion, an explosive appearance on the *Mike Wallace Show* (since almost completely erased from history) during which he said that he never killed anyone who didn't deserve to die, and a flirtation with evangelism and the Reverend

Billy Graham, by the end of his life, the once-feared mobster was making ringside appearances at major boxing matches, cheered as a celebrity.

Throughout his life, Cohen did everything and anything necessary to demonstrate his value as a man. He epitomized what is called *toxic masculinity*—an extraordinarily limited number of options for performing gender that oftentimes box men into a corner from which they feel they can only prove their manhood by taking risks and being violent. Few men in the history of crime were more violent or bigger risk takers than Mickey Cohen.

In this chapter, we will talk about the relationship between gender and crime in terms of how people age. How is crime different when we're young in comparison to when we're older? Why do we view the same act differently when it's done by a thirteen-year-old boy or a thirty-three-year-old man? Or woman? How do our relationships with our friends, family, neighborhoods, all potential indicators for developing criminality, and so on change over time? By addressing and exploring these questions, we'll get a better idea about how crime fits into the larger context of our lives—not only what happens to drive someone into a criminal lifestyle (or even just make one mistake), but also what happens afterward. If we want to understand why people take part in these behaviors, we can study all the theory we want, but it's helpful to try viewing crime in terms of the bigger picture too.

This way of thinking about crime, called the life course perspective (as discussed in the last chapter), was first articulated by Glen Elder Jr. (1994), though some have argued that the concept borrows heavily from developmental psychology. In short, the life course perspective argues that all the theories that attempt to explain why crime happens are right in some way. The old ways of thinking about crime, back in the dark ages of the 1990s, saw theorists pitting their ideas against each other in a sort of "two theorists enter, one theorist leaves" death match. There just wasn't room for more than one idea; the possibility that people with opposite ideas could both be right was impossible. Elder and subsequent life course theorists recognize that everyone can be at least partially correct. The larger point of the life course perspective is that whatever you think about the significance of any of the other theories that exist to explain criminal behavior, 100 percent of the human population shares one experience: aging. Yes, we're all going to grow old, and that process changes us biologically, psychologically, and socially. No amount of skin products or hair dye can change it, no miracle diet can fight it off, no pill can reverse it, and your Aunt Tina really hasn't turned twenty-nine for the past four years. So when we talk about age and aging, we have to ask ourselves how people are different at the various stages of their lives as well as how the various theoretical ideas meant to explain virtually all criminal behavior actually work at different stages. And finally, it's also important to look at how boys and girls progress differently through life, adding another dimension to our understanding of these processes.

Of all the crime in the United States in a given year, the majority is committed by young people. This has been true of crime for quite some time. The "original" age-crime curve plotted offenses by the age and biological sex of convicted offenders in England and Wales in the 1840s, and if we did something similar today, odds are it would look nearly the same: offending seems to start in the mid-teenage years and drops off by the early to mid-twenties (Hirschi and Gottfredson 1983). The original curve also showed males offending at a much higher rate than females, which also holds true some 150 years later. (Obviously this doesn't mean that no children or older adults commit crime or that no girls or women do.) The question is, why? What about this point in our lives makes us more likely to be involved in some kind of criminal behavior?

What Makes Juvenile Delinquency Unique?

Juvenile delinquency refers to, broadly, all crimes committed by persons under the age of eighteen. Because the majority of crime is committed by young people in general, this means that juvenile delinquency accounts for a good portion of all crimes committed: in 2013, of all persons arrested, 9.3 percent were under the age of

eighteen (UCR 2014). Why is it important to pay special attention
to the crimes committed by kids? Because kids are very, very different from adults. They have a different perspective on the world.
Their concept of stress is different. Their ability to exercise their
own agency is different. The amount of power they wield in society is different. For these reasons, crimes committed by juveniles
warrant special attention.

One thing that distinguishes juvenile delinquency from adult
crime is the status offense. A status offense involves an act that is
illegal because the person doing it is legally underage. Things like
drinking alcohol, smoking, and gambling (in places where it is permitted) fall into this category. Laws about how many people can
ride in a car, having to attend some type of school, and curfews are
also examples of status offenses. Status offenses are a category of
crime that applies only to young people; there is no crime that an
adult can commit that will be classified as a status offense.

For the most part, status offenses are not gender-specific, with
one exception: dress codes in schools. In many schools, the existing dress codes are much more punitive for girls than for boys,
demonstrating that these institutions don't really take the education of their female students very seriously. For example, in April
2015 the story of Macy Edgerly, an eighteen-year-old high school
senior from Orangefield, Texas, went viral after she was sent
home for wearing leggings and a long baseball jersey. A similar
incident happened to Emily Schaeffer at Brandywine High School
in Wilmington, Delaware, in 2014. In 2015, also in April, Jef
Rouner (2015) published an article on the *Houston Press* website
about a recent incident with his five-year old daughter being forced
to cover up at her school. These are just three of many examples
of girls being unfairly punished for dressing in the style of clothing deemed gender appropriate, and I'm guessing that some of
you have seen or maybe even experienced this firsthand in your
high schools, too. Many school administrators use the logic that
being dressed "inappropriately" creates a distraction for male students (and in a school district in Newfoundland, Canada, the argument was also made that it distracts male teachers), disrupting
their education. However, some male students routinely go unpun-

ished for walking around practically shirtless themselves, which, if we're buying into the logic that sexual urges are completely uncontrollable, would distract the female students as well. Then again, the idea that sexual urges are completely uncontrollable has only really been applied to boys. And for generations, schools haven't really taken girls' education as seriously as boys', so if the girls are distracted, it's OK. In reality, this sends the message to young boys that they're not responsible for their behavior—reinforcing a serious myth about rape and sexual assault that allows rape culture to persist in our society. These ideas may be unfamiliar to you now, but we will explore them in much more detail later in this book.

In any event, many of the crimes committed by juveniles are status offenses. On the flip side, a number of crimes can only be committed by adults (or are much, much less likely to be committed by a teenager). This is because a teenager, by definition, doesn't have the life experience, legal standing, social capital, education, power, or wealth required to commit the offense. A thirteen-year-old living in the United States is, by definition, incapable of committing marital rape or spousal abuse, for example. The majority of young people also can't commit child abuse because most of them haven't become parents yet themselves. Furthermore, most adolescents are incapable of embezzling millions of dollars from a corporation; if they did, they would likely be the subject of a major motion picture starting Jesse Eisenberg and treated like some kind of rock star genius outlaw hero. Some things that adolescents do wouldn't be socially acceptable for an adult to do. For instance, if a couple of sixteen-year-old kids skip school to go get high and watch bad movies all day, we'd get mad at them, possibly even furious, but it certainly wouldn't be the most unusual thing a kid did. However, if your parents decided to skip work and spent the day doing the same thing, then gave their bosses a vague excuse about a relative dying and got found out, they'd be seriously reprimanded—if not fired on the spot. This standard applies to university students and professors, too—skipping class to watch reruns of *Teen Titans* is acceptable for you (though don't let me catch you), but if I cancel class to do that, I'm the true villain.

Though this definitional twist separates juvenile delinquency from adult crime, we can still think about adolescent behavior sociologically and ask ourselves why kids become involved in these types of behaviors. Almost all the theories we discussed in Chapter 3 involved adolescent life in some way, but none of them focused explicitly on adolescent behavior; none looked solely at what it's like to be a teenager in American culture. On the surface this topic may seem very simple, but it is definitely worth exploring: What *is* it like to be a teenager in the United States? What has it been like to be a teenager historically? Are kids these days really destroying society, like the legion of cantankerous grandparents of the world would have us believe? The answers to those questions are hard. The fact of the matter is, not only are adolescents (together with young adults) responsible for most of the crime committed in our society, but they're also doing this in the context of one of the most difficult, awkward, and confusing periods in life.

Virtually all the theories discussed in Chapter 3 apply to adolescence as a stage in life and adolescents as a subset of the population, at least in part. Because these theories were designed to explain all crime committed by all people at all stages of life, nothing about them is completely unique to adolescence—they describe nothing that kids experience that adults do not. That said, we can look at these ideas and see some hopefully obvious ways that they work differently for young people than for adults. First, we want to think about some of the unique aspects of adolescent life, universal experiences that do not happen in adulthood. One obvious answer—with major gender ramifications—is the onset of puberty.

Summer Vacation and the Social Consequences of Puberty

The most awkward part of adolescence, easily one of the defining characteristics of this stage in life, is puberty. This biological transition can have massive social consequences for boys and girls alike, which in turn can promote or inhibit delinquent or otherwise deviant behavior. This speaks to an idea first proposed by Elder (1994): the timing of lives. Elder talks about the social consequences of transitions that most everyone makes and how their timing—whether they are happening earlier or later than average—can have serious consequences for the individual. Now, Elder uses marriage as his example, and some people obviously may never get married, by choice or otherwise. Puberty is different, though: all people make this transition, without having a say in it or being able to take part in the planning process, whether they're ready to or not.

It tends to play out something like this: the school year comes to an end, and everyone pretty much looks the same, and it's understood that the girls (and/or boys) are gross and the school would be better off without them. Then school breaks for the summer, which is great, because you can only take so much long division. Summer goes by too fast, as it always does, and when you go back, something seems different. Maybe the first sign is that kid you've known since first grade now has a magnificent mustache. Gym class, which might have been your favorite class last year, has become a disaster, as half the boys have suddenly lost much of their physical coordination because of a growth spurt. And then, in walk the girls. They're not so gross anymore, for some mysterious reason. Yes, this is the story of an emerging male heterosexual identity—but I'm guessing that similar stories, likely with a lot more tension and confusion, happen to all youth regardless of gender identity or emerging sexual orientation.

How do you think the timing of puberty can affect things? By timing, we're talking about the point at which a person enters into puberty, since obviously it doesn't happen to everyone at the exact same time. It might seem trivial, but in reality the timing of puberty can have monumental social consequences for boys and girls alike. For both, early puberty tends to equal greater popularity, though this could come at a cost, especially for girls, as we'll discuss momentarily. Late development can also have negative social and psychological consequences, as kids are more likely to be singled out as weaker and/or less attractive, which can be internalized and manifest as a sudden spike in depression or drop in self-esteem. This is a major reason why girls experience an enormous increase in depressive symptoms in adolescence (i.e., Wade, Cairney, and Pevalin 2002). It's also important to think about the consequences of being popular or unpopular—falling into either group can change a person's behavior. Look back at your own experience in high school. If you were one of the most popular kids, what do you think it would have been like to be one of the unpopular kids? Or the other way around? As we'll see, popularity might not be as awesome as people suppose.

The onset of puberty is also, obviously, the beginning of the development of our sexual identities. This is where sex and gender become intertwined, making it difficult for some people to really pull them apart. Remember the idea of gendered behavior—that nothing in our DNA compels us to behave awkwardly around people we're attracted to; no gene makes boys run awful pickup lines by girls or makes girls suddenly want to wear makeup. This is all socially constructed. These are just the rules of a ridiculous game we keep playing. As the game begins, we also see a social split open up between boys and girls because of differences in physical and emotional maturity. Here, we see the introduction of a high school archetype that many parents worry about: the dreaded older boy. Some of you may have known, dated, or been this boy. The older boy is so much cooler than any of the lame boys in your grade, he thinks he knows a thing or two about sex and has bad intentions. The onset of puberty gives girls entry into social networks comprised of older adolescents and can put them into sexual situations for which they are not psychologically or emotionally prepared. For boys, puberty much more rarely causes them to be viewed as sexually desirable by older girls.

The physical capacity for sexual activity develops at a time when the majority of people are not actually mature enough to make their sexual debut, and likely do not possess the psychological or financial stability to become a parent, should that occur. This is one reason why, for generations, people have been concerned about teen sex—why babies having babies is a national issue—because many people cannot handle this enormous responsibility. Historically, the issue of teen sexuality has been couched in moral and religious terms, leading to the creation of abstinence-only sexual education classes in schools across the country. The purpose here is not to debate the effectiveness of those programs (they aren't effective), but rather to point out that, outside those home economics assignments where you have to pretend an egg is a baby, kids don't really get a lot of exposure to the real-world consequences of sexuality.

What about the relationship between puberty and the onset of criminal behavior among boys and girls? It would certainly seem to make sense that puberty causes the onset of criminal behavior, since puberty occurs first and then delinquent behaviors happen immediately after. Felson and Haynie (2002) examined the onset of puberty and timing of pubertal development and their relationship to a number of types of delinquency: violence, property crime, substance use, and what they called precocious sexual behavior (in reality this is just a measure of virginity; they assume that any sexual behavior by any teenager is bad). Felson and Haynie show that puberty has a number of positive and negative consequences for boys. In terms of delinquency, pubertal development increases the likelihood of being involved in all four of the types of delinquency. The more mature boys were also happier and more popular and did much better in school—in fact, Felson and Haynie found that while grade point average (GPA) was a protective factor against delinquency (meaning that boys with a higher GPA were less likely to be delinquent), when pubertal development was factored in, grades didn't matter as much for the mature boys—doing well in school didn't necessarily shield them from delinquency.

What about puberty and delinquency among girls? Haynie (2003) looked at this relationship in terms of three types of delinquency, categorized by how bad the behaviors are: party deviance (i.e., smoking cigarettes or marijuana, lying to parents), minor delinquency (i.e., shoplifting, vandalism, stealing something worth less than $50), and serious delinquency (i.e., burglary, robbery, fighting). She also looked at puberty in terms of overall development and compared high and low relative development (in other words, those girls who developed much earlier or much later) to the average. Overall, Haynie found that early pubertal development is associated with a significantly higher risk of all three types of delinquency among girls. She also found that girls who develop earlier than average have a significantly higher risk of being involved in party deviance, while girls who develop later than average have a significantly lower risk. Any association between early or late development and minor or serious delinquency can be explained by the role of friends and family, so in terms of timing, there's no direct connection there, according to Haynie's research.

So, for both boys and girls, hitting puberty can increase the likelihood of involvement in some forms of delinquency. Certainly, outside social forces could act as barriers to prevent that from happening. Even still, the social forces that exist within the school setting are so persistent and powerful that even positive elements on the outside (i.e., family) might not be strong enough to stop someone from becoming delinquent in some way.

Another Brick in the Wall

Another universal aspect of adolescent life that contributes to delinquency is the changing relationship with parents and other adult authority figures. Now, this doesn't mean that adults don't answer to anyone (contrary to what you thought as a kid). We do. But the difference is, no matter how much the schedules, needs, and demands of other people seem to control our lives, we at least have some small freedoms that we allow ourselves. But while the lives of adults are very scheduled, the lives of children and teenagers are controlled down to the slightest details, with no questions asked. You have to go to school, wear this, eat that, do your homework, go to practice, share with that kid you hate, and be in bed by x time—and don't make me come up there. Adults tell each other that kids respond well to this, that they need discipline and structure, while leading undisciplined and unstructured lives themselves. This is David Greenberg's (1977) adolescent frustration hypothesis. Greenberg argues that delinquency stems from a lack of three things: respect, money, and employment. Basically, Greenberg says that because their lives are so completely regulated, youths view delinquency as a necessary way to make up for whatever is lacking and gain some control.

In a way, Greenberg's idea resembles Moffitt's (1993) typology of adolescent limited versus life course persistent offenders. According to Moffitt, life course persistent offenders seem, from childhood, to be constantly in some kind of trouble. They get detention in elementary school, suspended in middle school, and arrested in high school. As adults, they've got substance-abuse problems; they can't hold down a job—there's always something with them. Adolescent limited offenders, Moffitt says, make up most of the population. They were basically good kids, but got into some trouble in high school. For these people, delinquency is a part of becoming an adult—breaking the rules becomes a symbolic way to take back some control over their lives. The relationship between the two groups, Moffitt argues, is very complex: life course persistent offenders are unpopular children and unpopular adults, but they see a huge spike in popularity in high school because their rebellion is now cool. They become role models for those kids who want to break the rules and have fun too. But after high school comes entry into the adult world, be it work, technical school or college, parenthood, or some combination thereof, and with all of that comes more responsibility. For the adolescent limited offenders, delinquency drops off almost immediately, because they have a legitimate desire to take part in mainstream society and, thus, must stop doing all the bad things they'd been up to in the past. While this group is sobering up and settling down, the life course persistent kids are still getting in trouble and will continue to do so for most of their adult lives in some form.

Greenberg (1977) and Moffitt (1993) share the idea that many kids become involved in delinquency as a way to rebel against authority. However, we know that the rate of offending is much higher for boys and young men than it is for girls and young women, so does this mean that girls are less rebellious than boys? What do you think? Fagan et al. (2007) looked at gender differences in the relationship between crime and a number of risk factors, including rebelliousness, and found no difference—rebelliousness was associated with delinquency for both boys and girls. So in terms of crime, at least, rebelliousness is shared. But what about rebelliousness overall? Do you think that, in general, girls are less rebellious than boys? Or do you think that girls show rebellion in different ways than boys do?

Much of the research based on Moffitt's groundbreaking 1993 piece has attempted to confirm or disconfirm the existence of these two groups of offenders, or offense trajectories, and not much has been done on gender and any potential differences therein. What has been done has focused more on gender differences within the trajectories themselves. For example, Moffitt and Caspi (2001) found that far more boys than girls could be defined as childhood-onset offenders and that both boys and girls who offended came from high-risk backgrounds. However, the ratio of boys to girls offending for the first time dropped significantly in adolescence (there were still more boys than girls, though), and the role of coming from a high-risk family background was no longer relevant for female offenders. Odgers et al. (2008) looked for gender differences among life course persistent offenders and found that while more males than females fell into this group, their backgrounds and outcomes were virtually identical: by adulthood, the life course persistent offenders had serious mental and physical health problems as well as serious economic issues. What about the types of crimes being committed? Mazerolle et al. (2000) hypothesized that males would be committing a greater variety of crimes, simply because so many more males were involved with crime than females. Contrary to their expectation, their research found that while fewer females were involved in crime than males, there was no gender difference in the diversity of offending—meaning girls were committing the same types of crimes as boys.

Transgender Adolescents and Gender Fluidity

A growing issue among adolescents is the changing definition of gender. The term *transgender* refers to those people whose gender expression or identity does not match the societal expectations associated with their biological sex. This is different from being transsexual, which entails taking the steps necessary to alter oneself physically. Not all transgender people are transsexual.

Being gay was once considered a mental health disorder until homosexuality was reclassified as a legitimate sexual orientation; being transgender has recently undergone a similar reclassification. In the most recent edition of the *Diagnostic and Statistical Manual of Mental Disorders*, which is essentially the holy book of psychological disorders, the "official" term for being transgender was changed from "gender identity disorder," which phrases being transgender a problem that must be fixed, to "gender dysphoria," which now recognizes the enormous emotional struggle that comes with being transgender.

The growing acceptance of the transgender community has brought more attention to the process of coming out as transgender and making the transition, but a massive amount of transphobia exists in the United States. As a result, the violence experienced by transgender youths on a regular basis is being taken much more seriously. In January 2015, the Human Rights Coalition and the Trans People of Color Coalition released an issue brief highlighting the violence facing the trans community ("Addressing Anti-transgender Violence" n.d.). The Office of Victims of Crime report that over 50 percent of transgender people have been victims of sexual violence (Office for Victims of Crime 2012); over half of all members of the LGBTQ community murdered in hate crimes are transgender women.

In terms of the relationship between adolescent development and delinquency, remember the difficulty of going through puberty when your biological sexual identity and culturally assigned gender identity matched, and then think about how much harder it must be when that disconnect exists—and when expressing that frustration could get you killed. No doubt some of you reading this experienced that disconnect, and that disconnect was one of the defining parts of your adolescent life. When we talked about hate crimes in Chapter 2, I introduced you to the idea of the "gay panic" defense, used by the murderers of Matthew Shepard. A similar "trans panic" defense has been developed in cases where the victim is trans. As Wodda and Panfil (2015) describe it, the trans panic defense is rooted in transphobia, or intense prejudice against trans people. Just as the gay panic defense argues that violence is justified as a response to unwanted same-sex contact, the trans panic defense tries to justify and excuse violence on the theory that the offender was "tricked" into what he or she considered same-sex contact. Such violence, of course, is not excusable at all. Neither the "gay panic" nor the "trans panic" defense has held up in court. Wodda and Panfil argue that we should be thinking about transphobia at the institutional level—that it is woven into the fabric of our society and not a rare attitude among a few unenlightened people. As discussed in Chapter 1, we have been treating sex and gender as the same thing for a very long time, and the recognition that gender actually manifests itself in a lot of different ways is a relatively new development.

The Nightmare of High School

We've talked about high school as part of a larger network of social control in the lives of adolescents that many young people find so suffocating that delinquency becomes an attractive way to rebel and begin the process of becoming an adult. Later in this book, we will talk about the idea of the school-to-prison pipeline, which is a way of conceptualizing the criminal justice system. Before we get to thinking about schools as just another type of prison-like institution, we need to explore one very simple question: What's high school like?

We've already talked about the relationship between delinquency and pubertal development and some of the related social consequences. We won't repeat any of that here, though it might be useful to keep asking yourself what the potential trauma and anxiety of puberty could add to a situation for boys or girls. The first question we have to ask ourselves is, what happens in school? Yes, we know all about the academic stuff—the whole point, after all, is to get an education, and that's been true since you first toddled into preschool ready to get down with some finger paint. However, much more happens during our time in school than just learning about the marvels of the world around us. Our social lives begin in school. And for many people, regardless of gender, this can be a terrifying experience; they spend more time worrying about the way people think about them than focusing on the academic work at hand.

Derek Kreager has published several important studies focusing on some of the more nuanced factors of adolescent high school life, including the ways kids try to manage their reputation among their peers. This work is an extension of differential association (Sutherland 1947), social learning theory (Burgess and Akers 1966), and social bond theory (Hirschi 1969). Whereas these theoretical perspectives look at the relationship between delinquency and school in very sweeping terms, Kreager's work focuses on some of the more complex aspects of adolescent life and how delinquency shapes it. First, let's talk about the idea of being socially isolated. In general, we all know that some kids in school are much more popular than others. Countless people from all kinds of different industries have been trying for years to figure out what makes someone cool. But what about those kids on the other end of the spectrum? Why are some kids isolated? Kreager (2004) argues that kids become isolated for one of two reasons: either they choose isolation or they're pushed into it. Those kids who choose isolation have no real interest in the drama and the games—they've got other interests. Because of that, they're not going to be affected by anything happening in the larger social world of their school. Those kids who have been isolated against their will are disruptive to the larger culture of the school in some way, and have more or less become crusaders against that popular culture. For instance, chances are that someone who is aggressively antifootball at a school that lives and dies by the game will become isolated. These isolated youths are more likely to become involved in delinquency and start hanging out with kids who think the same way they do, in essence constructing their own delinquent and rebellious subculture within the school.

Isolation in school can cause kids to become delinquent in order to rebel or to try to gain some kind of popular status. Kreager (2007b) shows that, in some cases, being violent can be a way to gain positive status within school. First, Kreager demonstrates that boys and girls alike view a tendency toward violence as a negative character trait that they would not want to see in their friends. But then he shows that boys who aren't doing great in school generally consider violence a positive thing. Kreager found that the intersection of race and social class drove this effect:

> Moreover, because disadvantaged and minority males are less likely to be successful at school, they are at greater risk of turning to violence as a status attainment mechanism. The indirect effects of race and class on achievement and peer status may have important implications for the reproduction of social inequality. Future research may ascertain better whether those individuals who gain status from violence have lowered educational and occupational outcomes and whether these relationships vary by sociodemographic characteristics. (Kreager 2007b, 916)

This sounds very similar to an idea from Matsueda and Heimer (1997) that we'll talk about later in this book: Do boys value school and education as much as girls do? What do you think? Staff and Kreager (2008) found that boys who had a lot of status among violent groups in schools were at much greater risk of dropping out of school, which we know can lead to a whole laundry list of problems later in life (i.e., Hagan and Foster 2001).

In terms of how girls view violence among their peers, they generally don't support it across the board, regardless of any other factors, with one exception: girls who go to schools with high levels of violence have a less negative view of violence committed by other girls in their school (Kreager 2007b). Note that they still view it negatively—girls in general don't approve of or admire violence—just less than would be the case at a less violent school.

Finally, Kreager also looks at the relationship between involvement in sports and violence among high school students. Sports are tremendously important to many youths (more so than academics, in many cases), and our society has held them up as an extremely positive influence in a person's life. This is interesting because a lot of people see athletics generally as an unassailable, infallible, completely perfect institution, and if you dare criticize it, you're basically committing treason against the United States. At the same time, ask yourself how many student-athletes you've known or heard about who've gotten away with all kinds of bad behavior simply because they're athletes. Here, Kreager (2007b) wants to understand the relationship between involvement in sports in high school and violence among males. He finds that those boys who play football and are on the wrestling team are more likely to be violent than either boys involved in other sports or boys who aren't involved in any sports at all. Even boys who don't play football but are friends with boys who play are more likely to be involved in violence in some way. Kreager argues that this is because football (and the culture associated with it) socializes those boys who participate to be hypermasculine, and many boys overconform to this expectation, making them more likely to apply the qualities that make them successful in football to other aspects of their lives (in other words, they solve problems with intimidation and violence, conforming to an extremely narrow definition of what it means to be a man in the process).

If involvement in violent sports and associating solely with kids who play them can lead to off-field violence among boys, what do you think the relationship is between involvement in sports and delinquency among girls? Obviously most girls don't have the opportunity to participate in these contact sports in high school yet (though that could change in the future, with the rising popularity of women like mixed martial arts superstar Ronda Rousey and the viral sensation Sam Gordon, who made a name for herself running over the boys she was competing against in youth football, just to name two). Booth, Farrell, and Varano (2008) found that involvement in sports decreased the likelihood of serious delinquency for girls. Gardner, Roth, and Brooks-Gunn (2009) found that involvement in sports was not related, directly or indirectly, to delinquency among girls. Taylor et al. (2016) found that among girls living in rural areas, involvement in sports decreased the likelihood of gang involvement. In general, these studies suggest that girls' involvement in sports inhibits delinquency, drawing on social control theory.

This assumes that girls view their involvement in sports as positive and that girls and boys view their participation in sports similarly. Do you think they do?

In this discussion of the quest for popularity and how kids view violence among their peers, we've overlooked a simple question: Is it good to be popular? This is a good example of a sociological question that attempts to pull apart a seemingly obvious concept to see how it works. So, I'll ask you again: Do you think it's a good thing to be popular? Mayeux, Sandstrom, and Cillessen (2008) found that perceived popularity in tenth grade— perceived popularity being their attempt at creating an overall measure of popularity for each student in the school they studied by asking the students who participated in this survey to nominate people they thought were popular—was associated with an increase in sexual activity and alcohol use in twelfth grade for both girls and boys.

Similar to what we discussed before with unpopular kids looking for ways to increase their own popularity via negative behavior, Mayeux, Sandstrom, and Cillessen (2008, 67) have an interesting idea about how this "monkey see, monkey do" effect could have potentially serious negative consequences for the unpopular kids in comparison to the popular ones:

> As Cohen and Prinstein (2006) suggest, lower-status teens and those who experience depression or social anxiety may be particularly prone to emulate the risk behaviors of perceived popular teens in hopes of improving their own social standing. Lower-status youth, however, may not possess the same protective characteristics (prosocial skills, leadership abilities) that may naturally buffer high-status children from subsequent adjustment problems. Thus, even if experimentation with taboo behaviors does not pose personal risk to high-status teens, such behavior may spread to lower status teens who are not as well equipped to handle the attending risks.

In other words, when it comes to alcohol use and sexual activity and the possibility of negative outcomes in the future, the kids who are more popular may also have other things in their lives to help them deal with those problems. The less popular kids, who copy those behaviors to try to become popular themselves, may not have the same advantages to help them handle those problems. It's an interesting question, but doesn't it sound to you like they're saying that only rich and well-adjusted kids become popular?

Cillessen and Rose (2005) distinguish between kids who are well liked (who seem popular on paper) and those who are emulated (the truly popular kids, those whose behavior others mimic but who aren't really liked by many people). This makes us question the whole idea of popularity on another level—not just in terms of whether it's good to be popular but what being popular even means. And if boys and girls have a different view of violence as a means of becoming popular, but both see an increase in drinking and sexual behavior as associated with increased popularity, then what else could be going on here?

De Bruyn, Cillessen, and Wissink (2010) took this a step further by looking at the relationship between perceived popularity, peer acceptance, gender, and the risk of developing bullying behavior and being victimized. It might be hard to wrap your head around the idea that there is a difference between being popular and being well liked. Kids well liked by the other kids in their school were less likely to bully, while more popular kids were also more likely to be bullies. De Bruyn, Cillessen, and Wissink also found that kids who were popular and not well liked were more likely to be victimized than those kids who were popular and well liked. Not surprisingly, kids who were not well liked and not popular were the most likely to be victimized. What about differences between boys and girls in this popularity versus well liked idea? De Bruyn, Cillessen, and Wissink showed that the relationship between aggression and status was a lot stronger for boys than for girls, meaning that popularity as a cause of bullying was a bigger deal for boys, and being well liked as a barrier to bullying was less important for girls. In terms of the relationship between being well liked and being bullied among girls, de Bruyn, Cillessen, and Wissink found that girls who fell on the extreme ends of the spectrum—both not liked and very well liked—were at the highest risk of being bullied. Why do you think this is? The authors speculate that it shows how much more complex friendship networks are among girls than among boys, and that in order to avoid being victimized while simultaneously finding a place among their peer group, girls need to show some level of assertiveness. Note that this study doesn't say how these kids are bullying or being bullied (if it's physical, psychological, or what), just that it happens. Also note that this study looks at kids living in the Netherlands, so maybe the same wouldn't hold for kids growing up in the United States, but there really isn't any reason to think so—unless you can come up with something that sets apart American teenagers from kids growing up in other Western nations.

We've spent the last couple of pages talking about this idea of popularity being a central concern of adolescent life for both boys and girls. It turns out that there's a lot to unpack in terms of whether being popular is a good thing for kids. Many of you probably went into this discussion thinking that, obviously, being popular must be a good thing. I'll admit that I thought that same thing, too. It turns out, however, that the quest to gain and sustain popularity might not be the best thing for a kid to focus on. Research shows that kids who aren't popular might turn to delinquent behavior to become popular, especially if they're not doing well in school. Popular kids—and remember, they aren't necessarily liked; they are seen as the most dominant, the leaders, the ones to emulate (de Bruyn, Cillessen, and Wissink 2010)—are more likely to be bullies, more likely to be drinking, and more likely to be sexually active than kids who aren't popular. If violence itself isn't a way to become popular, then participating in what we might think of as acceptable violence, or school-sanctioned violence, is. As Kreager showed, participation in violent sports and hanging out with people involved in them increases the risk of becoming violent. In the majority of these findings, the relationships tend to be stronger among boys, because, as mentioned multiple times throughout this book, girls are in general involved in less bad behavior than boys are. So, in a way, a lot of what we're talking about might be overlooking some of the aspects of adolescent life that are unique to young women. Can you think of anything else that might be worth discussing?

"You're All Growed Up"

So far in this chapter, we've focused on experiences unique to adolescence that could contribute to the onset of criminal behavior: the social outcomes related to pubertal development, the awfulness of high school, the frustration at being stuck between childhood and adulthood. I hope that these made crime seem more relatable for you—not that I want you to go out and launch your own crime spree, just to have a better understanding of antisocial behavior. We've all felt some of the same angst and frustration as those kids when we were that age.

Having discussed things that are unique to adolescence and why people become involved in crime, if we go back to the idea of the age-crime curve, we know that some people involved in crime or delinquency eventually stop offending on their own, without getting caught. Moffitt (1993) called them adolescent limited offenders and said that their desistance—the process of stopping offending—was basically a natural process associated with the transition into an adult role. This is entirely possible, and we should talk about it here in more detail—especially in terms of the differences in how society views the roles that men and women take on.

As we discussed regarding Moffitt's work, one of the biggest reasons why people desist from crime is the boatload of responsibilities that come with adulthood. If you want to be successful, at least in terms of how society defines success, you need a career and a family, or at least one of them, depending on your circumstances. Sampson and Laub (1992) call this age-graded social control, meaning a type of social control that we can't possibly put on younger people for legal and moral reasons. Basically, the idea is that desistance occurs because people transition into roles that they would lose if they got in any trouble. I have a family and a career, and if I were arrested for anything, there's a good chance I'd lose both of them. I don't want to lose my family or my job, so I'm going to be a good professor. Actually, of the adult roles we transition into, marriage has the greatest effect on desistance (Sampson, Laub, and Wimer 2006). So in terms of policy, if we want to reduce crime in the United States, we should make people get married, right?

Of course not (you can take a breath now). After all, it's not the case that 100 percent of people who get married stop committing crimes. There are plenty of examples to the contrary. For example, in January 2015, Bryce and Jennifer Charpentier were sentenced to three years in California state prison for committing a series of burglaries and selling prescription drugs. One of the burglary victims was Jennifer Charpentier's own mother. What makes this story even more surprising, however, is that both husband and wife were members of the San Diego Police Department, and while they denied using their positions to bully or intimidate anyone while conducting their criminal activities, they were charged with breaking into someone's home while on duty.

On November 11, 2013, Troy LaFerrara was murdered by Miranda and Elytte Barbour after Miranda met LaFerrara on Craigslist and agreed to meet him for sex. This case captured the nation's attention, as Barbour claimed that she had killed "at least" twenty-two other people across the country. No evidence was ever found to support these claims—Troy LaFerrara was most likely the couple's only victim. Both Barbours were sentenced to life without parole in 2014.

Marriage not only did not prevent these crimes but may have played a part in facilitating them, as in both cases the married partners are literally partners in crime. Maybe these events wouldn't have happened had these couples never hooked up. Or maybe they would have, just with different spouses. These incidents don't disprove the idea that marriage causes desistance from crime; this is just how risk and probability work. In criminology, just like in the other social sciences, there's not going to be a 100 percent success rate for anything.

Some think marriage leads to desistance through the good marriage effect (Laub, Nagin, and Sampson 1998). It also explains why not all marriages create desistance. Essentially, there's a difference between being "married" and being "happily married"; people who are married and have a good relationship with their partner are more likely to desist than people who either don't marry at all or get married but aren't exactly thrilled with this change in their life.

Although the idea of marriage as a cause of desistance has been supported by subsequent research and is generally accepted, many scholars question the social control component. For instance, Giordano, Cernkovich, and Rudolph (2002) argue that because the data Sampson and Laub used in their study wasn't representative of the entire population (the respondents were entirely white men) and was culturally dated (the men in the study all reached maturity in the 1950s), we shouldn't buy into the social control argument wholeheartedly; maybe it just applies to white guys. Seeking to update the original work of Sampson and Laub using more up-to-date data, Giordano, Cernkovich, and Rudolph found that marriage and employment were associated with desistance for both women and men. Along the lines of our earlier discussion on Moffitt regarding gender similarities between life course persistent offenders, they also found a number of similarities between the male and female offenders in their research, including extreme poverty, problematic family and relationship histories, low education, and a history of run-ins with the criminal justice system. Instead of operating as a source of social control, Giordano, Cernkovich, and Rudolph argue, marriage and meaningful employment produce a cognitive shift in how the individuals think of themselves—so it's more complicated than control theory would have us think; there's more to it than someone just saying "I'm married, I want to stay married, I can't do this stuff anymore." In fact, many of the participants interviewed for this study indicated that they had tired of their old lives, wanted to stop offending, and viewed the new source of positivity, be it a partner or children, in their life as helping them make that change. In other words, they were taking a more active role in their conformity instead of passively adjusting like Sampson and Laub seem to suggest. Next, Giordano, Schroeder, and Cernkovich (2007) built on this by considering the role that our emotions play: if our way of thinking about ourselves changes as we age, then it seems to make sense that our emotions and how we react to the world around us must change too. They find that, in terms of marriage as a cause of desistance, the good marriage effect is perhaps better explained in terms of the positive emotions associated with being involved in a happy marriage. Here, the relationship balances or negates the negative emotions that existed previously and drove criminal behavior—being in a happy marriage helps the individual deal with the anger and depression likely experienced up until that point. As far as the relationship between emotional and cognitive change, Giordano, Schroeder, and Cernkovich (2007, 1650) argue that a happy marriage also gives the individual a positive role model to help him or her "embark on a significant self-improvement project." In terms of gender and the role of emotion and emotional growth, the authors found that depression was a greater emotional factor in the criminal behavior of men, but admit to not fully exploring gender differences and similarities as much as they would have liked. Unfortunately, not much work has been done on this subject since.

Another possible explanation for the marriage-desistance connection may have nothing to do with cognitive or emotional change in the individual and instead come about in a more practical way. Warr (1998) found that marriage was associated with a dramatic decrease in time spent with friends and therefore a decrease in criminal behavior. Think about it like this: in addition to the responsibilities, the shift in identity, and the increased social control, there's only so much time in a day to get into trouble, and only a fool is going to side with their good-for-nothing friends over their loving and adoring spouse. This is a very simplified way of thinking about the marriage-desistance link, but not out of line with the other ideas we've talked about. How do you think this would apply to gender, though? Do you think that the way men and women view their friends changes after marriage?

We could easily broaden the idea of a good marriage effect to fit more appropriately with the increased public acceptance of both same-sex relationships and cohabitation (living together in an intimate relationship without being married). In other words, does the good marriage effect apply in same-sex relationships? What about committed intimate relationships where the participants aren't legally married? Do you think that a sort of "good relationship" effect could build on the idea of a good marriage effect, or does marriage itself bring something to the table that encourages people to desist from crime?

Timing of Transitions

Earlier in this chapter, we talked about how becoming a parent too early in life can potentially cause a number of problems for the individual, regardless of gender. Having a child (or even becoming sexually active) when you're not prepared to do so is what life course sociologists call an early exit from adolescence. To better understand this, think about all the changes that have happened in your life: getting your driver's license, graduating from high school, and so on. Some of those may have seemed scary, exciting, or both as they loomed closer and closer. And now, looking back on it, maybe they weren't so bad. Think about what it would be like to see someone much older or much younger doing those things—a nine-year-old with a driver's license is terrifying, but that same nine-year-old who's already graduated high school must be some kind of genius. The timing of these transitions really do matter. Now think about the things in life that haven't happened to many of you yet: having kids, getting married, graduating from college. Maybe you have friends who have done some of these things, but you're still terrified of the idea. Look at your friends—your roommate can't wake up in time for a 2:00 p.m. class, but some day, somehow, that kid may possibly be someone's parent. The idea of early exits from adolescence looks at the relationship between criminality and the timing of these transitions. How do you think the two relate? What transitions are unique to boys and girls? How might they experience these transitions differently?

Hagan and Foster (2001) conducted one of the most important studies on this. Studying crime in terms of the life course instead of the other theories we've talked about means that we're no longer just trying to predict why crime happens; instead we are thinking about criminal behavior as one piece of a much larger puzzle. In their study, Hagan and Foster look at how experiencing violence—being a victim—can change the trajectory of a person's life. Specifically, they find that experiencing violence (including both verbal and physical abuse) in intimate relationships (i.e., dating) in adolescence significantly increases the risk of a number of bad outcomes later in life for both boys and girls, such as dropping out of school, running away from home, and developing depressive symptoms and suicidal thoughts. For girls who experience intimate partner violence as well as street violence, the risk of becoming pregnant goes through the roof—in the data used in this study, nearly 60 percent of girls who experienced both forms of violence became pregnant.

When we think about crime not as an act but as an experience that can disrupt the larger trajectory of a person's life, our ability to see just how massive the consequences can be grows tremendously. For instance, Kuhl, Warner, and Wilczak (2012) found that youth victims of serious violence are more likely to enter into a serious romantic relationship—either marriage or cohabitation—earlier than people who were not victimized. Kuhl, Warner, and Warner (2015) argue that being a victim of violence from outside the family during adolescence has a significant effect on the individual and that many youths are scarred as a result, potentially leading to future victimization in later intimate relationships.

Pairing this idea of early exits—which can include premature entry into serious romantic relationships—with the idea of the good marriage effect we talked about in the previous section (or the good relationship effect, if you want to broaden it) greatly magnifies the significance of both. It seems like truly good relationships are incredibly important, whereas hurtful ones are easy to slip in to, and it's not always clear whether a relationship is beneficial, at least in the beginning. When kids are exposed to violence, regardless of gender, we need to be alert to how they're handling it in the ensuing weeks and months. Acting like it's no big deal, especially with boys, isn't helpful at all. By treating the violence boys experience as inconsequential, we're saying to them that any of the emotions they're experiencing as a result of their victimization are not important, which can have damaging psychological consequences. It's also telling them that violence is a normal part of their lives, which can increase the chances that, should they ever have sons themselves, they may be more likely to pass on the idea that violence is a normal part of masculinity.

Prison as a Life Course Transition

Later in this book, we'll talk a lot about the relationship between gender and the different phases or levels of the criminal justice system, as well as what the experiences are like for men and women at each level of the system on both sides of the law. At this point, now that we know more about human development and the life course, let's take a few minutes to talk about going to prison as a sort of life course transition. Just as you can divide your life into before and after stages around certain major events—before and after high school graduation, before and after getting your first real job—people who have been to prison can mark their lives out in terms of before and after being convicted. We can think of incarceration as another type of transition.

We'll pick this up again in Chapter 8, but an interesting aspect of the prison system and how the entire criminal justice system works is the lack of public attention paid to prisons relative to the other levels of the system. Except when someone involved in a crime that captured national attention is executed, we don't really think about what happens to people—regardless of their celebrity— once they're behind bars.

Some of you might wonder how going to prison could be considered a transition with potentially bad outcomes for a person's life. Isn't involvement in whatever criminal behavior got the person arrested, convicted, and incarcerated the actual problem here? True, being involved in pretty much any type of criminal behavior can lead to some pretty major suffering in the future, regardless of whether you spend any time in prison (see, for example, Sampson and Laub 1997; Hagan and Foster 2001). Lanctôt, Cernkovich, and Giordano (2007) set out to determine whether being incarcerated had any effect above and beyond the already negative consequences that come with being involved in crime. They also wanted to know if, assuming being incarcerated had some effect on later well-being, it affects men and women differently in any way. Their findings indicate that, yes, having been incarcerated as an adolescent does cause problems later in life that cannot be explained solely by involvement in delinquent behavior. Kids who were incarcerated experienced "more socioeconomic difficulties, earlier and premature transitions to adulthood, more instability in work and romantic contexts, less caring and trust in their relationships with significant others, less emotional well-being, and more problems resulting from their involvement in anti-social behaviors" (Lanctôt, Cernkovich, and Giordano 2007: 148). In other words, not much good comes from being incarcerated.

So, we know that being incarcerated leads to a lot of problems in the future, above and beyond what happens as a result of being involved in crime itself. But does this happen to men and women, or just to one or the other? While incarceration negatively effects both men and women, Lanctôt, Cernkovich, and Giordano (2007) found that overall girls faced much harsher outcomes later in life. Many of these problems are socioeconomic; they rely the most on government assistance, have difficulty integrating into the workforce, and have often had a child as a teenager, which adds to their economic burden. Formerly incarcerated men also experience these problems, but, at least according to the research done by Lanctôt, Cernkovich, and Giordano, women experience them to a significantly greater degree. What problems, then, do men tend to face more? Whereas formerly incarcerated women weren't taking part in any kind of real criminal behavior (though they were using drugs and were more likely to use violence in their relationships), the previously incarcerated men were much more likely to be involved in criminal behavior, which further contributed to the laundry list of negative things currently happening in their lives. They were also much more likely than their female counterparts to have an alcohol problem.

As mentioned, we will be talking about some of these issues in more depth later. For now, consider this: What exactly is the purpose of putting someone in prison? The term *corrections* seems to imply the idea of making sure that people who commit crimes learn that they did something wrong and make the rational choice to never do it again. But if incarcerating people for whatever crime they committed actually makes their lives worse when they get out, how is that helping them become a better person? And, in the case of women, we are often talking about the lives of children who had nothing to do with the crime that their mom committed and are now also likely to be worse off because she was incarcerated. These are called collateral consequences. It isn't a huge jump in reasoning to see how those childhood disadvantages caused by mom's time as an adjudicated youth could lead to later offending as well, especially if mom is violent, being victimized, using drugs, and so forth. This is what Glen Elder (1994) referred to as linked lives: the idea that our actions and choices, as well as events and circumstances in our lives that are completely out of our control, for better or worse, will affect the people closest to us. If being incarcerated as a young person has this many negative outcomes associated with it, what's the point of locking up teenagers who have committed a delinquent act?

Crime Among the Elderly

It's appropriate in a chapter on crime at all stages of life to conclude with a brief discussion of crime committed by the elderly. As we learned earlier in this chapter, adolescents and young adults, basically high school– and college-aged people, commit the majority of crimes in the United States and other Western countries. Does this mean that they commit 100 percent of all crime in society? Of course not. Some older and elderly adults commit crime, too. But how much are they responsible for, and what are they doing?

According to the FBI's Uniform Crime Report (UCR 2014), a total of 984,404 people age fifty and older were arrested in 2014, accounting for approximately 11 percent of all arrests that year; of this group, 89,336 were sixty-five or older. The most common arrests were for driving under the influence, property crime (including larceny theft, arson, and burglary), and what the UCR refers to as "other assaults." (For the record, this list excludes the category "other traffic incidents.") Older adults committed violent crimes as well: there were 100 arrests for murder or nonnegligent homicide and 288 arrests for rape among persons age sixty-five or older.

So, while young people commit the majority of crimes, they obviously don't commit all of them. Why do you think the older adults who committed these crimes did so? Of the theories and other concepts we've covered, which do you think might best explain their behavior? They could certainly be life course persistent offenders, like the people Moffitt (1993) identified, or maybe they didn't make the good marriage that Sampson and Laub (1992) discussed. Maybe they've spent time in prison before, and prior incarceration largely drives their behavior (i.e., Lanctôt, Cernkovich, and Giordano 2007). Those could be possibilities. But what else do you think could be driving their behavior?

5

Gangs and Drug Violence

This chapter discusses urban crime. A more appropriate term might be *street crime*, since technically any kind of crime can happen in a big city. We're not talking about insider trading on Wall Street; we're talking about gang activities and violence, drugs, and vice. We're talking about the types of crime you're most likely to see at the center of any number of cable crime dramas and on local news stations across the country on a daily basis—the kinds of things that many of you have been taught to fear your entire lives.

In the first part of this chapter, we will discuss street violence and gang violence throughout the United States, with some background on how gangs as we think of them today developed in the United States. Next, we'll spend some time talking about drug use and dealing in the United States, including the reasoning behind particular drug laws and the impact of the "War on Drugs." Throughout these discussions, we'll see how gender manifests in these extremely intense criminal contexts—where it matters and where it doesn't.

Before we can talk about street crime, it's important to recognize that, obviously, the biggest cities in the United States haven't always been what they are today. Although cities across the country are home to gangs of all sorts, these gangs are not the only defining characteristic of cities—we aren't living in some kind of *Mad Max* type of world, at least, not yet. We need to understand that gangs are a unique and likely unanticipated outcome of the development of American culture and modern society. We need to remember, too, that New York City, Boston, Detroit, Chicago, Los Angeles, and so on, all have unique histories that give each city its character, as well as commonalities that allow us to talk about street crime on a national scale in very general terms. Even though every city has its own history, geography, and culture, the sociological forces, including gender, that drive crime and justice are constant.

I also want to note that it is difficult to talk about street crime in any form without also acknowledging the incredible effects of race and poverty. We will touch a bit on issues of racism, classism, segregation, and discrimination in this chapter; in the conclusion, we'll talk about the different ways in which gender intersects with other elements of the social structure. For now, let's focus on the role that gender plays in the types of crimes we see happening in our cities—specifically gangs and gang violence as well as drug use and dealing.

Where Did This Come From?
A Brief History of Gangs in the United States

Like the police,gangs as a criminal element have existed for much of the history of the United States, just not in the exact form they take today. The first gangs in the United States were an extension of conflict between immigrant groups and so-called Native Americans (a term that in this case refers to Protestants descended from the original colonists, not the land's indigenous peoples). The nativist gangs (the most famous of them was called the Know Nothings) clashed with immigrants streaming in from Europe over jobs, a sign of things to come. The immigrant gangs formed primarily along ethnic lines—Irish, Italian, and so on. Reflecting gender roles at the time, gangs predominantly comprised young men, though some women not only participated but more than held their own. For example, Hellcat Maggie, a member of a gang called the Dead Rabbits, allegedly filed her teeth into points and wore long metal finger tips, letting her literally tear anyone who crossed her to shreds (English 2005). Sadie the Goat was known for her vicious headbutts and for her rivalry with a woman known as Gallus Mag, who had a collection of ears she'd ripped off her opponents (Asbury 1927 [2008]; English 2005).

Early gangs, especially those in the nineteenth century, were incredibly violent, bordering on barbaric (Asbury 1927 [2008]; English 2005). They lacked the modes of transportation or types of weapons that gangs have today, making their violence that much more directly physical and brutal. As time progressed and police departments improved, gang violence diminished in brutality, at least publicly. In other words, the increased sophistication of guns and ammunition have tempered gang violence; we don't see many people filing their teeth into fangs so they can fight better.

Further complicating the story of gangs in the United States is their relationship to the police. In some cases, things back then were just like they are today—in some cities, emergency services and the police simply refuse to go to certain areas (English 2005; see also Venkatesh 2008). Gangs sometimes take their place—a strange contradiction we will discuss later in this chapter. There has also been a tradition of police corruption in the United States (see Buntin 2010 for an example of police corruption in Los Angeles). It's an uncomfortable reality that we have to accept. Police corruption hasn't disappeared, despite our best efforts.

As the European gangs all but vanished as immigrants assimilated into mainstream American culture and the core of the old gangs transformed into a more sophisticated system of organized crime, a new group of gangs emerged due to resistance their members encountered in their attempts to join the mainstream. The established powers refused to fully accept them without fear or hesitation. Many of the gangs we see today came into being for this reason. (I say many to account for neo-Nazi organizations and other white supremacist or white separatist organizations whose violence and drug manufacturing and distribution rival or exceed those of many gangs.)

Explicit and thorough rejection of African Americans throughout the early and mid-twentieth century by middle-class whites and
the laughable notion of "separate but equal" status blocked many
black youth from legitimate opportunities for success, pushing
them into poverty and, especially in cities, a search for alternative
ways to spend their time, express themselves, and develop their
identities and humanity. Does this mean that all black people are
poor and immediately picked up guns and started selling drugs and
killing each other? Of course not. That is a dangerous myth about
crime, and not at all true. After several generations of attempting
to assimilate and achieve equality, as the jobs and opportunities
that motivated their grandparents and great-grandparents to move
north passed them by, as even the social services designed to help
them find some way to surviveturned against them, gangs became
the obvious solution to some black youth.

Modern Gangs: Violence and Community Service

Enough history. What is the reality of gangs in the United States
today? The 2012 National Youth Gang Survey estimated that there
were 30,700 different gangs comprising 850,000 gang members in
the United States (Egley, Howell, and Harris 2014). This puts the
average at about twenty-seven to twenty-eight people per gang.
Remember, the majority of the people we are talking about here
are men—the National Gang Center estimates that over 90 percent
of all people involved in gangs are male and, depending on the
geographic context, likely to be adults. The gang-information site
maintained by the FBI as of this writing contends that there are
33,000 gangs with 1.4 million members nationwide ("Crime in
the United States" 2014), based on the 2011 National Gang Threat
Assessment conducted by the National Gang Intelligence Center
(NGIC). This discrepancy could reflect inclusion of prison gangs
or what law enforcement refers to as OMGs, or outlaw motorcy-
cle gangs. In any event, this is no small amount of people, and
some of you, who have perhaps heard of some of the better-known
gangs, like the Bloods and the Crips, may not quite comprehend

how there could be over 30,000 different gangs. As with most things related to crime, the problem is much more complex than most people realize.

With this many gangs and this many gang members, gangs must definitely be responsible for the majority of urban crime in America, right? It depends on how you look at it. According to the NGIC, gang activity accounts for an average of 48 percent of all violence (and up to 90 percent in some of jurisdictions). This is a very high number, but we need to remember how much violence this represents in reality: the 2012 National Youth Gang Survey, for example, shows that there were 2,363 gang-related homicides in 2012 (meaning that either the victim or offender was in a gang). The 2012 Uniform Crime Report indicates that there were 14,827 murders or nonnegligent manslaughters that same year. Assuming both numbers are correct, gang members were involved in 15.93 percent of all murders that year.

That said, this assumption rests on data collected by law enforcement—and law enforcement can't possibly know how much crime is happening in general, much less how many people are involved in gangs and gang-related activities. This is the dark figure of crime—the completely unknowable amount of crime happening in society. Across every period, the actual amount of crime happening each year and the number of people involved is higher than what official statistics report. This is why self-report data is a necessary and important part of the research process. Through self-report data, we know that the actual number of girl gang members is higher than official statistics would have us believe. For example, using data from the Gang Resistance Education and Training (GREAT) program, Esbensen and Carson (2012) show that the percentage of girls who are active gang members ranged from 31 to 45 percent across the five years of their study, a substantially higher figure than what we saw from the NGIC. Peterson (2012) argues that trying to pin down a number that represents the proportion of girls in gangs nationwide is problematic, because their involvement varies substantially by region and race/ethnicity. According to Peterson's findings, their membership is also contingent on the sex composition of the gang itself, with more girls involved in all-girl gangs self-identifying as "core" members (67 percent), as opposed to those in mixed-sex gangs (57 percent) and male-dominated gangs (39 percent).

Much of the information I've furnished about gangs thus far applies either explicitly or implicitly to male behavior. For many young men, joining a gang provides a sense of belonging—it is a chance to join a group that helps them find their place in the world. Gang life is attractive to some young men because it offers the chance for fun and excitement. For others, joining a gang provides protection from the violence in their community (Melde, Taylor, and Esbensen 2009). For others, a driving reason behind the so-called choice many young men make to join a gang is simple: there is no other choice—this is in keeping with Anderson's (1999) code of the street, discussed in Chapter 3. In the absence of opportunities to succeed in some mainstream, middle-class way in the long term and lacking any real meaningful short-term opportunities to get ahead (i.e., truly good schools), not to mention the very real fear of neighborhood violence (whether or not that violence is actually likely to happen doesn't matter), joining a gang not only becomes the only choice for so many young men, but it makes perfect sense. This is especially so when we remove the socioeconomic component and look at gang membership through the broader lens of systemic racism, systematic exclusion, and flat-out hatred. It's hard to believe that even if there was a way to balance the scales economically, America's racial tension would disappear and people—white people—wouldn't still be inclined to practice racism in some fashion. You can think of this argument as a sort of Marxist interpretation of crime (as per Chapter 2). We can think about gangs' criminal activities as a response to alienation from the larger economic structure and oppression by the powers that be; they offend because they are tired of the rest of the world having its foot on their throats.

I don't want to seem like I'm glossing over the role of racism here. As much as poverty contributes to the continued existence of gangs in American society and can be used to explain the criminal behavior that these young men and women continue to engage in—drug use and dealing, violence, sex work, and so on—racism is arguably the driving force behind all of this. For example, Brotherton (2008) theorizes that the framework used to analyze gang behavior in the past does not apply to gangs today and that contemporary gang behavior can be viewed as a form of resistance. From this perspective, gangs are a way for both individuals and the community to resist the dominant (corporatized) cultural influences in their lives that are working to keep them down. This perspective gives gangs and their surrounding communities substantially more credit than past research has, arguing that gang members are not just pathologically violent or hopelessly recreating their circumstances; rather they are aware of how the system is designed to oppress them and use the gang to rally resistance to that oppression.

When we look at the ways poverty seems to have changed the behavior of so many people—so many young men in particular—we have to recognize that poverty itself didn't just appear out of thin air. Poverty in the modern context has deep roots. Think about it like this: when the United States was colonized, there were no ghettos waiting to be populated. We have to ask ourselves how the ghettos developed. Where did poverty come from? While we will explore the intersection of race and poverty in more detail at the end of this book, I want to briefly discuss it here. Obviously, the United States has had a long problem with both race and immigration, since the country was first colonized and the Native Americans were all but annihilated. We have a long and storied history of othering people, of using the minor cosmetic differences between racial groups to create an almost insurmountable divide between people. While some groups that once experienced massive amounts of racial discrimination (for example, the Irish) have assimilated into the larger mainstream (white) culture, these cosmetic differences—especially skin pigmentation—have blocked others from doing the same on a large scale. This socially constructed difference helped mainstream culture completely demonize blacks in America, especially young black men. This vilification in turn helped justify economic mistreatment, job discrimination, denigration of welfare recipients, and mass incarceration. It helped create poverty, and the combination of poverty and systemic racism helped create and perpetuate gang behavior. All because people generations ago were scared of black men and that irrational fear has been passed on from generation to generation.

You may have noticed that the title for this section has something to do with community service. Maybe you thought that was another bad attempt at humor on my part. Sorry to disappoint. In actuality, gangs and gang members can fill some necessary and useful functions in their communities. The work of Sudhir Venkatesh (1997, 2008) provides a perfect example. Venkatesh (1997) identifies a complex relationship between one gang and its community, wherein some of the residents in a particular housing complex felt more compelled to go to the gang with their problems than to call the police. Venkatesh also shows how the gang, identified as the Saints, actively worked within the community to establish itself as a legitimate authority, playing the political games necessary with the powers that be to diminish criticism. This meant not only bribing key residents (at least, Venkatesh shows how the residents believed this was happening and accused each other of having taken bribes from the gang) but holding visible, public events in the name of "community building" as a sort of public relations move—for instance, staging basketball tournaments or organizing barbeques.

Beyond this public relations maneuvering, members of the community also knew that the gang's presence played a role in their own safety. One resident Venkatesh (1997) spoke to told him that the Saints regularly patrolled the buildings, which the police never would have done; ultimately, the resident said, if they ever did call the police over some instance of violence, at the end the police would leave, and the gang would still be there. Venkatesh (2008) substantially expanded on these themes in *Gang Leader for a Day*. Though he never explicitly says so, it seems likely that this second work discusses the same community Venkatesh was talking about in 1997—his stated entries into the communities are identical, the identification of both gang leaders is the same. The latter work gives us some significant insight into how the gang functions within the community. For instance, Venkatesh witnesses a meeting in which a community leader and a pastor attempt to broker a (temporary, if nothing else) truce between two of the gangs in the project. The two gang leaders meet face to face and air their grievances toward each other in an uncharacteristically calm way—then go about their business at the end. This is not the way we typically think of gang members—and men obsessed with honor—solving their problems (Venkatesh 2008).

Venkatesh's studies may not be generalizable to all gangs throughout the United States. They clearly discuss events in the same location, a unique geographic and cultural area in Chicago, and what happened in this housing project may not apply to the experiences of gang members and their communities in Philadelphia, Detroit, Los Angeles, and so forth. So we must ask ourselves a question: Since it is possible that gangs have a more complex relationship with their communities, as evidenced by Venkatesh's research, could there be some other ways that gang membership might entail benefits—as shocking as it might be for us to consider and accept the idea?

One benefit of gang membership that may or may not be obvious is this: it seems to have some significant mental health benefits for its members, especially those living in fear of violence in their community. As Melde, Taylor, and Esbensen (2009) show, we can think about gang membership in terms of fear of violent victimization. There is evidence to suggest a clear relationship between being violent and being exposed to violence and negative psychological outcomes, specifically an increase in depressive symptoms. But being violent in violent situations may help buffer that depression, especially for males (Latzman and Swisher 2005). Melde, Taylor, and Esbensen show that fear of violent victimization can lead people to join a gang for protection. Gang membership increases the likelihood that they will actually be victimized, but because they are now in a gang, someone will retaliate and go after anyone who commits any violence against them (a protection they likely did not have prior to joining the gang). Thus they feel better about their situation. This research doesn't look at gender differences in how fear of violent victimization can effect mental health outcomes or coping strategies, but that's an interesting question to explore. Based on your own knowledge of how men and women react differently to different types of stress, how do you think we might view gang membership as a positive (or, at least, useful) coping strategy?

Girl Gangs

So what about girl gangs and their members? Girl gangs have always been around in some form, and they've been somewhat overlooked as a criminal entity throughout the history of research on gangs in the United States. Venkatesh (1998), in a study of the rise and fall of Black Sisters United, a collective of girl gangs in Chicago, documents the multiple reasons for this: research done entirely from the male perspective, researchers viewing young women as untouched by the types of stressors that would push young men into gangs, the persistent idea that women join gangs solely to gain the attention of the leader or because they are tomboys, and so on. Similarly, Joe and Chesney-Lind (1995) caution against treating female gang members as hyperviolent, as accessories to male gang members, or as trying to break through some barrier into a male-dominated criminal occupation. This is important because the media present many violent youths as "superpredators." Although Joe and Chesney-Lind say we should not think about female gang members in these sexist terms, we should also be wary of stereotypes depicting violent youths as some heretofore unseen, out-of-control, insatiably violent subset of society. Depictions of youths as superpredators were common in the early to mid-1990s; a 1996 *Newsweek* article quotes then Cook County state's attorney Jack O'Malley as saying, "It's Lord of the Flies on a massive scale. . . . We've become a nation being terrorized by our children" ("'Superpredators' Arrive" 1996). This is a long way of saying that boys have been subjected to a problematic stereotype as well.

The NGIC estimates that 10 percent of gang members are female. However, as mentioned previously, information from the NGIC derives strictly from law enforcement encounters with gangs, and law enforcement has no way of knowing how much crime is being committed in a given community. The actual number of girls involved in gangs is much, much higher, coming close to 50 percent of all gang members in some areas (Peterson 2012; Esbensen and Carson 2012).

While past research has cautioned us against thinking about girl gangs as incredibly violent, we know that a desire to commit violence isn't the only reason people join gangs. Bell (2009) studied gender differences for gang membership, expecting to find significant differences in boys' and girls' reasons for joining gangs—instead, her research found a number of gender similarities. Violent peers, neighborhood disadvantage, school safety, and parental relationships were all significant risk factors for gang membership. Peterson (2012), in a review of research on why kids join gangs, argues that findings show neighborhood disadvantage and lack of pro-social friends affect girls more, which contradicts Bell (2009), so we still need to focus on gender differences in motivations to join gangs. These two factors also do not represent the entire universe of potential causes for joining gangs, of course. For example, Bjerregaard and Smith (1993) and Peterson (2012) note that failing in school, as a risk factor for gang membership, is particularly more important for girls than for boys. Why do you think that is the case?

We should also acknowledge that while there are similarities in the causes of gang membership, that doesn't mean boys and girls view these factors the same ways. For instance, research by Esbensen, Deschenes, and Winfree (1999) found that girls were more likely than boys to feel socially isolated and to have lower self-esteem. The idea of joining a gang for protection may also differ by gender, as the increased risk of sexual violence among girls may cause them to join a gang for protection (Venkatesh 1998), while boys seek protection from violence outside the home.

We should also be asking whether there exist gender differences in terms of what young men and women get out of gang membership. This means we have to revisit the idea of gangs as more complex social entities and social groups than the basic "gangbanging" stereotypes suggest. Some people struggle to understand this. Venkatesh (1998) argues that people have trouble wrapping their heads around this idea because the commonly held definition of a gang is itself very problematic. Venkatesh argues that to understand young women's motivation to join a gang, we need to think about gangs as more than purely criminal enterprises and consider their capacity to serve as a positive force in the community. We need to understand their role as a political entity in society, as gangs' more important functions can and do coexist with the more problematic (read: criminal) goals (Venkatesh 1998). This is another reason to question the NGIC estimate of the number of female gang members in the United States, because there likely exist young women affiliated with gangs who do not act in any criminal way and are thus not included in official government estimates. In other words, because the criminal justice system — by its very nature — has to think about gangs solely in terms of the bad things they do, it may be overlooking some gang members because, in the eyes of the system, they're not guilty of any wrongdoing.

Earlier, I mentioned the media frenzy in the mid-1990s over the new generation of "superpredators," or hyperviolent adolescents plaguing the streets and driving the crime rate through the roof. During this same period (roughly), the media also teed off on another narrative: the rise of violence among girls. Chesney-Lind and Pasko (2004) cite numerous news stories that reference a single instance of female violence as an example of a monumental increase in female violence in general, said to be driven by the liberation hypothesis (Adler 1975). This hypothesis argued that the increase in women's rights over the twentieth century, which led to increases in women's employment in traditionally male sectors and greater independence for women overall, had also resulted in their greater participation in criminal activities. Chesney-Lind and Pasko (2004) also note that this narrative has been largely debunked, but like many things in the social sciences, once the public latches onto an idea, it's almost impossible to get people to let go of it, no matter how false it is. In reality, Chesney-Lind and Pasko claim, the supposedly elevated levels of female violence do not exist; in many categories, female violence had actually decreased over this period. Further, in comparing the criminal behavior of female and male gang members, which shows that a greater proportion of girls have committed a homicide than boys, the numbers hide the reality: girls were only responsible for 8 of the 1,072 homicides attributed to gang members in the data. Overall, males commit gang violence almost exclusively, and gang membership does not appear to lead to any substantial amount of new instances of violence for girls. Chesney-Lind and Pasko go on to argue that girls and women could view gang membership as a potential solution to other problems in their lives, as we'll see in a moment.

So girls could be joining gangs for different reasons than guys and most definitely have different experiences than them. Venkatesh's (1998) study of Black Sisters United showed that the women involved joined not to engage in violence but because they were survivors of violence. In essence, Black Sisters United was a support group for women dealing with a number of different stressors and traumatic experiences who had nowhere else to turn. Individual group members engaged in criminal activities early on, but the group itself focused on social work and social activities—ranging from putting on fashion shows to helping survivors of intimate partner violence find shelter. Over time, according to Venkatesh, as the gang grew, so did interest among some of its members in participating in the drug markets. As members of Black Sisters United became more entrenched in the drug trade, they partnered with a male-dominated Chicago gang called the Saints to increase their share of the money. This decision marked the end of Black Sisters United, as a rift emerged among the leadership over the gang's direction and led to its dissolution (Venkatesh 1998).

Here we have an example of a girl gang that, at least at the outset, aimed to make its members' lives fundamentally better and only turned to criminal activities because of an inability to fund its legitimate operations legally. That seems like a pretty intense dilemma, so much so that some of you might find yourselves forgiving the gang girls' actions. Given their circumstances, if we found ourselves facing a similar situation, don't you think that crime (beyond belonging to a named gang, which is itself a crime) would be a reasonable, rational choice? This is what Chesney-Lind and Pasko (2004) were referring to when they said that girls might view gang membership as a solution to the multitude of barriers created by rampant sexism, racism, and classism. Though ultimately unsuccessful, for a time the Black Sisters United provided real support to women in their community.

But we're getting off track. The question is, was Black Sisters United an anomaly in gang culture or more typical of girl gangs? What do you think? Hansen (2005) found gender differences in gang members in New York City: while the girl gang members in her data were becoming more violent, they were also building more loyal relationships and more likely to view the gang along the lines of a family they got to choose, people who were there for them for more than just criminal purposes (Hansen 2005). This attitude resembles that of Black Sisters United (Venkatesh 1998).

It's also interesting to think about girl gang members in terms of how they negotiate their own gender identities. In other words, a lot of the gang research has focused on males and masculinity, and these stories portray women as playthings for the guys or as trying to emulate male behavior (i.e., violence). The members of Black Sisters United, however, didn't seem to be concerned with emulating masculine roles; quite the opposite—this black feminist organization pushed into criminal behavior to keep itself alive and only folded when some of the members chose to begin emulating the guys. So, in other words, how do women in gangs view themselves as women? How do they think about their own femininity? Laidler and Hunt (2001) explored this question and found that girl gang members must navigate a very complicated series of relationships with their parents, the guys in their lives, and each other, all under the larger umbrella of traditional gender expectations for their behavior. Laidler and Hunt argue that for the girls in their study, their biggest concern was respectability. Here, respect and respectability mean something different from Anderson's (1999) code-of-the-street idea of respect as a commodity worth dying for. For the girls Laidler and Hunt (2001) studied, respect and respectability had to do with how they carried themselves, their sexual reputations, and a larger idea of self-respect, self-worth, and independence. For these girls, completely succumbing to traditional gender expectations—and some experienced intense pressure to do so from their parents—would be a sign of weakness in the gang and all but guarantee serious problems for them in the future. In this case, emulating masculine behaviors became a survival technique rather than true imitation. These girls weren't bad and violent; they just needed to demonstrate that they could be violent to survive. In this case, we can see a parallel with Anderson's (1999) work, as this is code switching in a different context. Anderson distinguishes between "decent" and "street" families, noting that children from decent families have to be aware of the code of the street and adopt those behaviors as necessary as a means of survival. They aren't bad kids and don't wish to become involved in street crime, but they understand that to survive, they need to be able to change their behavior—to switch their personality—as needed.

Drug Dealing and Drug Use

Serious violent behavior aside, we almost always think about crime in urban areas in terms of drugs, including drug dealing, drug use, and drug-related violence. Many people think the urban poor and their neighborhoods are overrun with drugs. This popular perception has allowed politicians to pass laws requiring welfare recipients to be drug-tested as a condition of their assistance. (These mandatory drug-testing programs have caught very few drug users, but the politicians won't let the truth get in the way of a tried-and-true narrative and the myth of the welfare queen.)

Let's think about the realities of both drug dealing and drug use in these urban areas—focusing on the urban poor, for now—and the role of gender in pushing people toward or away from these behaviors. Do men and women living in urban centers use drugs for different reasons? Are they using at different rates? Does drug use affect their lives in different ways? There's clearly a lot to unpack here.

The overlap between drugs and violent behavior is very significant, and we need to spend some time talking about it. As mentioned, some of the violence in urban areas is related to the drug economy—typically violence that erupts over territory or distribution and not necessarily as a result of personal conflict. This violence is part of the drug business. But we can also think about the relationship between drugs and violent behavior in terms of the chemical effects of drug use and drug addiction warping our behavior and propelling some people into violent situations, which don't necessarily have to involve another person directly. For example, Sheehan et al. (2013) looked at gender differences in the presence of drugs in the systems of people who had suffered a violent death. They did indeed find a gender difference in the types of drugs present, which in turn correlated with greater risk of either homicide or suicide. Men were more likely to have marijuana, cocaine, or amphetamines in their system at death, drugs associated with a greater chance of homicide. Women were likelier to have opiates or antidepressants in their system at the time of death, drugs associated with a greater chance of suicide.

Rural Gangs

The number of gangs in the United States, north of 30,000, may be difficult for some of you to wrap your heads around because not all gangs exist in cities. Thinking about US residents in terms of people who live in cities versus people who don't is somewhat simplistic. In reality, gangs exist in all sorts of places throughout the United States, though the problem gets stereotyped as isolated to the poorest inner-city neighborhoods.

The fact of the matter is, we know that gangs do exist in other areas, but we don't really know much about them. The National Gang Center does have information on the demographics of gangs operating in smaller cities or in rural counties: they tend to have younger members, more female members, and somewhat different racial compositions than gangs in bigger cities do ("National Youth Gang Survey Analysis"). Weisheit and Wells (2004) posited that the number of rural gangs and gang members was on the rise and couldn't be explained using the same theoretical models as applied to urban gangs. They speculated that economic opportunity (as opposed to economic disadvantage) drove the rise in gangs in these areas, which reflected internal migration, but they also stated that the existence of rural gangs might be temporary. Weisheit, Falcone, and Wells (2005) expanded on this and suggested that gangs might also be cropping up in rural areas for a number of other reasons: (1) gang members growing tired of police efforts against them in urban centers and moving to places less equipped to combat their criminal behavior, (2) small-time drug dealers looking to increase their presence on the drug market and thereby bringing gangs into their town, or (3) juvenile offenders from rural areas being arrested and incarcerated alongside gang members and then bringing the behavior home with them upon their release.

Whatever the reason for the presence of gang activity in rural areas, the topic has been incredibly overlooked. Weisheit, Falcone, and Wells (2005) attribute this oversight to a difference in the types of gangs, with biker gangs more likely to reside in small towns and rural areas and are notoriously difficult to study. The rise of black and Hispanic gangs in these areas may also be so contradictory of the media depiction of, and existing stereotypes about, gangs that we flat-out refuse to believe this problem exists. Many of us, of course, are seeing gang activities in the small towns and rural communities where we live. What do you think about the idea that gangs in these areas somehow have different motivations than those in larger cities? Do you think gender could play a different role here?

That said, it is important to remember the importance of context. Klein and Maxson (2006) argue that the gang presence in rural areas is greatly overstated, because while it may exist, its prevalence does not come close to that in urban centers. In other words, what might constitute a gang in a rural space would likely not be considered a noteworthy threat in an urban center.

Klein and Maxson (2006) also question the above arguments regarding the migration of gangs from major urban areas into rural areas, arguing that this idea comes from law enforcement and not objective research. They argue that the increase in gang activity in rural centers is not because gangs are expanding; rather, these gangs are

> primarily home-grown gang problems, likely spawned by local community factors rather than instigated by the direct transfer of gang culture or recruitment by gang migrants.
>
> Minimal and, when evident, diffuse organizational affiliations with big-city gangs. There are very few examples of shots called by big-city gang leaders; closely connected satellites of major city gangs . . . are rare.
>
> Gang culture permeated through the popular media (movies, clothing styles, music) seems to have more influence on local gang activity than do big-city migrants. (Klein and Maxson 2006, 57)

This isn't to say that gang migration isn't happening. Klein and Maxson (2006, 58) characterize it as a "widespread yet shallow phenomenon," but they do say that the migration of gangs into rural areas has not been thoroughly researched.

Gang Membership as a Life Transition

As more criminological study places criminal behavior in a broader context and recognizes the value of longitudinal research, our thinking about gangs has morphed from a discussion of what gangs do and why people join them into a framing of gang membership as a turning point in the life course. For instance, Melde and Esbensen (2011) demonstrate that joining a gang is associated with changes in attitude, a reduction in informal social control, and an increased risk of delinquent behavior above and beyond those the new member may already have been engaged in. These changes have serious consequences for the overall well-being of the gang member throughout life; in a follow-up study, Melde and Esbensen (2014) show that even after leaving a gang, former gang members are at an elevated risk for antisocial behavior. This means that gang membership, even if limited in terms of time, clearly entails much more than we may think at first. Quitting a gang isn't like quitting a job or leaving your gym. The affiliation clearly sticks with a former gang member for a long time. So how does anyone ever actually get out?

Getting Out of the Game

In Chapter 3, we talked about the life course perspective and the concept of desistance. Remember that desistance is a complex process by which a person ceases to behave criminally. It can involve a change in life circumstances (marriage, employment), a change in the person's self-perception (greater maturity), physical change (growing too old to participate anymore), or even a lack of opportunity to commit crime. In that chapter we were talking about how men and women desist from crime in a very general sense. Now, let's think about whether desistance might differ in some way for people involved in the types of crimes we've been talking about in an urban context. In other words, what unique challenges might people living in urban areas face in ceasing violent behavior or getting out of drug dealing or drug using? What challenges might gang members face?

The idea of gang desistance is particularly interesting, at least to me, because of the group dynamic as well as the potential that membership provides a positive effect for the people involved (in their eyes, anyway—there is no net positive effect of gang membership according to the research). So how does desistance happen? The idea of desistance has been debated heavily over the past thirty years. Sampson and Laub (1992, 1993) insist that marriage is the driving force behind this process, while others seek alternative explanations beyond simple age-graded social control. Until recently, research framing gang membership as a pivotal point in the life course was relatively hard to come by. We do know—surprise!—that the process of getting out of a gang is more complex than just walking away, because, as a life course transition, gang membership seems to have a serious influence on behavior long after a person has quit (Melde and Esbensen 2014).

Leaving a gang is not the same as quitting a job and never talking to anyone you worked with again. Separating from gang life
takes time, and the transition is far from smooth and easy. As we
discuss the various reasons why people leave gangs, keep in mind
the question of whether these might vary by gender. Decker,
Pyrooz, and Moule (2014) talk about desistance from gang membership in terms of a shift in identity that can eventually lead to a
complete break from the gang. The process they identify is gradual,
with individuals first beginning to second-guess membership
because they see other gang members continually struggling with
poverty and crime and generally just not leading a life they envision
for themselves (Decker, Pyrooz, and Moule 2014). For some, a violent incident triggers the identity shift; others begin to see themselves as more important to their immediate family—especially
their children—than to the people in the gang. This raises one gender difference in desistance from gang life. O'Neal et al. (2016)
found that women were more likely than men to identify threats to
their families as reason to leave a gang. While Decker, Pyrooz, and
Moule (2014) show parenthood as a motivating factor in the desistance process for both male and female gang members, there may
be a question about which comes first—desistance or children—
especially for female gang members, who may not choose to get
pregnant until after they have left the gang and entered a presumably safer and more stable life stage (Varriale 2008).

One issue with desistance from gang activities has to do with
the larger social context in which these behaviors occur. For
instance, Decker, Pyrooz, and Moule (2014) state that one barrier
to desisting from gang activities has to do with whether the
gang—or rival gangs—will recognize the individual's new identity as someone who has gotten out of the life. Refusal to accept
that former members have quit could pull them away from a legit
lifestyle. There is also the issue of the intensity and embeddedness
of some of the relationships individuals might have with other
members of the gang. Decker, Pyrooz, and Moule highlight a few
people who have tried to desist from gang life and do not actively
participate in anything the gang does but may still consider themselves members of the gang all the same. Others may feel a need

to retaliate against rival gangs for any harm to former co-members about whom they still care. Finally, larger structural issue(s) of poverty, systemic racism, and poor police-community relations may have inspired them to join the gang in the first place, and unless things have improved (unlikely) or their perception of the problem or willingness to deal with it has improved (which, pessimistically, means accepting that things are stacked against them and learning to live with it, and what are the chances of that happening?), they may feel pulled back into the gang life (Decker, Pyrooz, and Moule 2014).

We need to talk about some other issues related to desistance from gang membership. Carson, Peterson, and Esbensen (2013) looked at different ways gang members might think about their own desistance from gang life and/or their own subjective interpretation of their membership in the gang. They then constructed three different definitions of gang desistance that required the youths in their study to admit to various degrees of past gang membership. The problem with this study is the way in which Carson and colleagues identified gang members. More respondents answered questions about their past gang life than actually admitted to being involved in a gang, which the authors think could show willful deception on the part of the respondents. More importantly, Carson, Peterson, and Esbensen identify some gender differences in how desistance works that cut across the gray-area definitions of gang membership they constructed. In general, they found that most kids didn't spend much time in a gang (around one year), eventually became disillusioned with gang life, and didn't face any real consequences if they chose to leave. However, males were more likely than females to experience violent repercussions for leaving, and they were more likely to report that a violent experience had motivated them to leave in the first place.

The last thing I want to talk about here is the possible relationship between gender and religion. In *God's Gangs: Barrio Ministry, Masculinity, and Gang Recovery*, Edward Orozco Flores (2014) discusses two programs in Los Angeles aimed at changing the behavior of young men in gangs. Flores argues that desistance from gang activity is difficult because there isn't exactly a soft landing spot for these guys once they leave—meaning there isn't really a dependable mechanism in place to help them make the transition back into normal life; there isn't an abundance of jobs out there that will provide these guys with both a meaningful identity and a living wage. Flores focused on the work of Homeboy Industries and Victory Outreach, each of which used a different religious background (Homeboy Industries is a Catholic-centered organization; Victory Outreach is Protestant-centered). In both cases, participation in the ministry served as a sort of substitute for gang membership in terms of involvement from a social control perspective and differential association from a learning perspective. The different religious perspectives, however, entailed different ways of transforming behavior. Victory Outreach, as I mentioned, employed a Protestant-centered approach, viewing God as transcendent and encouraging the transitioning gang members to strive to climb the hierarchy within the ministry so that they could rise above the chaos around them and become closer to God. Homeboy Industries, with its Catholic-centered approach, viewed God as omnipresent and encouraged its members to spread the gospel throughout the community.

On paper those might seem like small differences, but in practice, these were two very different organizations. Flores describes Victory Outreach as trying to instill in its members a sense of "hypermorality" that allowed the black men and disillusioned second-generation immigrants it worked with to see themselves as morally superior to the rest of the community. This sense of morality allowed these men to reframe how they saw themselves in terms of honor and respect—in other words, it changed their own view of how to attain and maintain these attributes, with moral supremacy now the center of their lives (Flores 2014). Flores also shows how Victory Outreach aggressively made its ministry and values central to the lives of its congregation, all but forcing its members to do away with any non-Christian cultural material (i.e., to throw away mainstream rap CDs and replace them with Christian artists), discouraging materialism, and even discouraging members from taking jobs that would prevent them from participating in church activities. The combination of hyper-morality and a centering of Victory Outreach's message in the lives of the congregation completely transformed the lives of these ex-gang members by dominating their time and reshaping their philosophy and sense of gender identity.

Homeboy Industries, on the other hand, took a very different approach to recovery. While Victory Outreach wanted to take these ex-gang members out of the corrupting world that had sent them down an evil path, Homeboy Industries viewed gangs and every-thing associated with them as the result of an unjust system and a heartless society (Flores 2014). Utilizing the motto "Jobs Not Jails," Homeboy Industries provided a number of employment opportuni-ties for its members, from landscaping to baking, as well as self-help workshops, tattoo removal, and legal services. While Homeboy Industries was more open spiritually, incorporating things like yoga or Native American symbolism in its teaching, its members also engaged in a similar type of "moral one-upsmanship" as Victory Outreach members, only from a slightly different perspective. Whereas Victory Outreach encouraged its members to find their masculinity and honor in moral superiority to the corrupt world around them, Homeboy Industries urged members to find strength and honor within an oppressive world that wanted them to become angry and to fail (Flores 2014). In other words, a central Homeboy Industries tenet was that oppression had led to gang life, but instead of getting mad at the government and police for creating these con-ditions, the best response was to show humility and peace. It is a bigger version of something that maybe some of our parents taught us as children: that the best way to get back at a person being mean to you is to be nice to them—it'll drive them crazy.

6

Relationship Violence

On October 3, 1995, the so-called trial of the century concluded. O. J. Simpson had allegedly murdered his ex-wife, Nicole Brown Simpson, and Ronald Goldman, a man in the wrong place at the wrong time. (Goldman had been returning a pair of glasses Brown's mother had left at the restaurant where he worked.) Simpson and Brown had divorced in 1992; Simpson earlier pleaded no contest to spousal abuse in 1989. The prosecution argued that Simpson killed Brown and Goldman in a fit of jealous rage. The jury disagreed with that version of events and acquitted Simpson of all criminal charges.

The most popular podcast of all time, *Serial*, debuted in late 2014 and covered the case of Hae Min Lee, a student at Woodlawn High School in Baltimore County, Maryland, who disappeared on January 13, 1999. Her body was found a month later in a Baltimore park. She had been strangled. Her ex-boyfriend, Adnan Syed, soon became the focus of the police investigation into Lee's death. He was eventually convicted of her murder and is currently serving a life sentence for it, though, as *Serial* documents, he maintains his innocence. The prosecution alleged that Syed was enraged over their breakup and that Lee had already started dating someone new, that this was an affront to him, and that he killed her to satisfy his anger and protect his honor. The jury agreed with this story.

Though there is a world of difference between O. J. Simpson and Adnan Syed, regardless of what you think about either man, their cases have a number of similarities—to each other and to so many other stories about domestic violence. Stories of men seeking to control their spouses and partners through fear and violence. Stories of men consumed with jealously. Stories of men so sexually charged that they don't care whom they target as long as they get theirs. Stories of men so depraved that they stalk women and children like a predator hunting down its prey.

How true are these stories, though? In other words, how do we separate the Simpson and Syed cases from the stereotypes surrounding them and discern the reality of the situation? In the next two chapters, we will cover two of the biggest areas in the field of gender and crime: relationship violence and sexual violence. These two topics overlap a lot, and finding a clear and obvious way to separate them may be difficult for some of you. Let's think about this in terms of the topics we will cover. First, in this chapter, we will talk about child abuse, stalking, domestic violence, rape, and the emerging area of same-sex violence. This seems to run the gamut of both topics, doesn't it? However, in the following chapter, we will focus on stranger rape, prostitution and other forms of sex work, and the emerging area of human trafficking—focusing explicitly on the sexual component of violence. In this chapter, as we'll see, violence that appears to be sexual in nature actually has nothing to do with sex at all.

Think about this chapter as covering all of the bad ways a relationship can go—between a parent and a child, between friends, between a couple married or cohabiting for twenty years. There is a major distinction between this and other forms of violence. Gang shootings, battles for drug territory, fights in a bar or at a party—these forms of violence happen out in the open. Relationship violence is much more nefarious, when you think about it, because it happens behind closed doors in the privacy of the home. Think about this in your own lives: if there was a fight in the middle of campus, everyone would know about it. But someone in your classroom right now could be fighting almost every day and putting on a brave face. You might never know what's happening to them.

Relationship violence can occur in myriad ways. Unlike the types of violence discussed in Chapter 5, relationship violence—regardless of the relationship between the people involved—doesn't necessarily have to be physical in nature. This isn't to say that relationship violence is never physical; physical abuse is definitely a major concern here. The difference is that relationship violence can also involve psychological or emotional abuse, making it much harder to detect and even define than other forms of violence.

The fact is, because relationship violence can occur in secret and involves more than just physical violence, it's a much more difficult crime to handle—it's so much more difficult to detect than more public or visceral forms of violence. And because some of these behaviors have their roots in traditional gender roles, some people in society do not view them as problematic. They might argue that it's a parent's right to discipline her child; it's a husband's right to have sex with his wife whenever he wants. These types of justifications or rationalizations illustrate how sometimes a behavior might seem obviously harmful to one person but acceptable to someone else. That said, for the purpose of this book, and being a decent citizen in general, let's go ahead and agree that all forms of relationship violence are wrong, that they are never justified or excusable, and that this is a type of violence that society needs to eliminate immediately.

Another issue we will explore in this chapter is the idea that men are always the perpetrators of relationship violence and only women are victims. Ask yourself, could this possibly be true? If so, why? If not, why is that belief so common? As social scientists, we know that it's impossible that men are the offenders 100 percent of the time and women are the victims 100 percent of the time. So who are the people who seemingly defy gender stereotypes, the male victims and female offenders? What are their lives like?

The Role of Power and Control

Before we begin to delve into the different types of relationship violence, I want to address the following question: Why do these different forms of relationship violence occur? What could drive someone to commit such an act—especially one as seemingly depraved as sexual abuse? While many of the broad theories we covered in Chapter 2 can and do apply here—the offender might lack self-control or be under immense strain or insufficiently bonded to pro-social institutions—the field of relationship violence gives us an alternative explanation for why it occurs. In many cases, relationship violence, regardless of the age of the people involved or the nature of their relationship, is all about exercising power and control over the victim. Abusive parents might be focusing on their children because, while they have no power in their jobs, they can exercise power over their kids. Rapists might see themselves as completely powerless in life, but in that moment with their victim, they are completely in control.

This need to feel power is associated with masculinity, and many men are socialized into it. Men learn as they grow up that you are not a real man if you are not powerful. Masculinity does not allow someone to be weak or vulnerable because that means you're not a man. Boys are exposed to this at a very young age. Being perceived as "girly" is a fate worse than death for many boys, who learn to demonstrate masculinity via expressing power and control over people around them. This is why sexual violence has nothing to do with the actual sexual experience but rather with the control exerted over the victim—it is an expression of power.

The idea of learning here also means that we learn ways to frame this behavior to make it socially acceptable. We will see the different neutralization techniques that people use to convince others that their behavior is not problematic. We learn how to deflect criticism of our behavior back onto the victim—he should have known better than to act like that, she led me on, and so on. Learning is the mechanism that drives relationship violence; rape culture is a main source of that learning; power and control are the primary motivations behind it; and offenders attempt to protect themselves and legitimize their behaviors using neutralization techniques.

Not only do sexually violent people attempt to rationalize their behavior, but society tends to accept their justifications, because we live in what is called a rape culture. This concept argues that the culture we live in replicates rape (and other types of sex crimes) by making people think that it's a normal and unavoidable part of life. Sexual victimization is going to happen to women no matter what, because that's just how things are, and that's how they're always going to be. This type of thinking—that things have always been this way and that it's not worth trying to change anything because it's always going to be this way—is a big reason why all of the types of crime in this chapter still exist. We are responsible for perpetuating rape by creating a culture that excuses these behaviors, that excuses rapists (especially if they're famous), and that makes jokes about rape while also blaming rape survivors for what happened to them. So when rape in the military can be partially attributed to commanding officers' failure to take sexual harassment seriously (Sadler et al. 2003), we can make the argument that those officers contributed to the rape culture of the military. College students who fail to take rape seriously (Armstrong, Hamilton, and Sweeney 2006) are contributing to rape culture on college campuses.

Understanding how the culture we live in affects our behavior can be very tricky for some people because we're so completely immersed in it that sometimes it can be almost impossible to see. The idea that elements of our culture can intentionally reinforce toxic behaviors is also hard for some people to accept, because nothing in our society is just pulled from thin air—someone is behind the production and distribution of our music, movies, books, and so on. How can this be?

Viewing culture in terms of the propagation of harmful and/or oppressive ideas is a Marxist perspective. Take, for instance, the song "Blurred Lines" by Robin Thicke. It's a generic pop song on the surface, maybe, but when you look at the lyrics side by side with things rapists have said to their victims, a whole other interpretation comes to the surface. Using images posted online by Project Unbreakable (http://project-unbreakable.org), an organization that gives voices to rape survivors, Sezin Koehler from The Society Pages (http://thesocietypages.org) did just this. The finding might be shocking to some of you, but in the end, "Blurred Lines" doesn't just promote rape culture, it's practically the rapists' anthem (even the title references the blurring of the line of sexual consent). For instance, the lyric "You know you want it" perpetuates the myth that all women secretly want sex and enjoy rape and that any resistance on their part is not real. Scully and Marolla (1984), in their interviews with convicted rapists, found that men commonly used this particular myth to justify their violent behavior. The lyric "The way you grab me / Must wanna get nasty" speaks to another justification the rapists in Scully and Marolla's study used: that it's the victim's fault, that women who are raped bring it on themselves by being too seductive. (For more information, see Koehler 2013.)

This song is a very obvious product of rape culture, and most cases aren't this blatant. Still, this should worry you, because even something as over the top as "Blurred Lines" still became very popular (albeit just for the summer of 2013), playing over and over, and it wasn't just adults who listened to it, either. This song helped perpetuate rape culture with kids, at least subconsciously. Plenty of other types of media normalize relationship violence and bolster this type of crime; for more, see Box 6.1.

Recognizing that we live in a culture that tends to downplay the seriousness of rape (and that is putting it extremely lightly) makes it easier to understand why so many people are so quick to blame rape victims for their victimization. The public response to widely publicized rape cases isn't to damn the actions of the rapists but to blame the victims for what happened to them. Rather than asking why a person (or group) would do such a horrible thing to someone, we ask, What was she wearing? Was she drunk? Was she high? Was she flirting with him? Was it a "legitimate" rape? Did she lead him on? And on and on. In the end, the story becomes more about all the ways the victim may have brought the attack on herself and less about the actions of the offender. As a result, rape becomes normalized, and any perceived mistake or misstep by the victim is amplified to the millionth degree. Do you think this could be why so many victims fail to come forward?

Box 6.1 Stephen A. Smith and the Ray Rice Controversy

Beginning in February 2013, the National Football League (NFL) and the world of sports media became embroiled in a domestic violence assault case involving Ray Rice and his (then) fiancée, Janay Palmer. The two were arrested on February 15 on simple assault charges involving an altercation at an Atlantic City casino. On February 19, four days later, TMZ released surveillance footage of Rice dragging an unconscious Palmer from an elevator. On July 25, following Rice's acceptance into a pretrial intervention program and a disciplinary meeting with NFL commissioner Roger Goodell, Rice was suspended for two games.

By definition, the sports media are equipped to discuss one thing, and one thing only, with any level of authority: sports. Asking them to opine on social issues is problematic at best. Following Rice's two-game suspension, ESPN personality Stephen A. Smith argued on air that women are responsible for their own victimization—and that it is on them to avoid provoking abuse. Smith's comments met with blazing criticism, including from other ESPN personalities, and he received a one-week suspension as a result. Why does this matter? Across all its television, radio, and Internet platforms, ESPN reaches millions of people daily, and presumably its audience is predominantly male (though that might be an unfair assumption). Though the network punished Smith for his victim blaming, his broadcast still went out and can't be unheard; to paraphrase Smith's own message, the damage had already been done. And therein lies the concern: the media have a tremendous ability to shape public opinion on social issues, for good or ill, and can transmit outmoded or incorrect values to impressionable people. How many young men looked at victims of domestic abuse differently because of this commentator's words—or, more likely, found reinforcement for their existing notions? Obviously, this isn't the first instance of a sports announcer spouting opinions in areas where he has no expertise. From Jason Collins's becoming the first openly gay professional athlete to the controversy surrounding the Washington NFL franchise, the sports media have a monumental ability to transmit ideas to audiences about subjects substantially more important than sports, and very little evidence suggests they handle it responsibly.

Child Abuse and Molestation

How much child abuse actually occurs in the United States? As with most crimes—especially those that fall under the rubric of relationship abuse—there is likely severe underreporting. This is especially problematic, because while many adult victims of relationship abuse may choose not to get help for a number of reasons, they at least have the power to report their abuse if they opt to do so. Not only might children not know they're being abused, but they may also be unaware of what to do about it.

Perhaps a better question is, how much child abuse do we know about? Who would have this information? Again we turn to the federal government. Information on child abuse throughout the United States is reported by Child Protective Services (and variations thereof), input into the National Child Abuse and Neglect Data System, and compiled by the Children's Bureau, an office of the Administration for Children and Families, which is in turn a part of the Department of Health and Human Services. According to the Children's Bureau, in 2014 there were an estimated 702,000 cases of abuse or neglect in the United States (Children's Bureau 2014). The most common form of victimization was neglect (526,744 cases), followed by physical abuse (119,517 cases), sexual abuse (58,105 cases), psychological maltreatment (42,290 cases), and lastly medical neglect (15,645 cases). Note that more cases are listed than victims during 2014. These numbers reflect the fact that an individual child can be victimized multiple times and in multiple ways. In other words, if a child is physically abused and neglected, both types of victimization would be counted even though he is only one victim. In terms of who committed these acts of abuse, the majority of offenders were the child's mother (247,616 cases), the mother and father together (129,599 cases), or the father (124,870 cases). Perpetrators defined as a nonparent were most commonly some other male relative (18,375 cases). This seems to contradict the supposedly "commonsense" notion that men are much more violent than women, further demonstrating, in the case of child abuse at least, that violence is context specific. Younger children were at much greater risk of victimization than older children. Over 25 percent of those children victimized were between the ages of zero and three; 20 percent were between the ages of three and five. If the reality of child abuse perpetration does line up with the numbers provided by the federal government (remember, we must take the statistics compiled by law enforcement with a grain of salt because law enforcement can't catch everyone), why do you think mothers are more likely than fathers to abuse their children?

What about the sex of the victims? According to the data, boys and girls are victimized almost equally. Of the cases in 2014, 50.9 percent were girls, and 49.1 percent were boys (Children's Bureau 2014). To put these numbers in perhaps more relatable terms, the rate of victimization was 9.8 per 1,000 for girls and 9.0 per 1,000 for boys.

In truth, Cashmore and Shackel (2014) show that much of the research on child sexual abuse tends to focus on the female-victim, male-offender dynamic. Society tends to view abusive situations, sexually or otherwise, in terms of the relationship between the victim and the offender as opposed to the nature of the act itself. As Cashmore and Shackel discuss, for girls and boys, their emerging gender and sexual identities play a key role in how their abuse is viewed. While both boys and girls are more likely to be victimized by a man, women can and do offend as well (although at a much lesser rate). What does this have to do with the gender and sexual identities of the victims? For boys, sexual abuse by a woman may be viewed not as abuse at all but as a point of pride—a "rite of passage" (Peake 1989; Spataro, Moss, and Wells 2001; Cashmore and Shackel 2014). Indeed, many men react to news stories in which a female teacher has had a sexual relationship with a male teenage student with something along the lines of "Good for him!" or "If I had her as a teacher, I'd study harder, too!" The abuse is treated as a joke, which means that a lot of people will tend to think that it isn't a big deal and shouldn't be treated seriously.

When the abuser is male, boys might experience psychological consequences that girls would not. An unwanted same-sex encounter, coupled with traditional male gender roles and an emerging sexual identity, can send many boys into a depressive spiral and cause them to question their own sexual identity (Crowder and Hawkings 1995; Dhaliwal et al. 1996; Dorahy and Clearwater 2012; O'Leary and Barber 2008; Rhodes et al. 2011; Romano and De Luca 2001; Cashmore and Shackel 2014). Furthermore, evidence suggests that boys experience much more physically violent sexual abuse than girls, which can include multiple perpetrators, repeat violations, and threatened or actual physical harm (Cashmore and Shackel 2014).

The relationship between abuse and future offending also differs by gender. According to research by Asscher, Put, and Stams (2015), female delinquents are more likely than their male counterparts to have a history of physical and sexual abuse. However, the girls in this study did not go on to become physically or sexually violent themselves—there is no direct transmission of violence. Boys who were victims of sexual abuse, however, were more likely to go on to become sexually violent themselves.

We can view the motivations of people who engage in child abuse in terms of how they justify their behavior to themselves and others. Sykes and Matza (1957) called these justifications techniques of neutralization. Basically, they argued that most individuals who engaged in crime and delinquency knew they were doing wrong but found ways to justify their misbehavior to themselves so they could continue with it, without having to think of themselves as bad people. We'll explore this concept in much greater detail when we discuss acquaintance rape, but it definitely applies to child abuse. For example, in the fall of 2014, when NFL star Adrian Peterson of the Minnesota Vikings plead guilty to child abuse after assaulting his four-year-old son with a switch, many people in the public defended him by saying that the switch method of discipline was acceptable and a part of "black culture" that people should leave alone. Thus defenders neutralize the behavior by turning the conditions of the argument around on the accusers and reframing the debate in those terms (Sykes and Matza 1957). Shockingly, few people instead realized, based on that incident, that they too had been abused as kids.

How can this possibly apply to child sexual abuse? Durkin and Bryant (1999) examined the rationalizations used by self-identified pedophiles online and found that they readily employed several of the techniques stated by Sykes and Matza (1957) and others who have further investigated this line of thinking. The majority of the abusers in Durkin and Bryant's (1999) study (approximately 70 percent) used one of two techniques: denial of injury or condemnation of the condemners. Condemning the condemners entails shifting the blame from the abuser onto the accuser. Child molesters commonly shift blame from themselves onto law enforcement, social workers, and so on. This means that rather than trying to defend or explain their own bad behavior, they instead try to refocus of the argument on the bad things that the people accusing them have done, real or imagined. For example, they will accuse the police of corruption or of sexual assault, or whatever, which in turn puts the authorities on the defensive and distracts from the real issue at hand.

Denial of injury is another way of saying that no actual harm was done—in other words, the whole incident was no big deal. Durkin and Bryant found a number of molesters who readily denied doing any serious physical or emotional harm to the boys they encountered. Another common neutralization strategy, though one not really used by the men in Durkin and Bryant's study, is to argue that the abuser is actually the victim—that the child seduced the adult, who is therefore not at fault for his or her actions (Mayer 1985; Lanning 1987). This may seem impossible, or dated, or both, but as recently as 2012, Father Benedict Groeschel, then the director for the Office of Spiritual Development for the Catholic Archdiocese of New York, wrote an opinion piece coming to the defense of convicted child abuser Jerry Sandusky, arguing that in many cases the child is sexually aggressive and the alleged abuser is anything but.

A final technique of neutralization worth mentioning here is called "basking in reflected glory"—BIRGing for short. This defense maintains that because revered historical peoples engaged in a behavior, it's acceptable. With regard to child molestation, BIRGing takes the form of arguing that because men like Socrates, Plato, Alexander the Great, and many others, engaged in it, it is perfectly acceptable (Durkin and Bryant 1999). Who are we to judge Socrates, after all? Through the use of these techniques of neutralization, child abusers justify their acts, at least to themselves. They aren't the only people who utilize techniques of neutralization to rationalize their actions either, especially not when it comes to the larger category of relationship violence. As we'll see, plenty of other offenders will try to manipulate the situation to frame it in a way that makes sense to them.

Incest, a sexual relationship (sometimes consensual, sometimes not) between blood relatives, is another form of child abuse that occurs in the United States but is rarely discussed openly. Of the forms of relationship violence discussed in this chapter thus far, incest is probably the least talked about, except in cases of child abuse. In that way, we have covered incest somewhat in this chapter already, in our discussion of child abuse and molestation. A sexually abusive relationship between parent and child would be defined as incest. This can also include sexual contact between siblings, half siblings, or perhaps cousins.

How much incest occurs where the assailant is someone other than a parent? Unfortunately, that's hard to say. Incest is so uncommon that many studies include it with other types of sexual deviance, like bestiality, or relatively harmless offenses that are technically criminal, like consensual sex between minors. Carlson, Maciol, and Schneider (2006) argue that because of a "dearth of research" on the subject, we can't even reach an agreed-on rate at which incest between siblings occurs, with some arguing that it is extremely rare, while others claim it to be much more common than father-daughter incest.

What *do* we know, though? Finkelhor (1980) surveyed 796 undergraduate students at six universities in the eastern United States and found that 10 percent of male respondents and 15 percent of female respondents reported some sexual contact with a sibling. Finkelhor classifies roughly 25 percent of those experiences as exploitative in that the respondent felt forced into the act and/or there was a serious age difference between participants. Furthermore, females were much more likely than males to feel negatively about the experience. Further still, women who did have this experience, regardless of whether they had a positive or negative perspective on it, were much more sexually active later in life. Unfortunately, Finkelhor's is the landmark study in sibling incest because it could very well be the only large-scale one of its kind; most research into this phenomenon involves either clinical studies or case studies. Krienert and Walsh (2011) argue that a major reason why we don't know more about sexual contact between siblings is because so many parents tend to think of it as completely normal, a sort of rite of passage. Because they think of it as normal sexual exploration and not dangerous abuse, it is rarely reported.

Stalking and Cyberstalking

Including stalking (and cyberstalking, a contemporary version of the same behavior that utilizes the Internet and smartphone technology) as a type of relationship violence may seem a little odd to some of you, especially as some types of behaviors that we would consider stalking were once considered perfectly appropriate ways to initiate a romantic relationship. What we think are stalking behaviors today may once have been thought of merely as strategies to wear down the resistance of someone you were interested in—as just another way to woo someone. The National Institute of Justice defines stalking as "a course of conduct directed at a specific person that involves repeated (two or more occasions) visual or physical proximity, nonconsensual communication, or verbal, written, or implied threats, or a combination thereof, that would cause a reasonable person fear" (Tjaden and Thoennes 1998). Again, because some people might consider stalking behaviors harmless or even flattering, the definition understandably accounts for the level of fear that a reasonable person should feel in response to this type of treatment. In other words, the too-friendly old man who always finds a way to seat himself in your section and stares a little too long is definitely creepy and inappropriate but may pose no real threat. When he starts bringing flowers or waiting by your car when your shift is over, his behavior has crossed the boundary between inappropriate and potentially threatening.

In their 2000 report on the findings from the National Violence Against Women Survey, Tjaden and Thoennes found that stalking was much more common than previously thought: 8.1 percent of the women and 2.2 percent of men surveyed reported being stalked at some point in their lifetime. The stalking behaviors the survey asked about included whether someone (aside from bill collectors or salespeople) had followed or spied on them, left unwanted items for them to find, showed up at places the respondent was at with no business being there, made unsolicited phone calls, or sent unsolicited written correspondence, among other things. Drawing on the National Crime Victimization Survey, Catalano (2012) estimates that 3.3 million people age eighteen or older were victims of stalking in 2005, roughly 1.5 percent of the population. In line with the findings of Tjaden and Thoennes (2000), more women than men were victims of stalking: 2.2 percent of women to 0.8 percent of men. These numbers may seem small, but remember, these percentages still represent millions of people, meaning that a significant number of people experience this form of relationship violence annually.

Cyberstalking is a relatively new form of stalking that began when access to the Internet became widespread. Though the term first appeared prior to the abundance of social media platforms that exist today, social media is perhaps the main area where cyberstalking occurs. Basically, cyberstalking is the Internet equivalent of physical stalking. Instead of calling you a hundred times a day, maybe someone is blowing up your messages on Facebook or constantly sending you direct messages on Twitter. Instead of vandalizing your property, maybe someone is slandering you online. Instead of sending you unwanted gifts, maybe someone is sending you unwanted pictures of him- or herself. Worse, because so much of our online lives are open to the public, cyberstalking becomes much more visible to people around us than offline stalking. This might be a good thing, because maybe we have support systems in place to help protect us or advise the stalker that his or her behavior is inappropriate. But offline, where no one might see the behavior happening, those support systems might not exist.

Another issue with cyberstalking and other forms of online harassment is whether they pose legitimate threats. Remember, the Internet affords a certain measure of anonymity—making it possible for many people to act in ways online that they would never dare in person. Because of that, we have to ask ourselves, should threats of violence posted online be taken as seriously as threats made, say, over the phone? Should I worry as much about a threat directed at me on social media as I would if someone made it to my face?

Does cyberstalking victimization mirror the same gender patterns as more typical stalking? Because there is so little research on the subject, it's difficult to say. Strawhun, Adams, and Huss (2013) found that women were more likely than men to engage in cyberstalking. In a predominantly male sample, Cavezza and McEwan (2014) found that the majority of cyberstalkers also employed more traditional stalking techniques. Finn (2004), looking at cyberstalking among a sample of college students, found no demographic differences in the risk of victimization other than sexual minority status—these students were more likely to experience abuse online. It may be that thinking about cyberstalking as a completely different type of crime is outdated; maybe now it's just another tool to engage in harassment, and its usage depends more on the personality and goals of the stalker than anything else.

Family Violence

Perhaps the most common form of relationship violence is also one of the most politically charged types of crime there is: domestic violence. Domestic violence is physical, emotional, psychological, and/or sexual abuse of a spouse or partner. Another term for domestic violence is intimate partner violence, which puts the emphasis on the relationship between the victim and offender and removes the emphasis on the idea that this happens in private and is therefore nobody's business.

Societal perceptions of domestic violence, long considered perfectly normal, went through a major transformation at the end of the twentieth century. The credit for this belongs entirely with feminist criminologists. No longer was it legally acceptable for men to physically dominate their spouses. No longer were laws or practices like the "rule of thumb" considered useful, much less humane. (The "rule of thumb"—a cliché people now use without realizing what it means—said that a man had the right to beat his wife with a switch no wider in diameter than his own thumb!) I say legally acceptable because obviously the laws have changed. Culturally, because we live in a rape culture, many people still see no problem with violence that occurs in intimate relationships.

Before we continue, let's talk about how common intimate partner violence is in our society. A common statistic that comes up over and over is that about one in four women will experience some form of intimate partner violence in their lifetimes. The National Violence Against Women Survey found that 22.1 percent of the women had been victims of intimate partner violence, compared to 7.4 percent of men (Tjaden and Thoennes 2000). It also demonstrated that intimate partner violence was the most common type of violence women experienced: 64 percent of the women who reported being physically assaulted, raped, and/or stalked since they were eighteen years old identified a romantic partner (ex-husband, boyfriend, etc.) as the offender, compared to only 16.2 percent of men.

Domestic violence is an excellent example of a criminal behavior that not all of society necessarily finds problematic. It's not that we believe the abuse should be legal, but many times we excuse the abusers. In many cases of domestic violence and/or rape, our attention turns to the behavior of the victim and not that of the offender. This is called victim blaming—saying the victim brought the victimization on him- or herself and simultaneously excusing the behavior of the attacker. People take the abuser's side and ask what the victim did to deserve such treatment. Was she talking back? Was he cheating? Were they abusive themselves? The abuser's behavior becomes secondary to the victim's actions that allegedly prompted it. This is especially difficult to talk about in a criminological context, because a major theory of victimology, called victim precipitation theory, tends to view a violent encounter as the end result of a chain of events potentially instigated by the victim. This does apply to domestic violence committed by women who attack their partners in self-defense (for example, he is choking her and she grabs a lamp and smashes it over his head to escape). In this case, the "victim" precipitated his victimization by trying to strangle his partner. This is really the extent of the usefulness of victim precipitation theory in terms of domestic violence, because applying it to individuals who have survived this type of abuse really just blames them for what happened to them. Victim precipitation theory as a method of explaining or describing why a violent encounter occurred tends to work better in discussions of other forms of violence that don't invoke the concept of power and control. We shouldn't think about relationship violence in these terms, because it is never, ever, the victim's fault.

As our understanding of the prevalence and seriousness of domestic violence has grown, the criminal justice system has been slow to catch up. Police departments and courts have in their own ways contributed to maintaining the status quo, intentionally or otherwise, by failing to take domestic violence seriously or, at one time, to allow abused spouses to explain themselves in court when they have become violent as a means of self-defense. Rachel Zimmer Schneider (2014) explored the incredibly difficult position abused women find themselves in when their victimization brings them into contact with the criminal justice system. Schneider focuses specifically on those women who felt so trapped that they murdered their abuser—usually simply because they wanted the abuse to end. Many of the women Schneider interviewed experienced the real-life consequences of the criminal justice system's failure to recognize domestic violence as a serious and unique problem that deserves a new approach—that the old ways of doing things, the status quo, won't help the victims in these cases, won't deter their abusers, and won't help society as a whole reduce domestic violence. First, as Schneider (2014, 32) shows, many women who called the police experienced victim blaming by the responding officers, who asked what they had done to bring this abuse on themselves; one officer even asked a victim "What did you do this time?" In another instance, the victim stood in her doorway next to her abusive husband, a knife sticking out of her back; not trained to recognize domestic violence as a situation worth investigating more thoroughly, the police believed her when (obviously coerced by her abuser) she said that she had slipped and fallen onto the knife. Unfortunately, the police have tended to believe that the key word in the phrase *domestic violence* is *domestic*, meaning it is a private problem and none of their business.

The second problem that Schneider (2014) explores is the inability of women in these situations—and please understand that though very rare, these cases are still worthy of our attention—to bring the full weight of their victimization to bear when they are put on trial. If we put ourselves in the place of these women and imagine experiencing the same level of physical, sexual, and emotional abuse they did—Schneider interviewed one woman whose abuser poured Drano down her throat; another was forcefully penetrated with a hot curling iron—it makes perfect sense that these experiences should be heard about in court, right? Well, the law isn't always about making sense. In this case, and in other self-defense cases, the law asks what would cause fear in a "reasonable person," which tends to be defined as a white, middle-class male. Supposedly a reasonable person would not shoot a defenseless, sleeping man for fear of abuse. A sleeping person is, by definition, incapable of striking fear into someone. Because of this, in the past, courts would not allow abuse victims who defended themselves with violence to share their stories, and many went to prison. This was obviously a problem. Because these women clearly deserved some consideration for their desperate circumstances, advocates created and introduced into the criminal justice lexicon the term *battered woman syndrome* (BWS), a type of post-traumatic stress disorder that also accounts for sexual intimacy issues and distortions related to physical ailments and/or body image (Schneider 2014). Still, many courts resisted it as a legitimate defense, with Ohio finally allowing testimony related to BWS in 1990, making it the last state to do so.

Think about that for a second. It's only been twenty-five years, as of this writing, since BWS was fully accepted as a legitimate legal factor in trials related to domestic violence (though many people likely weren't happy about it then and probably still aren't now). And how long do you think domestic violence has existed for? A thousand years? Two thousand? Since the dawn of civilization? And we've just now reached the point where we will consider the perspective and experiences of victims. It wasn't very long before the acceptance of BWS as a legal defense that the states began to recognize victims as legitimate parties in criminal cases—states didn't begin creating their versions of the victim's bill of rights until the 1980s. Sometimes it feels like the people working in the criminal justice system are the last to learn that something's changed.

Schneider's (2014) work shows that domestic violence is not strictly about men abusing women out of a need to express power and control. Women can also become violent, albeit typically in self-defense, either in the immediate situation or in the aftermath. This is especially true when the violence leads to the death of the abuser. Felson and Messner (1998) and Belknap et al. (2012) demonstrate that women who kill their partners are much likelier to do so out of self-defense; men killed in this situation are much likelier to have had a seriously violent background (Felson and Messner 1998), which suggests that a single instance of violence didn't provoke their partners to defend themselves with lethal force; rather, these men had a history of attacking and injuring them that led to this final critical moment.

I mentioned at the beginning of this section that domestic violence is one of the most politically charged types of violence there is. This is because of an ongoing debate centered on the context of these behaviors and how the behavior is being studied. Dutton (2012) argues that domestic violence is nowhere near as one-sided as I and others present it; he suggests that men are victimized at a much higher rate and women at a significantly lower rate than past studies have shown. Dutton argues that the actual number of "wife battering" cases is significantly lower than presented, and that overall male support for domestic violence is substantially lower than cultural critics would have us believe. Critics of Dutton have accused him of being antifeminist and an advocate for men's rights. I make no claim here about the legitimacy of either Dutton's ideas or his agenda and present them only as an example of the highly charged political climate surrounding the scientific study of domestic violence.

Like child molesters, many people who abuse their spouses or partners will also utilize techniques of neutralization to justify their behavior. Many times, they blame the victim for having done something to provoke their abuse, saying things like, "She knows to back away from me when I'm in that kind of mood." These techniques aren't used only by men, however. Abusive women are also likely to neutralize their behavior and place the majority of the blame for it on their victims (Hennig, Jones, and Holdford 2005).

Relationship/Acquaintance Rape

At the beginning of this chapter, I mentioned that certain behaviors that horrify one person may seem perfectly acceptable, even a source of pride, to another. I was talking about rape. Perhaps the ugliest form of violence there is, rape also seems to elicit the ugliest responses from people, who will go to great lengths to excuse the rapists while calling into question the victim's character. As mentioned, we live in a rape culture: rather than vilifying or demonizing a rapist as we might a murderer, aspects of a culture actually celebrate this crime.

Before we get any further into a cultural discussion of rape, first we need to talk about how much of it is actually happening. We don't actually know exactly how many rapes occur in the United States during a given year because so many victims choose not to report the crime to the police for a number of reasons. According to the Uniform Crime Statistics, 84,041 rapes, as defined by the "legacy" definition, were reported to police throughout the country in 2014. OK, but what is the legacy definition?

In 2013, the legal definition of rape was changed to reflect our growing understanding of relationship violence and sexual assault. The so-called legacy definition of rape is the one used by police before 2013. The legacy definition of rape was "carnal knowledge of a female forcibly and against her will." See any problems with that definition? There are a few. First, it characterizes rape as only happening to women, which is patently false. Men can be and are raped as well. Second, it defines the sexual aspect of rape in a very limited way, ignoring penetration using objects and assuming rapists are only interested in vaginal penetration. Obviously, this is not the case. The new definition of rape takes these problems into consideration. This definition of rape, which went into effect on January 1, 2013, says that rape is "penetration, no matter how slight, of the vagina or anus with any body part or object, or oral penetration by a sex organ of another person, without the consent of the victim" ("Frequently Asked Questions About the Change in the UCR Definition of Rape" 2014).

This change in the definition of rape means that we have to be especially dubious of the number of rapes reported under the legacy definition. Not only did that definition, by excluding roughly half the population, draw a very limited picture of what rape is, but it helped create the myth that men cannot be raped. And in those cases when men were victimized, because the government technically didn't take it seriously, ordinary people were also less likely to take it seriously. This may explain why prison rape, a massive problem in the criminal justice system and a clear violation of human rights, is oftentimes treated as the punchline to some twisted joke. Because of the legacy definition and the unwillingness of many rape victims to come forward, the disparity between the actual number of rape cases versus the number reported (traditionally, anyway) might be the biggest in any type of crime. Tjaden and Thoennes (2006) estimate that only 20 percent of rape victims actually report their victimization to the police, which would suggest that the actual number of "legacy" rapes in 2014 was closer to 420,000. Hopefully the modified definition helps us learn more about how prevalent rape actually is in our society.

As with other forms of relationship violence, most rape victims are female, and most of the perpetrators are male. *Most* certainly doesn't mean *all*. Stereotyping rape as a male-on-female crime not only denies justice to male victims but profoundly limits our understanding of this form of violence, which in turn limits our ability to do something about it.

In what situations, then, does rape occur? In the next chapter, we'll be talking about stranger rape, the least common form of rape but the most feared. In reality, women are most likely to be raped by someone they know—an acquaintance, a friend, or even a partner. In each case, the physical act more or less remains the same, but the relationship between the victim and the offender, as well as the social and psychological context in which the rape occurs, can be very different. The differences in these relationships and contexts have led to the creation of different categories of rape. And even though the trauma that the victims (or survivors) experience is enormous in every circumstance, this variation in the ways that rape can occur means we need more than one solution to erase it from society. A man who rapes his wife commits marital rape; a man who rapes his would-be girlfriend on their first date commits date rape; a male student who rapes another student he knows in any number of circumstances commits acquaintance rape. Sexual intercourse between someone of legal age and a person below the age of consent is statutory rape. If we're going to reduce or eliminate rape, then we need to talk about why it happens in married couples, between unmarried people, between people who barely know each other, and so on.

So, why does rape happen? As our societal discussion on the causes of rape continues, more and more people are moving away from a biological explanation of rape as a natural response to male sexual urges, toward a sociological explanation of rape as a learned behavior. In fact, contrary to what most people might think, rape has nothing to do with sex at all. Many of the core theories of criminology apply to this form of violence, but social learning theory seems the most useful today. But haven't I been arguing that rape is about expressing power and dominance over another person? What does that have to do with social learning theory?

Remember that social learning theorists believe that everyone is born with a blank slate and learn bad behavior over time. In this case, no one is born a rapist, and no one is born wanting to express power and dominance over other people to such an extreme. We, especially young men and boys, learn that this behavior is acceptable from the people around us. We could think of rape as one manifestation of learning that having raw power and dominance over others is good, desirable, and a source of pride. This speaks to the idea that we live in what's called a rape culture.

Violence in Same-Sex Relationships

While there is a great deal of research on relationship violence broadly, and domestic violence more specifically, violence that occurs in same-sex relationships has received little attention. Although domestic violence itself became a focal point of many social scientists beginning in the 1960s and 1970s, because of the taboo associated with homosexuality in the United States, violence among same-sex couples was oftentimes rejected as a worthwhile research topic. Drawing on stereotypes and playing off public concern and mistrust (in large part because of the AIDS epidemic in the 1980s and the moral panic associated with it), many viewed attempts to study violence among same-sex couples as a waste of time that might even legitimize these behaviors. This isn't to say that absolutely no work was done in this area. Adam Messinger (2014) recently published a review of thirty-five years of research on same-sex intimate partner violence that identifies the similarities in violence occurring in same-sex and opposite-sex relationships, while also outlining a persistent deficiency in the research. For example, not much work has been done on the state's response to these cases in terms of help provided to victims, because same-sex marriage was only recently legalized.

So what do we know about violence in same-sex relationships? The first step is to figure out how rates of intimate partner violence compare in same-sex and opposite-sex relationships. Frankland and Brown (2014) examined the available research on the topic and, unsurprisingly, concluded that the numbers are pretty inconsistent, with between 6.2 and 55 percent of couples engaging in physical violence (Turell 2000; Houston and McKirnan 2007;

Murray and Mobley 2009) and 21 to 90 percent of couples engaging in psychological aggression (Lockhart et al. 1994; Houston and McKirnan 2007). This is, obviously, a massive disparity.

In terms of why violence occurs in same-sex relationships, we again come back to the issue of power and control. Messinger (2014) finds a consistent similarity between same-sex and opposite-sex couples here. Regardless of sexual orientation, abusers manipulate and control their victims to maintain power over them, and the violence occurring in the relationship is an expression of this need to be powerful. Messinger also notes that the lives of victims are the same regardless of whether they are in a same-sex or opposite-sex relationship; they live in a state of constant fear and experience all the negative outcomes associated with that.

Messinger (2014) does highlight one difference: abusers in same-sex relationships may be violent because of their own internalized heterosexism. We live in a heteronormative society that views heterosexual practices as normal or natural and anything else as deviant, unusual, or unnatural. Heterosexism is the resulting discrimination against anyone who is not straight. In other words, a heteronormative society can cause some gay people to internalize homophobia, leading to self-hatred, and this hatred comes out in the form of violence against their partners. In addition to the possibility of heterosexist ideation, power can manifest itself in different ways that are unique to same-sex relationships. For example, people in opposite-sex relationships have never had to come out as straight; a heteronormative society like ours just assumes that everyone is straight. A person in a same-sex relationship who has not come out as gay may have this closeted status used against him or her by an abusive partner (Messinger 2014). Just as in opposite-sex relationships, power is the motivating force behind abuse, but how it manifests depends on the sexuality of the couple. This is further evidence that violence is substantially more complex than we tend to think.

7

Sexual Violence

Damon Wells, a thirty-seven-year-old man from Lake Winola, Pennsylvania, stood before a district judge charged with over 1,500 counts of rape and indecent assault of a child. He had allegedly engaged in these repeated acts with a girl beginning when she was seven years old and stopping only when she, at age fifteen, finally came forward. In court that day, Wells admitted to this relationship but said he was no monster—far from it, as a matter of fact. Wells claimed that he had never, ever touched the girl and that she had engaged in oral sex with him willingly. According to Wells, she sent him "mixed signals" (Nieves 2015). In this way, Wells framed himself as the victim—he had been misled—and so we should pardon his monstrous behavior. Wells remained in prison for over a year, unable to pay his $250,000 bail, and submitted a guilty plea in the summer of 2016 (Baker 2016). The court did not agree that he was the real victim in this case.

Stories like this are far too common in our society. We can go to any local newspaper or website anywhere in the country for proof of this—the story of Damon Wells is in no way uncommon. Whenever this happens, especially in cases involving children or adolescents, we say that we're horrified to live in such a society, denounce the evil in the world, and, hissing like angry cats, declare our thirst for vengeance and justice, and then . . . it happens again. And again. And again. (In 2014, 116,645 cases were reported to the police, according to the Uniform Crime Report [UCR].)

Sexual violence happens not only to children but to adults as well. And in some—perhaps many—of these instances, society finds ways to justify the offender's behavior and put the blame for what happened squarely on the victim's shoulders. What was she wearing? Was he drinking or using drugs? Had the victim been behaving flirtatiously and misleading the abuser? Ultimately, many people will bend over backward to find some way to blame the victim. This even happens when the victims are children. Some clergy accused of child molestation (or otherwise attempting to explain it) have painted a picture of children as intentionally seductive, luring poor, unsuspecting priests into sexual contact—a completely morbid and warped version of reality wherein the victims and offenders have switched roles. All of this is further evidence that we live in a rape culture that defends rapists and dehumanizes, delegitimizes, and all but vilifies rape victims, while simultaneously treating the offender's behavior as misguided—as a simple mistake that anyone could've made—instead of as a brutal act of violence.

In the previous chapter, we discussed specific types of relationship violence, their relationship to gender, and their consequences. In this chapter, we will discuss sexual violence, which we will treat differently from relationship violence, focusing only on those crimes where the offender and victim have no previous existing relationship. I want to make this distinction because, while these types of violence do overlap in terms of how they are motivated and carried out, I want to keep context in mind, with respect to all of the victims involved. In other words, violence happening within a family deserves as much respect as violence that's happening at a party or on a date; violence experienced by sex workers deserves the same attention as violence experienced by children.

That said, let's set this up. First, we will spend some time talking about the type of rape that people seem to think is the most common and fear the most: stranger rape. Just like in Chapter 6, we'll talk about how much of it actually occurs and in what circumstances, why it happens, and if it's any different from rape that occurs in a relationship. We're also going to spend some time talking about a relatively new type of rape, defined as party rape. We will also take some time to talk about rape that happens in a government context, specifically rape in prison and in the military. Next, we'll spend time talking about prostitution, or "the world's oldest profession." We'll also spend time delving into the broader world of underground sex work and explore how people enter this world and what their lives are like. Finally, we'll talk about sex work on an international level and human trafficking as an international crime happening all around us in ways we might not even realize. Of course, sex workers—willing or otherwise—are not all women, so we will spend some time talking about differences in the lives of male and female sex workers as well.

Remember the ideas we talked in the last chapter: that relationship violence is all about power and control, that children learn that being a man means being powerful, and that abusers tend to rationalize or neutralize their behavior. These ideas apply to our discussion in the first half of this chapter, too, with regard to the types of rape not covered in Chapter 6. You could even argue that power and control also come into play in prostitution and human trafficking. Remember, our discussion here complements that in the previous chapter, and it's important to recognize the suffering of all victims of sexual violence, regardless of their relationship to their abusers, the context of their victimization, or, clearly, their gender.

The Realities of Rape

As mentioned in the previous chapter, most rapes are committed by someone the victim knows. Also note that the 300,165 rapes reported by the NCVS is considerably higher than the UCR figure for the same year. The UCR reports that 113,695 rapes were reported to the police in 2013. That's 2.64 times as many rapes in one dataset as the other, and that should bother you, if not completely devastate you. Assuming none of the rapes were committed by serial rapists (which I recognize may not be the case), that

means that at least 186,470 rapists out there have never been challenged or punished and are free to continue to engage in this sort
of violence without fear of reprisal. That number is greater than
the individual populations of Providence, Rhode Island; Knoxville, Tennessee; and Fort Lauderdale, Florida—not a small
amount of people. That the behavior of these rapists has gone
unpunished not only legitimizes it to them but may also send a
message to the people who know about these incidents—friends
or family members connected to either the victim or offender—
that rape is a perfectly acceptable relationship technique, which in
turn could potentially lead to further sexual violence committed
by someone else in the future.

Because of the obviously overt sexual nature of the crime, it's
often very difficult for people to accept the fact that rape in general, and stranger rape in particular, is about expressing power and
exerting dominance and not about sexual pleasure. Convicted
rapists find this especially difficult to accept and tend to utilize
similar techniques of neutralization as child molesters. Scully and
Marolla (1984) found that the explanations of convicted rapists
usually fell into one of two broad categories: justifications and
excuses. Justifications for rape included arguments like, all
women eventually just enjoy it, "no" really means "yes," and nice
girls don't get raped. Through this framing, rapists hope to convince critics that their behavior is perfectly fine and that we're so
upset because we don't understand how the world works. Excuses
included blaming their actions on drugs or alcohol or on a mental
condition. Or they tried to convince the interviewer that while
they had indeed done something completely horrible, in every
other respect they were a nice guy and deserved the benefit of the
doubt. In other words, they tried to argue that while yes, they did
rape someone, they were really just nice guys at heart and
deserved a break. Keep in mind that several of the rapists interviewed by Scully and Marolla brutally assaulted their victims,
penetrating them in horrifying ways, and quickly took a very
blasé attitude toward their actions—as if assaulting a woman with
a broomstick is a perfectly normal thing. Given the horrific nature
of their acts, these attempts to justify or excuse their behavior, to

me, point to a larger problem with how we're socializing boys and men with regard to the right way to treat women.

In the previous chapter, we spoke to the idea that rape doesn't only happen to women, but it warrants repeating. According to data from the 2013 NCVS, 34,057 men reported being the victim of a rape or sexual assault that year. That number is approximately 11 percent of the total number of rapes reported in the NCVS. Because of the way the NCVS collects data, this figure includes men who were assaulted by either a man (or men) or a woman (or women), so it is an inclusive statistic in that regard. That said, it's important to remember that some participants in these types of surveys deny that they have been victimized in any way, so the actual number could potentially be much higher. This speaks to another major problem with men, masculinity, and sexual violence: not only is there a serious problem with how boys and men view rape specifically and view women generally, but men's reluctance to speak up when they've been raped themselves speaks to how deeply entrenched our gender roles are. Men aren't supposed to be rape victims. If I'm a rape victim and say anything about it to anyone, my identity as a man will be completely and utterly destroyed. For some, the fear of striding outside the narrow boundaries of hegemonic masculinity far outweighs the need for physical or emotional help or for justice. It's really quite sad when you think about it.

Clearly, how we socialize boys is problematic at best. This issue has cropped up previously in our discussion and will continue to do so as we explore other types of violence later in this book. You might call it a theme. The question becomes, how can we socialize our boys to have better attitudes toward women and to be less violent in general? Without getting bogged down in defeatist arguments that this is a waste of time, that boys will be boys, that aggression is an artifact of our biological makeup and impossible to change, what can we do better for the next generations of young men? I know this is an abstract question, so I want you to look at your own lives. What would you change about your own socialization? If you are a man, how do you define your own masculinity? If you are a woman, what do you think about the common conception (or misconception) about the inability of single mothers to correctly and fully raise their sons to be men? These might seem like fairly simple questions, but coming up with answers for them is much more difficult than it seems. We first have to agree that many men have not been raised to be emotionally healthy and have been cut off from a significant part of the human experience. Then we can rise to the challenge of raising our next generation of sons to be fully realized people, not just a fraction of a person.

Stranger Rape

It seems to be a common scenario: It's night, there's not a lot of light out, and she's walking alone—maybe across campus from the library to her dorm room, maybe through a parking garage, maybe walking home from a party. She's hurrying, but trying not to run, clutching her purse, because that feeling on the back of her neck tells her something isn't right. She makes it to her destination, but just before she can unlock the door, from nowhere, he strikes— and she becomes another statistic.

Of all the different types of rape we have talked about in this book, it seems that the type described above—typically referred to as stranger rape—is the one people fear most and think is most common. In stranger rape, the victim and offender have no previous relationship. Horror stories grow out of this type of assault—the man who jumps out of a dark corner of the parking lot or hides in your backseat, the sexual boogeyman who can pop out of anywhere at any time. It's the type your parents were most worried about and that talking heads on television wring their hands over the most.

While not as common as one might think, these types of rapes do happen. According to the National Crime Victimization Survey (NCVS), of the 300,165 reported rapes/sexual assaults in 2013, 57,136 were committed by someone the victim didn't know. That's just over 19 percent. Of those stranger rapes, 17,077 happened in a commercial place, parking lot, or some other public area. That's almost 30 percent of stranger rapes. Remember, as always with official statistics, the actual number is likely much higher because, especially with regard to sexual violence, victims choose not to report for a number of reasons: they are afraid, ashamed, or in denial. Stranger rapes obviously do happen, but strangers in parking lots aren't as common as we think.

Sexual Assault on Campuses

While stranger rape does happen, it's definitely not the only kind of rape. Obviously, as we saw in the previous chapter, rape can occur in the context of a married or cohabiting couple. But there is also a middle ground in terms of the relationship (or lack thereof) that exists between the victim and offender prior to the attack. Many times, there can be a very weak or distant relationship—the victim and rapist knew each other, but not very well, maybe only for a few hours. This type of rape has typically been called acquaintance rape, although recently, as our awareness of rape as a true epidemic on college campuses has increased, many social scientists now study party rape as a separate category. We'll talk more about that momentarily. Suffice it to say that many informal relationships in our lives—with a coworker, a study group partner, a friend of a friend—can potentially lead to a rape. In all honesty, I wish that I could say some relationship existed without the potential to become sexually violent, but if I did, I'd be lying.

The epidemic of rape and sexual assaults on college campuses has led to the creation of another contextual definition: party rape. Let that word sink in: "epidemic." In other words, this type of rape is widespread on college campuses throughout the United States. A party rape occurs at a party, as the name implies. Armstrong, Hamilton, and Sweeney (2006) published the definitive modern study of rape on college campuses. Unlike rape in other situations, they argue, party rape occurs, in part, because of anticipatory socialization (Merton 1957), the idea that most kids come to college with expectations about the experience that include a lot of drinking, a lot of partying, and a lot of casual sex. Partying also gives college students a method of bonding during a period of incredible uncertainty and loneliness in their lives; instead of figuring out what to do with the rest of their lives, or what kind of person they want to be, they can party and drink their fears away. Partying is a method of gaining acceptance, making friends, and

giving everyone something to do and look forward to, which is
why college students are incredibly resistant to efforts to eliminate party rape—because the party might stop (Armstrong, Hamilton, and Sweeney 2006). That's an incredibly sad thing, if you
think about it: partying has become such a vital part of college
culture that, even though it can entail a devastating form of violence, the notion of eliminating it to protect themselves is terrifying and therefore not an option. What has college become? What
does this say about the nature of higher education? Has it always
been like this? What can we do differently? There are so many
difficult questions here.

Armstrong, Hamilton, and Sweeney (2006, 492) summarize
party rape and its difference from other forms of rape thusly:

> Party rape is accomplished without the use of guns, knives, or
> fists. It is carried out through the combination of low level
> forms of coercion—a lot of liquor and persuasion, manipulation
> of situations so that women cannot leave, and sometimes force
> (e.g., by blocking a door, or using body weight to make it diffi-
> cult for a woman to get up). These forms of coercion are made
> more effective by organizational arrangements that provide men
> with control over how partying happens and by expectations
> that women let loose and trust their party-mates. This system-
> atic and effective method of extracting non-consensual sex is
> largely invisible, which makes it difficult for victims to con-
> vince anyone—even themselves—that a crime occurred. Men
> engage in this behavior with little risk of consequences.

That rape on college campuses seems an acceptable consequence
of a larger cultural process, an agreed-upon part of a game that
all students feel compelled to play, makes it incredibly difficult
to eradicate. That it is so entrenched in college culture is very dis-
heartening and serves as even further evidence that we live in a
rape culture.

It's important to highlight the gender roles that both male
and female students gladly assume in this context. Neither sex
has any issue (overall) with the existence of this culture: it's better to have something to do, even if it is dangerous. Female stu-

dents tend not to object to their objectification; some male students may passively reject being labeled as a threat, but there exists no real active pushback against this idea. Nor is there a sizable resistance to rape culture from many male students. In this case maybe, given the enormity of the larger college culture, it's not quite accurate to think of men as the offenders and women as the victims. For instance, same-sex rape that happens at fraternities in the guise of hazing could potentially fall under this umbrella, but maybe not. This is why context is such a vital part of trying to understand why all violence, not just sexual violence, happens.

We can try to better understand the motivations behind and occurrence of party rape by going back to our sociological roots and asking a question that I've kind of been dancing around here for a minute: What are college students like? How are male and female college students similar and different? Look at yourselves and each other. How do you react to all the push-and-pull forces in your lives—work, sports, dating, establishing independence from your parents—and how does that affect your coursework?

Finding a solution to rape in general is an overwhelming task; trying to find a solution to it in any of the context-specific scenarios I've laid out for you in the previous chapters is much harder. When virtually everyone agrees that a lifestyle is desirable, how on earth can you get them to behave some other way? If we're going to put an end to party rape on college campuses, then we must completely change how we conceive of and run colleges and universities. It is clear to me that simply saying that we'll ban parties or punish rapists severely will not make a difference. Ending party rape means fundamentally changing how higher education functions, and that's going to be an incredibly difficult task to accomplish.

Rape in Government Institutions: Prisons and the Military

One form of rape that rarely gets much attention is prison rape. As the name suggests, this is rape that occurs inside a prison (or any correctional facility). While many of you probably think of prison rape as occurring between two men, it isn't exclusive to male prisons. Nor does it only happen among the incarcerated; it can also include rape of inmates by prison staff. How much does it go on? In 2003, the Prison Rape Elimination Act (PREA) mandated that the Bureau of Justice Statistics (BJS) and the National Institute of Justice begin collecting data on this problem. Because of the enormity of the criminal justice system, this was a lot easier said than done (PREA mandated that information be collected at the federal, state, and local levels, which is the equivalent of your math professor assigning 17 million homework problems every week and writing them in a secret code that only she knows). The BJS rolled out several different data-collection projects aimed at different segments of the population at different times. That said, according to its most recent report, there were 8,763 allegations of sexual victimization in 2011, according to the administrators of the nation's adult correctional facilities, approximately 10 percent of which were substantiated (meaning that the subsequent investigation concluded that the sexual assault did occur). The remaining 90 percent of alleged cases either didn't have sufficient evidence (the most common finding), had been falsified, or were still under investigation (Beck, Rantala, and Rexroat 2014). Of the 8,142 alleged instances of staff sexual misconduct in adult facilities (which includes rape, bargaining for sexual favors, invasion of privacy for sexual gratification, or intentional touching or grabbing of body parts for sexual gratification) reported during the period of 2009 to 2011, 1,034 were substantiated (Beck, Rantala, and Rexroat 2014). That's 12.7 percent of all cases. We're all smart enough to know, however, that just because a case was unsubstantiated doesn't mean it didn't happen. Perhaps more shocking, this number is substantially higher than the number of nonconsensual sexual acts that occurred between inmates: of the 7,791 alleged incidents, 624 were substantiated (Beck, Rantala, and Rexroat 2014). That's just over 8 percent, and the same caveat about unsubstantiated cases applies here as well. It is important to point out that the nature of prison life doesn't really allow prisoners to violate each other's privacy the way that a correctional officer can. Staff can sexually victimize a prisoner nonconsensually in many more ways than a prisoner can victimize another prisoner. That difference definitely accounts for some of the difference in the numbers of substantiated cases.

Prison rape must only be a problem in adult facilities, right? Wrong. Analysis of a random sample of youths in state facilities across the United States found that 7.7 percent of respondents—young people incarcerated in juvenile facilities—reported that they had been sexually assaulted or raped by staff (Beck et al. 2012). They were also victimized by other youths: 2.5 percent of respondents reported being sexually victimized by other inmates (for lack of a better term) in their facility (Beck et al. 2012). Just like adult respondents, adolescent inmates reported a much higher level of victimization perpetrated by staff than by other inmates. This seems to go against the stereotype of prison rape—that it's all done by big dudes who trade other inmates for a few packs of cigarettes. And that certainly does happen, but nowhere do staff members enter into the stereotype. There is a gender difference in the risk of victimization in juvenile facilities as well: more males are victimized by staff; more females are victimized by other inmates (Beck et al. 2012). As with the adult version of this report, it is safe to assume that many sexual victimizations don't get reported and are not reflected in this data. I do want to point out that there are far fewer youths in these data sets than in the adult version of the report—in terms of the actual sample sizes that these statistics were derived from, and in terms of the larger pool of incarcerated persons that could have been included.

The final area we'll talk about in this section is rape in the military. Rape in the military is, in some ways, similar to rape in prison, because both prison and the military are what sociologists call total institutions, meaning they control every facet of the lives of the people involved (for the most part). There is growing awareness of, and concern about, rape in the military among members of the media as well. So how much of it is actually going on? If you thought that was difficult to address in regard to prison rape, military rape is a whole other animal. In 2013, President Barack Obama requested that Secretary of Defense Chuck Hagel provide a report on the efforts of the Department of Defense (DoD) to reduce sexual assault in the military. The subsequent data collection showed that in fiscal year 2014 (October 1, 2013–September 30, 2014), there were 5,983 reported sexual assaults in the military (Sexual Assault Prevention and Response Office [SAPRO] 2014). This is more than double the number of reported assaults since fiscal year 2007 (SAPRO 2014), which the DoD would argue indicates a greater willingness among the branches of the military to treat sexual assault cases within their ranks as a serious crime (here, sexual assault refers to a number of sex crimes, including rape). This is interesting because using the military's own estimation of how many service members actually experienced some sort of unwanted sexual contact, over time the number drops drastically: from approximately 34,200 total cases in 2006, to 19,300 in 2010, to 26,000 in 2012, and to 19,000 in 2014. This isn't really a downward trend, though hopefully the more immediate downward trend means that the amount of sexual assault continues to decline. Of these (estimated) victims, the DoD does show that women are more likely to be victimized by men, but again, that doesn't mean that there aren't any male victims of sexual assault in the military. In 2014, 4.3 percent of women and 0.9 percent of men in the military reported unwanted sexual contact (SAPRO 2014). Again, those numbers only represent reported offenses, not the total number of assaults or rapes that happened.

As with any other type of rape, underreporting is a serious problem concerning rape in the military. That's why the DoD can only provide us with those estimates of how much unwanted sexual contact occurred during those time frames. Like other survivors, rape victims in the military have a tremendous fear of reporting. What about other similarities between rape in this context and others? Sadler et al. (2003) found that among other things, a permissive attitude toward sexual harassment by one's superior officer(s) helped contribute to a climate that made rape permissible.

Violence in Sex Work

Think about the stereotypes associated with female prostitutes. Aren't they almost always negative? Something along the lines of: she's dirty, she's trashy, she's older, she has bad teeth, she smokes a lot, she's always walking the streets, she probably has a drug problem, and so on and so forth. People who buy into this vision of prostitutes might not have empathy or compassion for them. Now, think about stereotypes associated with being a male prostitute. Undoubtedly, some of you have jumped right to the film *Deuce Bigalow: Male Gigolo*. The theme here is that male prostitutes are attractive men who get to travel the world in the company of rich, older women. That they are being paid for sex is not a source of shame; rather, male prostitution is stereotyped as a glamorous lifestyle full of travel and adventure. For many people, the image of male prostitutes walking the streets dressed as women never comes to mind.

Prostitution is commonly referred to as the world's "oldest profession," but people seem to know very little about it—about who's doing it, why, how they got into it, and so on. Let's spend some time getting to know these people better. As simple as the idea of trading sex for money might seem, it's actually deeply complex, complicated by both its illegality and its popularity. The world of prostitution is very similar to the drug trade in this regard. And like the drug trade, with its wide variety of ways that a person can be involved (as a major supplier, a small-time dealer, or a petty user), prostitution entails its own continuum that makes it impossible to talk about in general terms. Furthermore, prostitution has not been treated consistently across the years, as you will see in Box 7.1.

Current research on prostitution tends to frame it in one of two ways: as either a major form of exploitation or not. People who talk about it as one of society's major evils subscribe to the oppression model of prostitution (Weitzer 2007). This approach draws attention to the worst of the worst cases and presents them as the norm: children pushed into prostitution, passed from one violently abusive pimp to the next, addicted to heroin, dead before

166

Box 7.1 The World's Oldest Profession: Prostitution in US History

When we talk about prostitution today, we tend to think of the stereotypical streetwalker trying to survive a brutal existence or the high-class escort flying all over the world and living some sort of glamorous lifestyle in the (figurative) lap of luxury. But like most types of crime we've talked about in this book, prostitution isn't anything new. Maybe you've heard jokes about prostitution being the world's oldest profession. So what was prostitution like in other periods of history?

Prostitution wasn't always illegal in the United States. In some parts of the country, it was quite prevalent. There are stories of prostitutes being an integral part of the American Revolution, intermingling with the army and boosting morale while simultaneously spreading venereal disease. Prostitution was not only legal but also found in abundance in some interesting places. In New York City, for example, prostitution and the larger sex industry formed a thriving part of the economy, conducted openly and without shame (Gilfoyle 1992). That isn't to say that it was accepted by everyone. In his book on prostitution in antebellum New York City, Timothy Gilfoyle (1992) talks about mob violence directed at brothels and other houses of ill repute, where the rioter's main goal was to destroy property (not persons) and force the establishments out of business.

That antiprostitution sentiment grew, and attitudes toward the work and the women involved in it changed considerably over the next century. For instance, William Sanger, a medical doctor, published a book in 1897 (reprinted in 1939 as a testament to its legitimacy), detailing the entire history of prostitution across the entire world. Describing prostitutes' lives, Sanger (1897 [1937], 486) writes, "In addition to the physical dangers must be considered the mental anguish they undergo, which inevitably preys upon the constitution. In the earlier stages of their career is an agonizing memory of the past; thoughts of home; the grave, a nameless, pauper grave, yawns before them; thoughts of the inevitable eternity intrude; and a past of shame, a present of anguish, a future of dread, are the subjects of thought indulged by many who would never be suspected by the gay world of entertaining serious reflection."

This is quite a different picture from that painted by Gilfoyle (1992) nearly a hundred years later. Our society went from open prostitution to pearl clenching quite quickly, relatively speaking.

age twenty. No doubt, this can and does happen. Perhaps it is a common way to become involved in prostitution. But does it apply to the life of every prostitute? Does every prostitute have this story to tell? Not likely. There are people who turn to prostitution of their own accord for a number of reasons.

Anyway, the idea of selling sexual favors for money sounds pretty simple. Advocates of viewing prostitution as a victimless crime would argue that it involves the entry of at least two consenting adults into a formal business arrangement, wherein the parties agree to an exchange of money for services. This view presents prostitution as a very straightforward transaction. The idea of the stereotypical prostitute makes it seem like a full-time job: always walking the street, working the corners, working bars and clubs, looking to get paid. These types of prostitutes do exist, but what about the woman who is only out on those corners one night a month? Or one night every six months? What if she isn't doing it to make a living but because her rent check is late, or she doesn't have enough for groceries this month? These women are prostituting themselves, but should we treat them the same way we do stereotypical streetwalkers? Further, the oppression model of prostitution doesn't necessarily explain their motivations—they aren't being forced to do this by a pimp or madam who is controlling and exploiting them.

Let's explore this idea of exploitation a little bit further because, from the critical perspective, even though people who voluntarily prostitute themselves are not being exploited by a pimp, one could argue that they are being exploited by an oppressive economic system in which their only means of survival entails prostituting themselves to their landlords. Capitalism is an economic structure that relies on the existence of the poor to stoke the fire of competition among the middle and upper classes and to serve as a source of cheap labor. This system regularly exploits the poor. Someone who prostitutes him- or herself because it's that or wind up homeless is being exploited by an economic structure that does not value the individual.

Sudhir Venkatesh (2013) raised the idea of sex as currency in *Floating City*, which explores the underground economy of New York City. This is an incredibly fascinating look at the sex and drug trade in New York and the lives of the people swept up in this wildly unpredictable and dangerous lifestyle. Venkatesh encounters many women who are prostituting themselves but don't really consider themselves prostitutes. I bring this up not to raise the question of whether or not they are, because that's irrelevant. For the purpose of this discussion, it's more important to show that there are different degrees of prostitution.

We also need to distinguish where the prostitution is occurring: indoors or outside? Weitzer (2007) shows a substantial difference in the lives of women working in the two environments. Weitzer argues that women who fit more into the streetwalker category have much more dangerous lives than women who work indoors (in brothels, massage parlors, or bars). The latter experience violence at a substantially lower rate than their outdoor counterparts. Harcourt and Donovan (2005) conducted a meta-analysis of 681 articles on prostitution and created a distinction centered not on geography but on how overtly sexual the relationship between client and worker was. Direct sex work is much more upfront about what's going on. The category includes any context in which sex in some form is the immediate goal of everyone involved, regardless of whether it happens on the street or in a hotel or bar. Indirect sex work includes those situations where the relationship between client and customer isn't overtly sexual, but sex can be negotiated under the table, so to speak. This includes working to advertise different types of alcohol at bars, being hired solely as a social companion at a public event, exchanging sex for drugs, or using sex as a survival strategy or something to barter with.

So, sex work—prostitution—can happen in a variety of different contexts that have varying degrees of safety (Weitzer 2007) and secrecy (Harcourt and Donovan 2005). It isn't unique to the United States (Harcourt and Donovan 2005). Why would anyone choose to get involved in the first place? In terms of the indirect sex workers Harcourt and Donovan (2005) describe, I suppose it makes sense that these people could be lured by the idea of making money on the side, or the thrill, or maybe they're—gasp—genuinely attracted to the other person and have no moral problems with hooking up. I can't cite for you any research about this part of the underground sex trade. We just know that it's there.

But what about the people who are more obviously and openly prostituting themselves? How did they find themselves there? Looking at the relationship between prostitutes and pimps is a classic approach to studying prostitution and a major theme in the literature on the oppression model. Here, we see pimps as vicious predators looking for vulnerable and naive girls whom they can transform with some combination of drugs, money, and empty promises. Pimp-controlled prostitution accounts for roughly 50 percent of all prostitution, with many more prostitutes than that indicating they've worked for a pimp at some point in their career (Williamson and Cluse-Tolar 2002). In other words, it's quite common, but certainly not the only way that prostitution manifests itself in society.

A pimp gets a woman to work for him by "turning her out" and thereby transforming her from a noncriminal into a criminal (at least in terms of sex work). Being able to do this is a required skill for any successful pimp. To turn a woman out, he must be not only physically attractive but exciting and able to offer some hope of a better life (Williamson and Cluse-Tolar 2002). He must be able to quickly identify and home in on a woman's weaknesses and vulnerabilities, convincing her to use sex not only to improve her circumstances but to earn him money and make him proud of her (Williamson and Cluse-Tolar 2002). It's all about manipulation, down to how a woman working for a pimp relates to the other women working for him. This is interesting, because part of the pimp's ability to turn a woman out stems from his ability to win her affections (or infatuation), to the point where many women see themselves less as employees than as the pimp's girlfriend. The presence of other girls in the "family" isn't always viewed as a direct threat—many women refer to them as "wives-in-law" and may take pride in training them. Rather than leave the relationship, they compete for the pimp's time, money, and affection (Williamson and Cluse-Tolar 2002). This speaks to the charisma and manipulative powers of the pimp—the turning-out process can clearly render these women completely dependent on him and nothing more; it blinds them to their situation.

This is a relatively simple explanation for why some women become involved in prostitution. It's a classic tragedy of a woman with seemingly no hope being preyed on by someone with anything but her best interests in mind. When you factor in the physical and emotional violence that some pimps use to maintain their dominance, it's easy to see why those researchers espousing the oppression perspective would see prostitution as an absolute evil. However, not all women are turned out; many work independently or in small groups, without any kind of pimp driving their behavior. They're basically independent contractors. So if not manipulated into joining the game, why did these women make the choice to become prostitutes? Money and drugs are still a primary focus, just without the violently manipulative pimp. Williamson and Folaron (2003) found that many women became prostitutes either as a means to support themselves and their families or because it seemed like a quick way to make a lot of cash. Venkatesh (2013) has a similar perspective on some of the women in his study: sex work offers excitement, can pay well, and provides a level of independence that most other jobs don't. Venkatesh's study is especially insightful in this regard, as he interviews women on both ends of the economic spectrum—poor, uneducated, immigrant women and rich, white, college-educated women—attracted to the lifestyle for similar reasons. The allure of the easy payday and constant party can attract women (and men) from all walks of life.

The research on the lives of prostitutes tends to focus on women working the streets, essentially bolstering the stereotype of the poor streetwalker. We know that there are male prostitutes too, though, both on the street and in more private, upscale settings. What about these guys? What are they like? As with so much of the research on prostitution and sex work, part of the issue has been in framing the behavior. Because we live in a heteronormative society, male prostitutes have until recently been treated as doubly deviant: prostitution is illegal and therefore deviant, and because mostly other men solicit their services, their perceived homosexuality is also viewed as deviant (Scott et al. 2005). As with the total body of research on prostitution, research on male prostitutes has begun to move away from this negatively judgmental language toward a more sociological approach that asks, simply, who these men are and why they engage in this behavior.

As our perception of female prostitutes has changed over time, so has our perception of male prostitutes. We now understand that drug addiction or a history of abuse does not necessarily drive all cases of male or female prostitution (Scott et al. 2005). We know that there are different types of prostitutes, based on both location and clientele (Scott et al. 2005; Weitzer 2007). We know some men, just like women, get into prostitution on their own, without being turned out, and view it as a viable career (Scott et al. 2005; Venkatesh 2013). In reality, nothing shocking or surprising about male prostitutes sets them apart from their female counterparts. Some have found themselves in an impossible situation and are selling sex to survive. Some simply find it appealing. That's it.

That said, one gender difference is worth exploring, and that is how men and women have been socialized to think about work. Until recently, men were expected to structure their identities around their careers, and women were expected to structure their identities around their families. Those were really the only options. The moral majority could label a woman who prostituted herself (or otherwise engaged in some element of sex work) as a failure because she wasn't living up to her feminine duties. But because women's work has always been seen as supplementary, or unnecessary, it's possible that all the anger over prostitution has more to do with women choosing to work in the first place and less with what they choose to do professionally. With men, though, I think it might be a little different. Because the male identity is so intensely focused on career, how do male prostitutes find their way into a vocation that brings so little status and so many other risks? Do they take the same path as men in other low-paying, low-status occupations? Or is something different happening altogether? Cates and Markley (1992), in a small psychological study comparing a group of adolescent male prostitutes to a group of "normal" adolescent males, found some differences in their backgrounds. First, perhaps not surprisingly, the prostitute sample had a family history of drug and/or alcohol abuse and struggled with substance use and abuse themselves. Second, the guys in the prostitute sample reported that they had significantly lower career aspirations than the guys in the comparison group. It is worth pointing out that just because the individuals in the comparison group were not prostitutes themselves (were "normal"), that does not mean they had no issues of their own. That is, we should not assume that the opposite of a prostitute is someone who is not deviant in any way.

Now, this idea may be applicable to all male prostitutes, but it is more likely unique to the thirty people in this study—it is difficult to generalize psychological findings to the entire population when you're using such a small sample. In fact, Bimbi (2007) cautions that much of the research on male prostitutes—or as he calls them, male sex workers (MSWs)—is problematic for this very reason. Bimbi argues that times have changed, sex work for men has become legitimized, and the Internet has provided new opportunities for sexual deviance and/or sex work, so we too need to adapt. Whereas past research focused largely on male streetwalkers to the exclusion of men who worked strictly in other areas, the Internet has created a world in which MSWs have numerous new ways to ply their trade. Because of this, Bimbi argues that we need to think about them not as listless deviants but as men who have chosen a legitimate career path. This point holds not only for male sex workers but for the entire sex-work industry.

Many discussions of prostitution look at how and why people (usually women) become prostitutes and never ask why anyone would want to buy their services. It's as if everyone agrees that paying for sex is acceptable, but selling it is morally objectionable. Researchers in this field argue that the focus is on the prostitutes rather than the johns because some people think that seeking out prostitutes is a normal part of male sexuality (Carpenter 1998; Weitzer 2000; Monto 2004). Some place the blame for male deviance on the prostitutes themselves (N. Davis 1993; Monto 2004). Johns are also a difficult group to study because they're hard to find—many men who solicit prostitutes don't want to draw attention to themselves, for obvious reasons. Monto (2004) tries to assess from existing research how many men actually do visit prostitutes in the United States, concluding that between one-fifth and one-sixth of adult men have likely been with a prostitute in their lifetimes; that said, less than 1 percent of adult men indicate having been with a prostitute in the past year. This means that soliciting a prostitute isn't nearly as common or normal among men as people might think. Granted, Monto's study is over a decade old, but I don't think that in the intervening thirteen years there's been a massive spike in the number of men soliciting prostitutes. Plus, you have to think about what that percentage really means—in a country as large as the United States, 1 percent of the adult male population is still a fairly large number of people. Let's do some crude math to look at this: If we estimate the population of the United States to be roughly 312 million people, then subtract children and adolescents, we're looking at roughly 120 million adult males and 120 million adult females. If between one-fifth and one-sixth of all adult men have been with a prostitute at some point, we're talking about between 20 million and 24 million men. If 1 percent did so in the past year, we're talking 1.2 million men. Again, these numbers are just crude hypotheticals to suggest how many people we're talking about. One percent still amounts to quite a few people, but certainly not enough to say that this is a normal part of the male sexual experience.

If this isn't part of a normal, healthy sex life, why do these men do this? Do men who solicit prostitutes differ in any way from "normal" men? Again, their secrecy and elusiveness, due to the illegality of their behavior, not to mention any associated shame or stigma, makes this pretty hard to figure out, because they're not very willing to identify themselves. Monto's (2004, 169–170) review of the research draws the following conclusions:

(1) Though a significant proportion of customers are married (Freund et al. 1991; Jordan 1997; McKeganey 1994), customers are less likely to be married than noncustomers and more likely to define their marriage as unhappy or unsatisfying (Monto 1999); (2) although there may be some overrepresentation of non-Whites, customers generally reflect the ethnicity of the cities and locales in which they live, with minority prostitutes more likely to serve minority customers (Armstrong 1981; Lever and Dolnick 2000; Monto 1999); (3) although age ranges vary depending on the type of prostitution, and men of all ages can be customers, the combination of most studies would place the average age of customers in their late 30s. (Faugier and Cranfield 1995; Freund et al. 1991; McKeganey 1994; Monto 1999)

In other words, men who visit prostitutes tend not to be completely normal, at least in terms of their home lives. This might seem like a relatively minor distinction, but it's important all the same. Prior research into prostitution tended to characterize johns as sexually deviant or otherwise lacking socially or psychologically (Holzman and Pines 1982; Monto 2004). Are these men really just not satisfied in their marriages? Hardly. Again, Monto (2004) finds that reasons for visiting a prostitute are actually quite varied, including, but not limited to, awkwardness, promiscuity, thrill seeking, and a desire for sex but not the responsibility of a relationship.

If research on why men buy sex is limited, research on women who patronize prostitutes is virtually nonexistent (Weitzer 2005). This is important, because there's no reason to think that such women don't exist anywhere. We know from prior research that some sex workers do primarily serve women (Harcourt and Donovan 2005; Weitzer 2009). We know nothing, however, about women who solicit female prostitutes. Since we know so little about these women, we're forced to speculate about who they are and what motivates them. Let's revisit what we know about men:

they tend to be unhappy in their marriages and/or seeking some kind of emotional companionship or sexual release. Isn't it possible that women who solicit prostitutes could have the same motivations, or do you think otherwise?

The phrase *sex work* sometimes feels like a code word for prostitution. We all know that we're talking about prostitutes, but because we're trying to be polite or sound sophisticated, we say *sex worker* instead. Obviously, prostitution is not the only type of sex work that exists in society. We commonly talk about it in criminology because it is illegal. But there are also legal forms of sex work, and we should spend a little time talking about the relationship between gender and that economy as well.

More than you might think falls under the umbrella of legal sex work. Pornography probably comes to mind immediately for most of you, so let's focus on it. We're kind of in unknown territory. As Weitzer (2009) points out, very little sociological work has been done on this industry. This isn't because pornography is completely taboo—Weitzer points out that in 2002, 34 percent of men and 16 percent of women had viewed some pornographic material in the previous year, and one can only imagine what those numbers look like today, given how much the Internet has changed our lives since then. Pornography isn't so rare that sociologists and criminologists have been unable to study it. They just haven't. We do know that there are laws governing pornography—for example, any pornographic images or videos involving children are illegal (we'll go into in more detail about that shortly).

Instead of focusing our attention on the people who participate in the production of pornography, because that world is pretty much blocked off to us, we can briefly talk about gender differences in the consumption of pornography and what (if anything) happens to people when pornography becomes a regular part of their lives.

A major area of inquiry is the relationship between pornography use and sexual aggression. A review of the existing literature conducted by Malamuth, Addison, and Koss (2000) suggested a strong correlation between sexual aggression and frequent pornography use. This association was especially strong when the pornography in question was violent or the men in the study were already at risk for sexual aggression. However, much has changed since this study was published, especially regarding technology—and as mentioned earlier, the availability of pornography has substantially increased with the growth of the Internet . We also know that the amount of money made by the pornography industry has skyrocketed, surpassing $13 billion annually (Foubert, Brosi, and Bannon 2011). So, what's been happening since this article was published in 2000?

Short et al. (2012) analyzed a decade of research on Internet pornography and found some pretty major inconsistencies across studies. They demonstrate differences in how studies define, measure, and assess pornography in terms of both negative or positive outcomes that could stem from its use. Wait, positive outcomes? Short et al. argue that evidence suggests that consumption of pornography could result in a healthier sex life, making viewers both more knowledgeable about sex and more comfortable with it. But given the wild inconsistencies across different studies, who's to say what the consequences are.

We know that recently there have been fundamental changes to how the pornography business operates. Foubert, Brosi, and Bannon (2011) highlight research that speaks to this; unprecedented growth in the ability of pornographers to peddle their wares created an unbelievable amount of demand for content, which has engendered a wide variety of newer forms of pornography (including violent pornography) and led some pornographers to resort to human trafficking to find enough actors. As we'll see momentarily, human trafficking—a type of violence largely experienced only by women and girls—is another major problem related to sexual violence.

Research has looked extensively at the consequences of watching pornography. This area of study has focused on how exposure to pornography—especially violent pornography—can alter the way that people think. Specifically, exposure to violent pornography can change whether people consider rape a crime worth caring about, as well as reinforce many of the existing rape

myths that act as a barrier to reducing and eliminating this particular form of violence. We've talked about party rape as an epidemic on college campuses. Foubert, Brosi, and Bannon (2011)
looked at violent pornography use among fraternity members,
specifically examining a sample that comprised 62 percent of all
fraternity brothers (not pledges) at a large, public, midwestern
university. Their findings were universally negative for anyone
who might be in the pro-porn camp, as the results "showed that
men who viewed pornography, particularly rape and sado-
masochistic pornography, report a greater likelihood of raping,
committing sexual assault, higher rape myth acceptance, and
lower willingness to intervene in a sexual assault situation" (Foubert, Brosi, and Bannon 2011, 225).

That's not great news for anyone trying to market this new
world of pornography as positive. Now, for a critique of this particular study: perhaps something distinguishes fraternity brothers
from other men on campus, giving rise to a selection effect—
because of the party culture that most likely exists on this campus and the negative stereotypes associated with Greek systems
already, maybe the guys in this particular study were predisposed
to having negative attitudes about women. Certainly, women
would react differently to this, right?

Finally, I want to clarify something I mentioned earlier about
how much truly falls under the umbrella of sex work. In short,
any job for which attractiveness is a job requirement could be
considered sex work, because the business expects any potential
client or customer to indulge in an unspoken sexual fantasy
regarding the employee. Restaurants do this all the time. Some
barbershops now do this. Women representing alcohol companies
and working crowds at popular bars to get people to drink that
brand are a part of this. Even clothing companies may do this;
Oliver Bateman (2014) wrote about his time working at Aber-
crombie and Fitch and the company's practice of grading how
attractive their employees were. This obviously isn't sex work to
the extent of pornography or prostitution, but in a roundabout sort
of way, it could fall under the same rubric.

Child Pornography

Pornography featuring adults is by no means the full extent of the material that exists. Child pornography as a dimension of the underground economy has generated some research into who seeks it out and the risk these people pose to the community. For instance, Wolak, Finkelhor, and Mitchell (2011) looked at changes in the number of arrests for possession of child pornography and the nature of the material itself from 2000 to 2006, using data provided by over 2,500 law enforcement agencies. There were over twice as many arrests in 2006 as in 2000 (3,672 versus 1,713), suggesting that child pornography was on the rise. Of greater concern was the change in the severity of the materials seized; in 2006, a larger portion of the pornography featured children under the age of three, more of it was traded via peer-to-peer networks online, and the materials were more likely to be violent. Because this study only tracked changes in child pornography at two time points, I'm reluctant to draw any absolute conclusions about what is true ten years later. My guess, however, is that, because of the opportunities the Internet has given people to expand their sexuality, the nature of child pornography in 2006 is quite possibly the same in 2016.

What about the types of people who are into this type of pornography? Webb, Craissati, and Keen (2007) compared convicted child molesters to persons convicted of possessing child pornography to determine whether these behaviors stem from the same character traits and could thus be treated the same. Their findings indicated that while child molesters and Internet offenders (their phrase for persons involved in online child pornography) shared many similar background traits, their long-term risk to the community varied significantly, with Internet offenders posing much less risk of recidivism than child molesters. However, Webb, Craissati, and Keen did note that 14 percent of the Internet offenders did overlap in some significant ways with the child molesters in their samples, suggesting that there may be a subgroup of offenders who present an exceptional threat to society due to their involvement in both forms of child abuse.

However, further research comparing these two types of offenders conducted by Bourke and Hernandez (2009) found contradictory results: in their comparison of child molesters and persons merely "collecting" child pornography, they found that the pornographers were significantly more likely than not to have abused a child. They argue, "We have found that exposure to child pornography, as well as the cultural and technological context in which it is exchanged, has an insidiously deleterious effect on them. It normalizes child/adult sexuality, dehumanizes children, and desensitizes the offender to the harmful consequences of child victimization. These effects are further exacerbated by the offender's immersion in cyber-communities of similarly socially marginalized and sexually deviant individuals." (Bourke and Hernandez 2008, 188)

The overlap between mere consumers of child pornography and those who actively engage in child abuse and molestation does seem to be an area of future research, especially with regard to the onset of these behaviors and how online communities act to legitimate them. It may also be interesting to think about how status operates in these communities (relative to how you think about status in your own lives). For example, Quayle and Taylor (2002) found that willingness to distribute material, the volume of a collection, and possession of highly valued, rare, or sought-after pieces led to an increase in status within the community, which in turn helps to further legitimate these behaviors.

This line of research into the world of child pornography, in my opinion, pairs well with some of the research we were just discussing on the consequences of regularly watching extremely violent pornography, in terms of how it works to alter participants' view of the world around them. I don't think that it's any stretch of the imagination to say that the people viewing these forms of pornography are mostly men; so, here we have an example of a massive form of media that puts women and children at greater risk of victimization by some form of sexual violence. If pornography influences people in such a negative way, it would make sense to make all pornography illegal. My question to you is this: Besides the massive amount of money involved—no small amount of which goes to otherwise legitimate companies that you might think of when we say pornography is a multi-billion-dollar industry (including the various Internet service providers and credit card companies)—why might someone say the entire industry cannot and should not be shut down?

Human Trafficking and the International Sex Trade

I mentioned earlier in this chapter that the incredible growth of the pornography industry in the past decade has created instances where pornographers are turning to human trafficking to find enough actors to meet demand. In truth, any discussion of pornography, prostitution, and the larger field of sex work in the United States is incomplete without a discussion of the international sex trade (IST). The IST is responsible for bringing women and children into the United States for sex work against their will. It is sex slavery, plain and simple. The IST has also created an underground economy where people—again, presumably mostly men—travel to other parts of the world to have sexual encounters that they couldn't engage in back in the United States, oftentimes with children. Southeast Asia is a particularly popular destination for these people, and a thriving sex tourism economy has developed there as a result.

Sex slavery and sex tourism are two sides of the larger issue of human trafficking. It's one of the darkest topics in this book. Most Americans think slavery ended when Abraham Lincoln issued the Emancipation Proclamation, and that was that. Slavery was legal in this country so long ago that many people (incorrectly) think it is irrelevant and nonexistent today (spoilers: it is relevant and it exists). The truth of the matter is, there are roughly the same number of people trafficked into the United States for various forms of labor each year as there are homicides; there could be as many as 60,000 people living in slavery in the United States today. Worldwide, the number could reach the tens of millions. Besides sex work and domestic labor, people may also be enslaved to do forced manual labor. Forcible recruiting of children into guerilla military organizations to work as soldiers represents another form of slavery, which I point out to make sure you know that it's not necessarily all about sex work.

That said, for the purposes of this part of this chapter, we will focus solely on the IST. I want to talk about how and where these organizations operate, because odds are it's happening much closer to any of you than you realize. It's also important to talk about how the women and children being trafficked find themselves trapped in these awful situations, as obviously no one volunteers to become a slave.

Since no one in her right mind would voluntarily subject herself to the kinds of abuse and violence that sex slaves endure, how, then, does it happen that these women (and children) find themselves in this situation? You might think it's similar to what we talked about with prostitution and the turning-out process, whereby pimps—through sheer force of personality—convince women they meet to prostitute themselves for them. In truth, that practice is limited to prostitution. Sexual slavery involves far more deceit and is much more brutal. Consider, for example, this story from the Coalition to Abolish Slavery and Trafficking, about a woman named Maria:

> Maria was taken from her hometown in Mexico at the age of 15, with promises of a well-paying job as a housekeeper for a family in California. Instead, the same woman who offered her the job sold her into slavery to a single, white older male for $200. For five long years she was raped and beaten. She was forced to clean 18 to 20 hours a day while her "boss" dug her own grave, reminding her of what would happen if she tried to escape. After five years, she was freed when her boss was killed by another man. That is, she thought she was finally free, only to learn that she was to be held responsible for his death. ("Maria" n.d.)

Stories like this are quite common in human trafficking, be it for sexual slavery or some other type of forced labor. Young people in bleak situations are promised meaningful work or the opportunity go to school in America and eventually to bring their families to join them. The wealthy Americans making these promises will say anything to get them to agree, and they seem so sympathetic, their victims think they are saviors. However, in America, things end up quite different—as they did for Maria. Typically, the woman being trafficked is told that she has amassed a lot of debt and must pay it off. More likely, though, the entire charade is dropped as soon as she is in the United States, and she is put to work immediately in some sort of brothel. Many times, these brothels masquerade as legitimate businesses—massage parlors, for instance. The women are constantly watched, and in some cases, their captors will move them from one brothel to another to keep one step ahead of law enforcement and confuse the women: if they do escape, they will have no idea where they are or what to do. The language barrier in cases of international trafficking only adds to these women's isolation and protects the brothel owners.

Now, it isn't always the case that women being trafficked from other countries are outright tricked into it. Sometimes the path is much more direct, depending on how desperate the family situation is. For example, Kieu, a twelve-year-old girl in Cambodia, was sold into slavery by her mother to attempt to pay back loan sharks (Hume, Cohen, and Sorvino 2013). Kieu's mother said, "Selling my daughter was heartbreaking, but what can I say?" What, indeed.

So, in terms of how people find themselves in this situation, there is obviously a great deal of manipulation, just like in the turning-out process. It definitely takes a charismatic person to accomplish this. But human trafficking differs from prostitution in the level of manipulation. Does this mean that no victims of human trafficking were ever turned out? Of course not. There are many stories of women who have fallen in love with the greatest man on the face of the planet, only to have him brutally rape and beat them and then sell them to someone else. It can happen.

Sex Slavery? Not in My Backyard

A problem with combatting human trafficking and sexual slavery is that so many people still stubbornly continue to think that it isn't

happening near them. In reality, many if not most of you reading
this book have likely seen an establishment that deals in sex trafficking without realizing it. People in rural or suburban areas might
think this only happens in big cities; people in big cities might think
it doesn't happen in their city. Nobody thinks it's happening in their
backyard. That is definitely not true. For example, in my state,
Pennsylvania, there have been 2,624 calls to the National Human
Trafficking Resource Center since 2007 ("Pennsylvania" n.d.). Of
those calls, 551 cases were opened, and 592 "high-risk" victims
were identified (meaning the characteristics of the case most certainly pointed to human trafficking). That the number of victims is
greater than the number of cases speaks to the fact that multiple
victims of trafficking are being held by the same person(s). Now,
you might look at that number and say, well, Pennsylvania is on
the East Coast; it's so close to New York City, this must just be a
spillover. Certainly a state in the center of the country would not
have this problem. So, let's look at some of the other states that we
might assume would have no human trafficking. Since 2007, South
Dakota has had thirty-six cases of human trafficking with fifty-nine
high-risk victims ("South Dakota" n.d.). In that same period, North
Dakota had fifty-five cases with forty-seven high-risk victims
("North Dakota" n.d.). Wyoming had twenty-six cases with fifty-
one high-risk victims ("Wyoming" n.d.). Finally, Idaho had forty-
seven cases with seventeen high-risk victims ("Idaho" n.d.). So, the
notion that human trafficking only happens in faraway places is
patently false. It could be happening in a business near you right
now, without anyone being any wiser.

It's also not the case that the victims of sexual slavery come
entirely from other countries. Take, for example, the story of fifteen-
year-old Debbie—not her real name—who was abducted in front of
her home in the Phoenix area and kept in a dog cage for forty days,
while her captors and countless other men who had seen her advertised online gang-raped her (ABC News 2006). Or nineteen-year-old
Miya, who, while working at a mall (also in the Phoenix area), was
approached by a couple about a modeling opportunity and ended up
being peddled as an online escort. Luckily for Miya, she escaped
after "only" six days (ABC News 2006).

The numbers can be frustrating. It might look like few cases are happening near you, and yet we know that so many people are dealing with this worldwide. It seems like a faraway problem, but it's happening right around us. It seems to target poor, unfortunate women and children from impoverished countries, but it is also happening to women and children in the United States. The question I have for of you now is this: What can be done to stop human trafficking and sexual slavery? Can you think of anything that you can do in your community to try to prevent it? What if we broaden the scope away from sexual slavery and focus on all human trafficking. Do you think if you changed the stores you shopped at, restaurants you ate in, and brands you purchased, anything would change? The cynics out there are saying, no, nothing will work. Actually, you can make a huge difference here, even if it's just changing where you shop. This cuts into the profits of companies that directly or indirectly employ slave labor—food companies, electronics companies, hospitality companies—and motivates them to follow more humane employment practices. Going back to sexual violence, though, what do you think you could do in your own communities to reduce this specific type of violence in your area? What do you think local and state governments could be doing to achieve that goal?

8

Gender in the System

In *All God's Children*, Fox Butterfield (1995) sits down with one of the most notorious criminals in the history of New York City, Willie Bosket, to discuss Bosket's own criminal history as well as the past transgressions of several generations of men in his family, going as far back as the antebellum South. Butterfield concludes that at least some of the causes of Bosket's own criminality were set in motion decades before he was born: Willie Bosket was the product of institutional and systemic violence and racism, adherence to toxic standards of masculinity, and allegiance to the demands of bureaucracy, all of which are prevalent in the United States.

Bosket's criminal history is extraordinary. At age nine, he cursed out a Manhattan family court judge and ran out of the courtroom, only to be later apprehended by his own mother as he was holding a knife on another boy near the store where she worked. By adolescence, Bosket had lost track of the number of robberies he had committed, and as an adult, New York prison officials considered him one of the all-time most violent inmates they had ever encountered. By the conclusion of Butterfield's time with him, Bosket had been sentenced to consecutive twenty-five-to-life sentences for his repeated and unrepentant criminal behavior in prison, the final act being the attempted murder of a prison guard using a shank he fashioned from a piece of a typewriter.

Though extraordinary, Bosket's case illustrates quite well the relationship between the criminal justice system as an institution and future criminal behavior (it also exemplifies a number of other criminological concepts, such as Butterfield's argument that the code of the street originated with the idea of honor and respect embedded in southern culture). It's true that Bosket may have ended up in his current situation regardless of how the system handled him, but as he recounts his experiences with a number of people at all stages, it's hard to deny that the system compromised Willie Bosket's well-being severely.

If Bosket's case is too extraordinary, then consider the lives of so many other children whose criminality blooms while they're in school. Remember, as we talked about in the chapter on juvenile delinquency, there is a fundamental philosophical difference in how we treat juvenile offenders in comparison to adults: kids can be changed; adults cannot (remember, this is according to the system and may not be true—there's plenty of evidence that adults can change, too, but we won't get into that here).

In this chapter, we will look at each phase of the criminal justice system, with a special focus on the differences between adolescent and adult behavior, in addition to the larger theme of gender that we've been exploring throughout this book. Because we're including young people in this discussion, we'll start with how a person becomes formally labeled a criminal during his or her time spent in school. Next, we'll talk about the relationship between the police and everyday citizens. Finally, we'll examine the role that gender plays as the accused navigates the legal system and is acquitted or convicted. We'll also spend time discussing a revolutionary new model of justice being utilized more frequently throughout the United States.

In terms of gender, we will see one theme over and over throughout this chapter: because the legal system views boys and girls differently and men and women differently, it treats people differently based entirely on their gender. Here again, we're using the ideas of gender and sex interchangeably, which isn't appropriate, but because this is how the criminal justice system tends to view things, we must too. Much of this relates to labeling theory—the idea that people behave in accordance with what they believe is expected of them based on labels they've been given formally or informally. An informal label can be thought of as similar to a reputation or a role: someone is labeled informally as intelligent, funny, an athlete, and so on. A formal label involves official branding by some authority figure: someone who is arrested and convicted of a crime is formally labeled as a delinquent or a criminal.

The relationship between labeling theory and gender is twofold. First, we must consider gender in terms of the expectations society places on males and females, as well as the ways individuals internalize these expectations. In other words, I know that many people in society expect me to behave a certain way simply because I identify as male; whether I conform to those expectations is my choice. Many people cannot bear the pressure to conform. Others attempt to defy gender norms and then conform when they experience a backlash for being different. Still others revel in making people uncomfortable. Second, we must consider labeling and gender in terms of how agents of the criminal justice system perceive us. I've already mentioned that, typically, the system views gender and biological sex as the same thing, so it's already operating in a way that puts people at a disadvantage. Think about it like this: You hear that someone was murdered. How will your reaction differ if you find out the alleged murderer is a man or a woman? Or a boy or a girl? Or a transgender person? How do you think the prosecution will approach the case depending on the accused's gender? How will gender shape the defense?

Teachers and Students

For many people, their first encounter with the criminal justice system does not involve the police. Instead, the first step in transformation from ordinary citizen to convicted offender happens in school. Think about the relationship between a student and the typical authority figures at school: teachers, vice principals, and principals. These authority figures can impose informal or formal labels on a student. This applies doubly to teachers, who deal with students on a daily basis. How teachers interact with students, especially those who are disruptive, can generate labels for these kids.

Consider the following example: A student in the fourth grade is being very disruptive during class. He keeps talking out of turn and elbowing the student next to him. The teacher's solution is to move the student's desk away from the rest of the class, putting him in a place where the other students can see him. He is on an island now. The teacher believes she has settled the problem: no more elbowing or talking. But by isolating the disruptive student like this and putting him on display for the rest of the class, the teacher has effectively placed an informal label on that student: he is now the bad kid. Even the act of telling a student to cease bad behavior could potentially create an informal label, because it signals to the rest of the class that this is a bad kid, or a weird kid, or an otherwise different kid.

Should this disruptive behavior become more serious, the informal label can become an official label with punishments like after-school or weekend detention, in- or out-of-school suspension, or even expulsion. These penalties go in the student's file (the mythical "permanent record") and could follow him or her from school to school. The existence of this formal label means that teachers and administrators at other schools might form opinions about the student before even meeting him or her—especially in cases of expulsion—which could then create a sort of self-fulfilling prophecy: I expect you to be a bad kid, I treat you like a bad kid, and so you act like a bad kid. This is the key idea behind labeling theory.

How teachers discipline students, how they react to mistakes made in class, and whether they reinforce positive behavior or simply just punish bad behavior can all go a long way toward fostering juvenile delinquency. Navigating and cultivating these relationships can be incredibly difficult. Remember, teachers are people too, capable of the same mistakes and misjudgments as everyone else. People working in education seem especially prone to frustration and alienation as well. So in situations that call for disciplining a student for whatever reason, with the rest of the class watching, there's a lot of potential to make a mistake in the heat of the moment.

These mistakes might happen because the teacher has labeled the student as bad, but they likely also happen because of the gender of the student. After all, can't we think of gender as a label too? Teachers may approach discipline differently based on the (presumed) sex of the student. The gender of the student might even affect whether the teacher perceives behavior as good or bad to begin with. Maybe behavior that calls for harsher punishment gets chalked up to "boys will be boys." Maybe behavior that should be ignored is punished because it's inappropriate or "unladylike." Bartusch and Matsueda (1996) found that parents were more likely to falsely accuse their sons than their daughters of delinquent behavior, so it's not unreasonable to suggest something similar could be happening in schools, if we view teachers as sort of surrogate parents.

Beyond delinquent behavior, teachers might also treat students differently in other areas, based on their gender, which can have indirect effects on delinquency in adolescence or criminality later in life. A big issue recently has been a double standard regarding the dress code in high schools. More often than not, girls are punished for how they dress, the argument being that even the slightest bit of exposed skin will distract the boys in class, interfering with their education. However, when male students come in with as much exposed skin, if not more, they receive no punishment. What does this have to do with crime and delinquency, you ask? It treats students differently based on their sex, gives males clearly preferential treatment over females, and reinforces the idea that, when it comes to sex and sexuality, male behavior is uncontrollable. Such lessons, instilled at a young age, must, one would think, play some part in perpetuating a culture of victim blaming regarding sexual assault. If a student can say that he did badly in math because he was distracted by the exposed shoulder of the girl sitting in front of him, then he can say he raped her at a party for the same reason, right?

Labeling in schools has created one of the biggest problems with the public education system in America today: the school-to-prison pipeline. This refers to the process by which young people—especially young black and Hispanic males—become incarcerated due to zero-tolerance disciplinary practices, engendering an atmosphere of exclusion rather than inclusion. Put simply, many schools have ramped up their disciplinary practices, making them harshly punitive to the point of cruelty. Price (2009) documents a number of cases in which students were severely punished for inexplicable reasons; the police were even called to deal with five- and six-year-old girls having temper tantrums (in both cases, the girls were handcuffed).

Let's talk about the process in more detail and try not to dwell on the horror stories it has created. Because school is the first place where many young people are formally punished, it is also the first place where they might encounter someone from the criminal justice system acting as a law enforcement agent rather than a school officer. In the past, some of the more minor acts of delinquency might be handled in-house; a student caught with a small amount of drugs might be suspended. With the presence of uniformed police officers on campus, however, that student might now be arrested and convicted of a drug offense. That conviction could possibly include incarceration in a juvenile facility, which would entail the student's removal from the public school system for a number of years and receipt of the formal label "juvenile delinquent." While that label can eventually be removed, its consequences cannot without considerable work. The student's risk of offending again is now much higher, as is the risk of rearrest and reincarceration.

Alternatively, the constant threat of excessive punishment for relatively minor offenses might also render some students less inclined to go to school at all. How would you view college if you saw one of your classmates charged with a felony because he looked at someone else's paper during an exam or showed up to class late? Such an environment would not promote learning and intellectual growth. How can a student possibly develop as a human being when challenging a teacher on an academic level could be construed as making a terrorist threat?

This is the school-to-prison pipeline: the inclusion of formal legal authorities in lieu of informal school authorities has created a system in which many high schools are no longer places of learning; rather, they have become a point of entry into the criminal justice system. Now, ask yourself what role gender plays when we think about delinquency in terms of the school-to-prison pipeline. Specifically, how do you think boys and girls view school in general? What do we do in school? What do we get out of it? Matsueda and Heimer (1997) argue that young women and men differ in terms of their appreciation for the value of education, with girls valuing it much more than boys. Matsueda and Heimer argue that boys are more concerned with being perceived as tough or violent instead of smart. If that's the case—and remember, we're talking in general terms—then everything begins to fall into place. We have boys not interested in becoming more intelligent who view school as an arena to develop a violent or tough persona. We have school officials who, rightly or wrongly, may be more likely to perceive male students as bad, which could further push those students away and cause them to devalue their education even more. Conflict is natural in education, but it should not get to the point where neither party wants anything to do with the other, right? This, coupled with the existence of harsh punishments and zero-tolerance policies, seems to have perverted and warped many schools.

The transformation of many schools into war zones raises a number of questions: Why did so many schools choose to take this hyperpunitive approach? How did this transition occur? What was the reasoning and rationale behind it? How did the criminalization of relatively common (albeit deviant) behaviors happen? How did students become prisoners-in-waiting? Hirschfield (2008) argues that there is nothing really new about this—that discipline has always been at the foundation of the educational philosophy in schools serving children from poor and working-class families. But, again, what changed to make the traditional disciplinary style so much more extreme? According to Hirschfield, it stems from the economy's moving away from its industrialized, manufacturing-based structure toward a focus on information and service; this "shifted impacted schools and their disciplinary practices from productive ends toward a warehousing function[. T]he

ensuing criminal justice expansion . . . deprived schools of potential resources. Aided by a crime-fixated and punitive political climate, these changes helped reorient school actors more toward the
prevention and punishment of crime, and less toward the prepa-
ration of workers and citizens" (Hirschfield 2008, 81).

It is scary to consider that for many poor and working-class
students, school is no longer a place to learn; it's a place to be
monitored so that even the most minor act of delinquency can be
immediately caught and punished. Many young men are living
under a microscope, with every move analyzed for a potential
threat, every aspect of their behavior compared against the labels
assigned to them, until the prophecy of their bad behavior comes
true. It's no wonder so many schools perform so poorly. It's no
wonder so many students leave.

Cops and Citizens

Just like teachers and school administrators, police can make
decisions based on gender. It stands to reason that police officers
assigned to schools might view male students as more likely than
female students to cause trouble. We know that throughout the
population men are more responsible than women for crime, so
why wouldn't the same hold true among boys and girls in school?

Of course, the police are responsible for so much more than
just patrolling schools and dealing with disruptive youths. A few
different styles of policing dictate what the police do on a daily
basis—how they approach the duty to protect and serve the community. Police departments that utilize a law enforcement strategy
simply react when someone breaks the law. In some cases, police
might respond only once the crime has been reported to them. In
others, they might actively seek out people who are breaking the
law—for example, when undercover officers arrest drug dealers.
In the latter instance, a crime has occurred, but no one has
reported it. In another style of policing, called crime prevention,
instead of reacting to crime that has occurred, the police (with
assistance from other public or private organizations) try to inter-

vene in some way to prevent crime from happening in the first place. You could think of the police as playing the role of social worker or counselor and of police departments as analytical bodies, examining data on past crime to prevent future crime. You could think of the people associated with this approach as political lobbyists or advocates, championing solutions to the crime problem in the hope that future legislation will reduce crime in some form. This proactive style of criminal justice uses the resources of the system (and its affiliates) to fight crime head-on. In some ways, it resembles the idea of restorative justice, which we'll discuss later in this chapter.

One tool that can be utilized in a crime-prevention approach is community policing. Community policing harkens back to the days of police officers walking their beats, getting to know the people in their assigned neighborhoods, and building and maintaining a relationship with them. Why should that matter? According to the philosophy of community policing, these relationships have a lot of power. A good relationship with the neighborhood police officer means you will be more likely to call the police for help or to report something you see going on than you would if your contact with police was restricted to a squad car with tinted windows driving through the neighborhood without stopping. Community policing also allows the police to demonstrate a commitment to helping the people in the community, which in turn can go a long way to helping them do their job better. For instance, in May 2015, members of the Chicago Police Department (CPD)—which has a notoriously bad reputation for too many reasons to list here—threw a daddy-daughter dance for the community. A CPD officer escorted those girls who wanted to attend but whose father was absent (for whatever reason) or otherwise unable to participate (Keady 2015). Taking the time to do that for those girls showed that those officers had a stake in their well-being, not just whether they'd done anything wrong.

That said, for better or worse, many police departments have focused on law enforcement rather than crime prevention for the past several decades. There are a lot of political reasons for this, which we won't dwell on here. Suffice it to say, the "War on

Crime" and the "War on Drugs" have a lot to do with it—you don't go into a war worrying about the well-being of people who could conceivably be the enemy.

Returning to the role of gender, when law enforcement, not cultivating positive relations, is the primary goal of the police, then both the police and community members will rely more on labels than facts to predict behavior. This means that the police will use profiling. It's very easy for officers to make decisions based on stereotypes about the people they're observing. When it comes to profiling the community at large, police officers might use racial profiling, meaning that they will tend to assume blacks and Hispanics are generally guilty (even responsible for all crime) and so deserve mistreatment, whereas they usually assume whites to be completely innocent and treat them with respect. Could gender profiling exist? Unfortunately, there has not been much research on this subject. Visher (1983) developed the chivalry hypothesis, which says that women who display traditional gender behaviors (submissiveness, demureness, weakness, etc.), even after being caught committing a crime, are likely to receive better treatment because the officer (presumably male, though much has changed since Visher collected the data for this study) will take pity on them and their circumstances. Visher also found that older and white women were more likely to receive beneficial treatment. Think of the stereotype of the woman crying to get out of a speeding ticket: her doing so will likely invoke a very different emotional reaction from the officer than if, say, I turned into a sobbing mess. I'd probably be cited for a noise complaint too. Speaking of which, Smith, Makarios, and Alpert (2006) examined the relationship between the police and gender in this very context in their study of over 66,000 traffic stops in Miami-Dade County, Florida, and found that police were less suspicious of female drivers than of male drivers, which meant that they arrested more men than women during these stops. Strangely, a number of studies focus on gender profiling exclusively in terms of traffic stops (Ikner, Ahmad, and del Carmen 2005; Scheb, Lyons, and Wagers 2009), and even these may couch gender in terms of profiling in general, not as a unique aspect of it. Stolzenberg and D'Alessio

(2004) used data from the National Incident-Based Reporting System to demonstrate that, in general, women are less likely to be arrested than men (black women are more likely than white women—race is an important factor in this study), which the researchers attribute to a general leniency shown to women by criminal justice agents.

Even with somewhat limited research on gender profiling and the chivalry hypothesis, it makes sense that the police would consider gender in their treatment of individuals. In *The New Jim Crow*, Michelle Alexander (2012) quotes David Cole on the profiling of drug couriers. Cole argues that the police are trained to look for any indication that someone is running drugs—including whether the individual is acting nervous or calm (either can be an indicator of wrongdoing). If these contradictory mindsets can be used to profile people, certainly gender must be involved somehow. Sounds like an idea for a paper, doesn't it?

If the research on how police view people differently based on gender (if they do) is somewhat limited, what about gender differences in how people view the police? Much of the existing research on this topic tends to focus on the influence of age and race on perception (see Brunson and Weitzer 2009). In their study of youth perceptions, Taylor et al. (2001) found that girls had a higher opinion of the police than boys across almost all racial and ethnic categories (there was no gender difference among Native American youths). Nofzinger and Williams (2005) also show that women have a higher opinion of the police then men. Gabbidon, Higgins, and Potter (2011) found that in a nationally representative sample of blacks, women were less likely than men to report being treated unfairly by the police. This is an interesting approach to citizens' perception of the police: asking not whether the police are good or bad or display gender bias but whether they have been fair; asking not if they did their job wrong but if they did it properly. Moreover, Halim and Stiles (2001) found that men were more supportive than women of aggressive police behavior—including violence—across a variety of different contexts. So, perhaps we should be asking whether there are gender differences in what people want from the police instead of assuming everyone agrees about how they should behave. This is an especially relevant question given the current climate of police-community relations in cities across the United States today.

The idea that men have a worse opinion of the police than women do, coupled with the idea that the police tend to treat women better than they do men, creates an unwinnable situation for everyone involved. Regardless of whether they have a law-enforcement or crime-prevention mentality, police officers have to deal with people every day. Going into a situation already believing that the people you're dealing with are bad will drastically change how you approach them. And if they also have a preconceived negative opinion of you—like we said, men tend to have less favorable views of the police than women—then the potential for escalating hostility is that much greater. Add in other sociodemographic factors that shape how people view the police and vice versa, like race and age, and the situation could quickly become one that will benefit no one. When the interaction between the police and the community becomes hostile, both sides return to their camps with further evidence that the other is in the wrong. This can generate confirmation bias or selection bias, whereby we seek out information that supports our viewpoint and ignore alternative explanations.

What about gender differences among police officers themselves? Do men and women view their jobs differently, or can gender explain any unique experiences they have? In their study of the risk of job burnout, McCarty, Zhao, and Garland (2007) found that the violence associated with the job—making violent arrests, attending the funerals of other officers—affected female police officers more than their male counterparts and significantly contributed to their burnout. Rabe-Hemp and Schuck (2007) found that female officers were more likely than their male peers to be assaulted when intervening in a family conflict. This means that, when called to a fight between husband and wife, for example, female officers were more likely than a male officer to be attacked physically by either the husband or the wife.

Ivie and Garland (2011) examined the role of military experience as a resource against stress and burnout among the police and found that female officers without military experience did experience a higher level of stress than their counterparts who had served in the armed forces—but note that this study focused on only one department. Gächter, Savage, and Torgler (2011) found that female officers experienced more physical strain—including dizziness, chest pain, and nausea—than their male counterparts, and that female officers needed more social capital and a greater sense of fairness at work than their male counterparts, not only to cope with stressors but to also handle some of the unique aspects of being a female officer, such as tokenism. Tokenism is the practice of including one or two members of a minority group in an organization historically made up of members of the dominant group; because police departments have traditionally been mostly male, the presence of just a few female police officers could be considered tokenism if they do not get the same rights, privileges, and opportunities as their male peers. In case it isn't yet obvious why being the token female officer would be problematic, Wertsch (1998) outlines some of the issues these women experience: in addition to being isolated socially, they face the dual pressure to exceed at the job while also being pushed into tasks that fall into the category of "traditional" women's work. In other words, they might be expected to be a superhero on the street and bake cookies for the boys back in the office simultaneously—a ridiculous and impossible dichotomy to live with. Wertsch concludes that because of tokenism—combined with the structure of the institution and the personal lives of female officers (we still live in a society that expects all female employees to fully commit to motherhood and a career, which is virtually impossible for many women)—fewer female officers received opportunities for promotion, which perpetuates the status quo of tokenism and discrimination in those departments where they are rampant. (Remember that we're talking about this in general terms, so we can say that many police departments have historically had a problem with the treatment of women in their ranks, but we shouldn't conclude that 100 percent of the officers in 100 percent of police departments are misogynists. We can still speak to a larger cultural problem without singling anyone out.)

What about how male and female officers interact with each other? Vega and Silverman (1982) found that many male officers had no use for their female counterparts, who, they suggested, were not physically or emotionally strong enough to perform the job. Interestingly enough, female officers also indicated that their female peers might not be capable of performing well in this line of work. Exploring the idea that female officers are unwilling or unable to use coercion, either verbal or physical, Paoline and Terrill (2005) found no gender difference between police officers in either Indianapolis, Indiana, or St. Petersburg, Florida, in terms of willingness to use coercive techniques. Again, note that this study's geographical reach is limited.

Gossett and Williams (1998) conducted a qualitative study of policewomen in the Southwest and found that the majority reported experiencing discrimination from their male peers (other officers, administrators, or superiors) or from citizens (male or female). However, the policewomen interviewed did indicate that they felt things had substantially improved. Archbold and Hassell (2009), in their study of promotion procedures among police departments, found that female officers were blocked from opportunities for promotion based on their marriage to another officer. Again, the number of policewomen interviewed was extremely small, and I offer the study result here not as a generalizable truth but for your consideration.

All of this research suggests that female police officers have a more difficult time on the job than male officers, but what about their ability to perform the job? Franklin (2007) argues that women might be able to perform the job better than men when confronted with a situation in which communication—and not violence—is the best solution. We'll see this theme again when we discuss prison life. Gender socialization that encourages women to be more communicative and empathetic can help diffuse situations that, were aggression used instead, could become violent. This does seem to contradict the idea that female officers are more likely to be attacked when they intervene in a family conflict. Some pioneering criminology student could clearly explore the topic in more detail.

So what can we conclude about the lives of female officers relative to their male peers? There's no evidence to suggest that they cannot do the job as well as men or that they get into police work for different reasons. Substantial evidence suggests, however, that they still aren't a welcome part of the force, having more negative experiences inside and outside the police based on their defiance of and deviation from traditional gender norms.

Courts and Defendants

The final branch of the criminal justice system that we'll discuss in this chapter is the courts. As with the police, people think they know a lot about this branch, having spent so many holidays binge-watching *Law and Order*. And, like the police, this branch of the system is incredibly misunderstood because of the media. I'm sorry, but odds are that the assistant district attorney in your area, though talented, probably doesn't have the sheer force of character of a television lawyer.

As with schools and the police, when talking about gender and the courts, it is important to think about gender differences in the application of justice. I want to draw your attention in this section to the importance of the phrase *application of justice*. When we think about how the criminal justice system operates in other areas—schools, police departments, prisons—we know people make mistakes. If we're going to be realistic, we also know that some people are biased in some way or another and that their behavior will reflect those biases. No one is perfect, and we can really only hope to minimize the number of mistakes, then move quickly to take responsibility and correct them. A mistake in the criminal justice system, however, could put someone through a lot of unnecessary pain and stress. When it comes to the courts and the application of justice—weighing the evidence and the facts of a case to determine whether someone has broken the law and, if so, what their punishment should be—there should be zero room for error. Justice is supposed to be blind. If people are treated differently by members of the court simply because of their demographic status, for instance, then how can we say that we truly live in a just society? Unfortunately, this isn't just a rhetorical question; bias is a very real part of the legal system today.

Biases based on both race and gender can emerge almost immediately in court. Before the accused stands trial, he or she goes through what is called the pretrial phase. The accused hears the charges and enters a plea, and the judge decides whether he or she will be released pending trial, the amount of any bail, other conditions of release (i.e., electronic monitoring), and so on. On the surface, this seems obvious and routine; we've watched it hundreds of times during those *Law and Order* marathons. However bias can creep in here in the form of what Steffensmeier, Ulmer, and Kramer (1998) describe as perceptual shorthand. These are the stereotypes judges will use in their decisionmaking process—either based on the demographic characteristics of the defendant, or the details of the case, or both. Demuth and Steffensmeier (2004) argue that perceptual shorthand gets used because, during the pretrial phase, in making their decisions, judges know only the nature of the crime and the basic characteristics presented by the accused. That said, Demuth and Steffensmeier found that women received better treatment or had a better outcome than men in every measure used to describe the pretrial phase: being detained, being denied bail, getting a financial versus a nonfinancial release option, the bail amount, and even their ability to post bail.

Does it really make a difference if women receive better treatment than men in this part of the trial process? The pretrial phase is overlooked and underappreciated and can have serious implications for the future well-being of the accused. Think about it in terms of your own life. You've been arrested and accused of a crime. During the pretrial phase, the judge takes one look at you and orders you held on bail that's so high, your family would have to take out three mortgages to make it. How well could you put together your defense from prison? If released, you'd theoretically be able to meet with your legal team every day in either their offices or your home, rehearse your testimony in front of your bathroom mirror, and, if nothing else, enjoy the comfort of sleeping in your own bed. In prison, you might be limited in the amount of time you're able to spend with your lawyer and members of your family, your only legal resource is the prison law library, and you're definitely not sleeping in the most relaxing environment. In the end, it stands to reason that more lenient pretrial sentencing can lead to a stronger defense during the trial itself, which should lead to a greater chance of acquittal.

Doerner and Demuth (2010) found that on the basis of gender alone, women receive better treatment during the pretrial phase, with their odds of incarceration 42 percent lower than for men. So in sum, women receive better treatment than men in the pretrial, trial, and sentencing phases. Why do you think this might be? Remember the chivalry hypothesis that Visher (1983) talked about regarding how the police tend to treat women better than men? We can apply some of the same logic to the courts. Keep in mind that we're talking about the way that the courts perceive gender here, so we don't want to put too much importance on the role of the jury, though obviously it is a critical factor in this process. At the pretrial phase, as Doerner and Demuth (2010) among others mention, the perceptual shorthand utilized by judges in determining the risk of releasing defendants back into society follows three broader concepts: their blameworthiness, protection of the community, and any other practical constraints. In all three categories women are viewed more favorably: they are viewed as less physically threatening, less culpable, and less likely to reoffend and benefit from the public perception that separating children from their mother is problematic. In other words, the perceptual shorthand used by so many judges considers stereotypes of women and assumes that because they are (supposedly) weak, timid, and passive, they could not have committed the crime or must have been tricked into it. While clearly this sexist attitude is not based on fact, this is how the system tends to view women. As a result many women benefit from these stereotypes. Conversely, this perceptual shorthand uses negative stereotypes to justify treating male defendants more harshly: men are supposedly more violent and aggressive, more likely to reoffend, and less involved in their families and communities, so giving them harsher sentences is justified.

We should also look at gender's intersection with other sociodemographic characteristics—specifically race—to better understand its effects on sentencing decisions. It'd be foolish to think that gender bias is the only type that exists in the court, especially when we've seen evidence to suggest that the police engage in racial profiling.

In the pretrial phase, there is evidence to suggest that racial discrimination is also present. Blacks and Hispanics tend to receive worse treatment than white defendants, with Hispanic defendants receiving the worst treatment of any group based on their perceived outsider status. An inability to speak English fluently and a lack of basic understanding of the criminal justice system tend to make this discrimination worse (Demuth 2003), likely because judges engage in confirmation bias. So how does this racial bias match up with how the courts view men and women? In some ways, these biases stack—in the pretrial phase, Demuth and Steffensmeier (2004) find that Hispanic males receive the worst treatment among blacks, Hispanics, and whites, while white women receive the best treatment.

Restorative Justice

Historically in the United States, there have been two models of justice: retributive justice, which emphasizes long prison sentences, capital punishment, and other harsh penalties, and rehabilitative justice, which attempts to fix problems in the lives of the incarcerated, which could include providing mental health care and job-training programs. Many criminologists believe society swings like a pendulum from one style of justice to the other based on public opinion. When we embrace an extremely retributive model, over time support erodes as the number of people in prison increases, punishments become harsh, police become increasingly detached from the community, and so on. More areas then embrace the rehabilitative model, but that, too, eventually loses public support, as people begin to feel that the "free" job-training programs, GED classes, and even college courses made available to inmates are undeserved and unfair. Why should the average twenty-year-old college student have to pay tuition to take this amazing criminology course, while someone who committed some awful act and hurt society gets to take it for free? And the pendulum swings the other way.

This description, of course, oversimplifies the relationship between retributive and rehabilitative justice. The point is, regardless of the model utilized, it is difficult to say that it has worked. Ask yourself this: What is the purpose of justice? What is the purpose of punishment? Regardless of the model of justice or punishment, isn't its purpose to reduce the amount of crime in our society? Why, then, has the number of people incarcerated in the United States skyrocketed in the past thirty-plus years (Alexander 2012)? We have to question whether or not the system works.

It would be foolish to think that only these two modes of justice and punishment are possible. And it would be foolish to continue to implement practices that clearly aren't working. An alternative style of justice is slowly spreading throughout adult and juvenile systems in the United States: restorative justice, a model championed by John Braithwaite (1989, 2002). Braithwaite (2002, 11), quoting Tony Marshall, defines restorative justice as "a process whereby all the parties with a stake in a particular offence come together to resolve collectively how to deal with the aftermath of the offence and its implications for the future."

How might restorative justice relate to some of the connections between gender and crime discussed in this book? It depends on the type of crime. Braithwaite (2002) argues for the use of restorative justice in areas outside of the criminal justice system (for example, schools—which has been done with some success). Because of the nature of this approach, however, it just isn't feasible in every situation. Take, for example, the types of crime we discussed in Chapters 6 and 7: relationship violence and sexual violence. In the case of intimate partner violence, restorative justice has provided a successful alternative to previously utilized models. In some cases, abusers are ordered to participate in some type of restorative program; in others, they're given the option.

Restorative justice as an approach to handling cases of intimate partner violence is not without its critics. For instance, Coker (2006) and Stubbs (2007) both caution that because domestic violence is unique in comparison to other forms of violence and its causes are deeply rooted in patriarchy, a restorative approach emphasizing forgiveness may end up reinforcing the abusive behavior and placing additional stress on the victim. Specifically, if the abuser is allowed to downplay the seriousness of (typically) his behavior and is not forced to confront the pain and suffering he has caused his partner, then there will be no growth, and the program instead becomes an easy way to avoid prison time and continue the abuse once everyone is back behind closed doors.

The restorative justice approach would also be extremely problematic in cases of sexual violence. If a core goal of restorative justice is to bring victim and offender face-to-face in an attempt to resolve conflict and, as much as possible, to restore the status quo that existed before the offense, then forcing the victims of sexual violence to confront their attackers and accept their apologies will likely do immeasurable psychological damage to the victims more than anything else. Put simply, it is asking the impossible of a woman who has been raped and is dealing with the harm associated with that trauma to suggest that she sit down in a conference room with her rapist and talk about the assault in front of a group of strangers, with the understanding that she should listen to and eventually accept his apology.

Prison Life

The final step in the criminal justice process is incarceration and, in many cases, a period of supervision following that. This chapter focuses on prison as an institution and explores the differences between male and female prisoners and the lives of male and female correctional officers. The next chapter will pick up with what happens after release from prison, as well as the impact of incarceration on the families and communities of inmates.

I want to start by discussing prison first because it's the stage in the system that gets the least attention, especially from people not interested in crime. Think about any case that's gotten national coverage in your lifetime: Michael Vick and the Bad Newz Kennels dog-fighting ring in 2007; the death of Caylee Anthony and the trial of her mother, Casey Anthony, in 2011; the Aurora, Colorado, movie theater shooting in 2012; the Boston Marathon bombing in 2013; the attack on a Pennsylvania State Police outpost by Eric Frein in 2014 (which has not yet gone to trial as of this writing). The list goes on. In such events, the public avidly follows the manhunt, the investigation, the gory details of the case, and the day-to-day happenings of the trial. And once the prosecution is over, and justice has allegedly been served, we move on to the next tragedy. The people at the center of the story are forgotten. Once they have gone to prison, they are out of sight, out of mind.

For the prisoner, now removed from the public eye, life also goes on. In reality, prison can be an extremely miserable experience. Kenneth Adams (1992, 275) writes that "although incarceration is punishment, and punishment is meant to be unpleasant, the fact that prisons will always be unattractive places does not mean that all inmate difficulties can be ignored."

McClellan (1994) studied prison discipline and the treatment of male and female inmates who have broken a rule in an environment that demands absolute compliance. She found that female inmates were much more likely than male inmates to be cited for much less serious offenses. She also found that punishment for these transgressions tended to be harsher for female inmates than for male inmates. Jiang and Winfree (2006), however, showed that female inmates have a higher level of social support within prison and in what remains of their lives on the outside, which the researchers believed helps them adapt to prison life and makes them less likely to be written up for some misconduct violation. While Jiang and Winfree demonstrated that female inmates do have a larger social support structure than male inmates, this network has no significant bearing on whether they receive conduct violations. The key gender difference, according to Jiang and Winfree, is the effect of marriage: married male inmates are less likely to be written up than unmarried male inmates; marriage has no bearing on the risk of being written up for female inmates. This means that having family outside—and we will go into this more in the next chapter—impacts how the inmate adjusts to life on the inside. Jiang and Winfree only talked about this variable in terms of prison misconduct, but maybe we could think in other ways about the relationship between family on the outside and life on the inside and how it might affect male and female inmates differently.

What about the lives of prisoners prior to their incarceration? Sure, we talked about some gender differences in the theories of crime way back in the beginning of the book, but we know that not everyone who commits a crime is either caught or incarcerated. Might male and female inmates have unique attributes? McClellan, Farabee, and Crouch (1997) compared male and female inmates incarcerated in Texas and found that the women in their study reported significantly higher rates than men of childhood maltreatment; this abuse was significantly linked to future depression and substance use, which in turn was linked to criminal behavior. This finding supports the notion that men and women have unique pathways into crime, based on any of the existing criminological theories. Mullings, Hartley, and Marquart (2004) also show a connection between childhood maltreatment and later alcoholism among female inmates and demonstrate that these women were more likely to grow up in homes where alcohol abuse was common. This suggests a longer-term role of alcohol in criminality that taps into the life course perspective: in other words, alcoholism may be situated in a much larger context than we tend to think, potentially having a negative effect on the next generation. In a study of inmates in federal prison, Langan and Pelissier (2001) found that women had also abused serious drugs at a higher rate, increasing the risk of a myriad of negative long-term outcomes related to education and family life.

What about the lives of male and female prison guards? They aren't completely the same, but they aren't absolute opposites either. Zimmer (1987, 421) looked at how gender roles allowed female correctional officers to change the way that they did their job, noting, "Some women play a mothering, nurturing role vis-à-vis inmates, a role that is in direct contrast to the macho, competitive role typical of men guards. Women guards are also more likely to have a social worker's orientation toward the job and to spend a great deal of time listening to inmate problems, discussing their family relationships, assisting them in letter writing, and helping them make plans for their release."

This didn't mean that female guards in Zimmer's study necessarily had a different perspective on their work than male guards did. In fact, Zimmer found that male and female guards had the same motivation for getting into this line of work. Gender socialization and gender roles shaped their approach to the job, though Bierie (2012) found that women staff may perceive potentially violent incidents differently than men do, making them more willing to communicate than men because they might not see a situation as potentially explosive. Lawrence and Marian (1998) found that women guards faced the most resistance from male guards with the most job experience (which is to say, the older male guards). Despite this resistance, the women in their study viewed themselves as every bit as capable as the male guards. This largely parallels what we saw with male and female police officers in terms of their motivation to do the job, the unique skills they bring to it, and the resistance women experience in the workplace.

What other challenges or stressors are unique to working in a prison? In our discussion of sexual violence, we talked about sexual assaults, up to and including rape, in adult and juvenile correctional facilities. We talked about this in terms of either inmate-on-inmate or staff-on-inmate violence. Left out of that discussion was the potential for staff to be victimized. Gordon, Proulx, and Grant (2013) studied the risk and fear among female prison guards of multiple types of victimization, including both sexual violence and more ordinary violence. Risk was measured in terms of the likelihood of such an event, while fear was measured in terms of how afraid they were of it happening. Female guards were significantly more fearful of inmate victimization than male guards, but in terms of staff-on-staff violence, there was no difference. How common is violence perpetrated against prison staff? Sorenson et al. (2011) found that, at least in the prisons they studied, serious physical violence against staff was extremely rare, especially violence against female staff members.

9

Life After Prison

I present to you here a tragic but not uncommon story:

> On April 22, 1983, Bruce and a female friend pulled up in front
> of Monte Carlo liquor store in the Bronx. Bruce parked the car
> and followed his friend inside to buy wine. There he encoun-
> tered pandemonium. Tyrone, a man Bruce had never met
> before, had cornered his friend and was making sexual
> advances toward her. The girl screamed, but the man persisted.
> The scene sparked a fight between Bruce and Tyrone. The fight
> spilled out onto the street, and Bruce shot Tyrone. (Heinlein
> 2013)

Over several years of conversations with Bruce, Sabine Heinlein gradually got him to open up about why he killed Tyrone and
talked to him about some of the challenges he's facing now that
he's back on the outside. His reason for killing Tyrone had less to
do with defending his friend and more to do with something we discussed earlier in this book—Bruce was, at that point in his life, a
firm believer in the code of the street. It's that simple: Bruce basically thought he had no other choice. What makes his story more
interesting is the relationship of his time in prison and transition
back into the community to another aspect of his identity: Bruce is
somewhat of a foodie.

Bruce shared with Heinlein examples of how he honed his cooking skills in prison. Specifically, he developed a reputation for his cheesecake—not something most people would associate with a convicted murderer. One of Bruce's biggest concerns on his release from prison as he transitioned into a halfway house was not whether he'd be able to find work and make a new life for himself while staying away from the old habits and people that sent him down the wrong path, but whether he'd be able to make his cheesecake in a real oven—he was very relieved when it turned out just perfectly and was well liked by the other people in his halfway house.

Most people wouldn't think of such a small thing as a source of anxiety for someone who has just gotten out of prison, but it was hugely important to Bruce. After all, he didn't really have much else going for him besides his interest in food; he didn't really know anyone, and the people he did know represented a past he was unwilling to go back to. Try to put yourself in Bruce's shoes: You've eaten the same diet, more or less, for twenty-four years, and you've developed a whole catalogue of tricks to make that food palatable. And now you're suddenly taken out of that world. Like Bruce, you probably wouldn't even really know how—or what—to eat anymore.

We've covered a lot of ground so far. We've talked about gender and multiple types of crime and how these things manifest over a lifetime. We looked at gender and the system, beginning with school and moving on to the police, then the courts, then prison. It only seems natural, then, to finish that journey talking about issues surrounding reentry, recidivism, and the various struggles that men and women face when returning to their lives after prison.

This is an incredibly important topic because we have so many people in prison, and the vast majority will return home at some point—obviously, not everyone in prison is going to be spending the rest of his or her natural life there. According to the Bureau of Justice Statistics, 636,300 inmates were released from prison in 2014 (Carson 2015). This number does not include people being held in local jails, juvenile homes, halfway houses, or any other part of the penal system. Were we to include them, then the number of people transitioning back into their communities would be much, much higher. We expect that incarceration will help them become better people, or at least convince them to not do again what got them sent away. As we'll see, however, prison doesn't really work very well in that regard. I can't stress enough how important this is. If the purpose of prison is to correct bad behavior so that offenders can be better members of society, why don't we bother to see if it is accomplishing this goal?

Recidivism: What Is It and Why Does It Happen?

The fact of recidivism demonstrates a fundamental problem with the setup of the criminal justice system. Recidivism occurs when someone who has committed a crime and been punished for it—thereby paying his or her debt to society and supposedly learning that crime is bad—proceeds to go out and commit another offense. Well, people make mistakes, I suppose, and I guess you can't expect everyone to walk the straight and narrow on release, right? And since prison is such a brutal place, surely few people really do recidivate, right? Well, about that. Beginning in 2005, researchers tracked the behaviors of over 400,000 newly released inmates in thirty states. Their findings were surprising: within one year, 56.7 percent of the offenders (over 229,000) had been rearrested; within three years, 67.8 percent had been rearrested (over 274,000); within five years, 76.6 percent had been rearrested (over 309,000) (Durose, Cooper, and Snyder 2014). Over three-quarters of the released offenders found their way back into the system! That's incredible! It's also clear evidence that the system doesn't really work the way we want it to, which we'll get to momentarily.

What about gender differences in the recidivism rate itself? Are men more likely to recidivate than women, or vice versa? What about being male or female could influence how well one responds to discipline or experiences the process of having his or her behavior corrected? Is there any tangible difference at all?

Surprisingly, research on gender differences in the recidivism rate is almost nonexistent. Perhaps this stems from a basic truth about gender and crime. We know that men commit crime at a higher rate than women in general, and nothing suggests that going through the justice system will suddenly erase that discrepancy or cause women to recidivate at a higher rate than men. Instead, research on recidivism tends to focus on other potential influencing factors, the effects of different types of punishment, or differences across categories of crime. We'll be talking about the first two of those issues in this chapter, but I will leave the question of differences in the recidivism rate across types of crime as a research project for you.

Before we get into those points, I want to spend some time thinking about why people recidivate in the first place. It's one thing to point to the exceptionally high recidivism rate and clutch our pearls because the system isn't working. I want to take things a step further and try to figure out why people recidivate. What causes them to offend again, even after they have been formally penalized for past bad behavior? Is prison not harsh enough punishment, or is something else going on here? Are prisons bad, or are people not fixable? This is a very important question, because if there will always be some whose behavior can't be corrected, then a subset of the population will always be in prison, and eliminating crime is impossible. That said, if people recidivate because the system isn't working correctly, then it seems to me that we should scrap the system and start over from scratch. What is the purpose of doing something over and over and expecting different results? Isn't that the definition of insanity?

It turns out that the answer to this might be simpler than you think. In a meta-analysis of 131 studies related to recidivism, Gendreau, Little, and Goggin (1996) found that the majority tended to identify similar causes—specifically, offenders' age, race, gender, history of antisocial behavior, association with antisocial people, substance use, social achievement, and other family factors. In other words, pretty much every identifiable theoretical cause of crime that we've talked about thus far plays a part in why people reoffend, even after being punished for committing a crime. That might seem like an obvious point to some of you, but I want to make sure that it sinks in: the system of punishment does not take into consideration any of the major theoretical causes of crime we've talked about in this book, and those very same factors prevent the system from working the way it is intended to.

It'd be easy to say that the system isn't working because we're blind to these causes and foolishly sticking to the narrative that crime is very simple, but I don't want to go into that so much. Instead, let's step back and focus on a core principle of American culture: individualism. A major problem with the structure of the criminal justice system and how we conceptualize and implement punishment in the United States is that an intense focus on the individual leads us to do absolutely nothing to change the circumstances that the inmate is returning to. It puts the responsibility for changing those conditions—which is much easier said than done—on the released themselves. Our intense focus on the individual and on individual rationality has created a system of punishment that happily incarcerates people for violating the law but does nothing to change their behavior, other than hoping that the threat of further punishment will cause them to make the choices necessary (however possible) to change their own lives. This gives rise to situations like that faced by Bruce. The only people he could reconnect with were involved in crime, and he had to make a conscious choice not to rejoin them. Bruce is an atypical case in this instance; once released from prison (or jail or juvie), most people have no choice but to tumble headfirst back into the circumstances in which they got into trouble in the first place. And because the circumstances of life back home haven't changed, the likelihood that they will commit another crime and go back to jail is pretty high. For some people, the deck is eternally stacked against them.

Changing offenders' circumstances to reduce the likelihood of recidivism—or guarantee desistance from criminal behavior—is often referred to as the "knifing-off" process (Laub and Sampson 2003). This entails complete separation of offenders from those prior influences, which allows them to begin reshaping their identities and reframing past experiences in a negative light. This can happen in a few ways; Laub and Sampson suggest joining the military or getting married as two, but these options (especially the military) may not be available to some offenders.

In general, the theoretical predictors of crime will still have some effect on ex-convicts even after their release from prison, unless they go through this knifing-off process (Laub and Sampson 2003). Do certain theoretical predictors work differently for male and female offenders after release? In other words, might gender differences in the risk factors lead to recidivism?

Benda (2005) examined six hundred offenders—three hundred female, three hundred male—to determine not only what risk factors affect men and women differently, but also whether any differences in those forces prevent offenders from recidivating. In terms of risk factors, Benda found for both men and women a number of criminogenic factors—alcohol use (men), selling drugs (women), being with a criminal partner (women), having criminal friends (men)—which, in my opinion, overlap quite a bit. More interesting are the psychological and emotional differences in risk. Depression, stress, suicidal ideation, and fearfulness are more likely to cause female ex-offenders to recidivate; aggression is much more likely to cause male ex-offenders to recidivate. Because of this, it appears necessary to develop gender-specific reentry programs, because men and women face unique challenges on leaving prison, and a "one-size-fits-all" approach might not help them fully reintegrate into society.

In terms of those factors that inhibit recidivism, Benda (2005) finds that education and job satisfaction ward off recidivism for men—though neither is an absolute guarantee—while relationships and number of children reduce the likelihood of recidivating for women. This makes the relationship between gender and recidivism much more interesting, because stereotypical gender issues and gender roles reduce and increase, respectively, the risk of recidivating for both men and women. Negative emotions more commonly associated with each gender can lead to reoffending; adherence to gender roles commonly (or stereotypically) associated with masculinity and femininity can reduce the risk of reoffending.

My next question is, could we argue that going to prison actually increases the likelihood that someone will commit another crime? In other words, what if the US system of punishment actually does the opposite of what it's intended to? Anecdotally, we know that people in prison are exposed to all sorts of opportunities to learn about other types of crime; as the social learning perspective would say, they're spending most of their time around bad people, learning techniques and motivations that not only reinforce whatever bad behavior got them there in the first place but open up a whole new world of offending. Could prisons actually be contributing to the crime problem? Mears, Cochran, and Bales (2012) compared the consequences of going to prison to the aftereffects of other forms of punishment, specifically jail or prison time (prisons are run by the state, whereas jails are run by local law enforcement), traditional probation, and intensive probation. Their findings have interesting ramifications for the utility of the criminal justice system. First, they found that prison itself does appear to increase the risk of recidivism, meaning that people subjected to a prison term instead of traditional or intensive probation are more likely to offend again (as were people who went to jail). However, this only applies to drug and property crime—meaning that prison does not increase the chances of future violent offending. Second, they found that this effect works for both men and women but holds especially true for women with regard to property crime. Mears, Cochran, and Bales argue that this means that, overall, prison may have a greater deterrent effect for women than it does for men, as women tend to be the primary caregivers in their families; the researchers also acknowledge that, overall, this paints an unsettling picture regarding the utility of prisons. Essentially, we're lying to ourselves if we think prison is an effective deterrent, at least among those most likely to commit crime. I think we've known this for a while but haven't been willing to say it out loud yet. The threat of prison may deter the population in general but actually exacerbates criminality for the subset that it doesn't inhibit. This should really bother you, because the purpose of incarceration is to correct behavior—that's why prisons are part of the Department of Corrections and not the Department of Making Matters Worse.

Taken as a whole, not only does prison do little to address why people committed whatever crimes got them there, it fails to help them learn to make better choices or find ways to get their lives back on track, but it actually seems to have the opposite effect and increase the chances that they will offend again. In this way, prisons are really just a warehouse for this segment of the population, whose members revolve in and out, never getting a legitimate opportunity to make something of their lives. This also means that the people to whom they matter most—their partners and children, friends and family—experience a constant cycle of arrest and incarceration, seeing their loved one(s) ripped out of their lives, dropped back in, and ripped out all over again. No wonder so many people have a serious disdain for the criminal justice system. It doesn't do anything to make their lives any better.

Reintegrating the Family

As mentioned, the criminal justice system assumes the individual, having made a rational choice to commit a crime, is solely responsible for his behavior, and so it does nothing to change any of the circumstances in the offender's life. As we'll see, returning to those circumstances can seriously sabotage the efforts of the recently released to fully find their way back to a life of righteousness.

When we talk about incarceration and reentry into the community, most people think that we're only talking about the accused. Actually, more than a few people are possibly effected by the offender's going away, and many people refuse to talk about this, much less consider it important. I'm talking, of course, about the offender's family—especially any children.

Incarceration and reentry punish not just offenders but the people in their lives. Now, you might think, who cares? If parents had a hand in raising a criminal, maybe they're not the best people in the world, and we shouldn't be losing any sleep over them. And who's to say the friends are not criminals too? Don't birds of a feather flock together?

Fair enough. What about the well-being of the children of the offender? What do we do with them? What happens in their lives after a parent is sent to prison? Do we just assume that they'll be OK with the remaining parent or that some other arm of the state will intervene to help them out? Does anyone ever think about them?

Some might say that by incarcerating that parent, we're actually doing a service to the kids involved, because how could a criminal possibly be a good parent? But remember, not everyone in prison is violent or incarcerated for child abuse. In fact, in 2014, 50 percent of men and 59 percent of women in prison were there for drug offenses (Carson 2015). Coincidentally, over half of all inmates are parents too (Travis, McBride, and Solomon 2005).

The fact of the matter is that decades of the "War on Drugs" and the "War on Crime" have torn many families apart, and that isn't something to take lightly. If we think about this in terms of low-level drug dealing or some property crime, we're seeing kids dependent on whatever money was coming punished by the system. Even in the most brutally violent situations, we're seeing children lose a source of emotional and/or financial support in their lives.

Some of you may rightfully be asking what this has to do with problems associated with reentry. The separation of parent and child can actually make reentry much more difficult, depending on the timing of the separation, because it's going to have a different effect on the child, depending on his or her developmental stage. This can lead to anything from a poor parent-child bond if the parent is incarcerated while the child is an infant, to impaired coping skills if the child is in middle childhood, to imitation of bad behavior if the child is in late adolescence (Travis, McBride, and Solomon 2005). So, depending on their age when the parent is taken away, children are at risk for a whole list of problems. This means that when the parent comes home, while hopefully welcomed back with open arms, he or she is now thrust back into a parent-child relationship that could very quickly become very strained. Coming home from prison and having to discipline a moody teenager who harbors resentment about your arrest sounds like a source of tension (Agnew 1992). If you're struggling to recreate and rebuild a strong emotional bond with your family as you reenter society, couldn't things get bad for both your children and you (Hirschi 1969)? I'm sure you can imagine plenty of scenarios in which a returning parent might be pushed back into criminal behavior because of a strained relationship with a child following incarceration.

Some people might put the responsibility for this on the incarcerated, though. If a poor parent-child relationship could prevent successful reentry after incarceration, why not do more to maintain contact with children and family members while inside? We know prisoners can make phone calls, send and receive snail mail and e-mail, and have visitors, so isn't it their own fault that this happened? Actually, visiting people in prison is much harder than you might think. Not all people serve their sentences in institutions geographically close to their family, which can make it difficult, if not impossible, for loved ones to visit them. If I am sentenced to ten years in a prison several hours from my family, they are not likely to be able to come and see me every weekend.

In addition to potentially damaging the parent-child relationship, the removal of the offender from the family alters the entire family dynamic altogether, especially if he or she is incarcerated for a significant period (Travis, McBride, and Solomon 2005). People have to get on with their lives and can't just sit around because a parent or spouse has gone away. The remaining parent must take on the other's responsibilities—or family members or friends might step in to help out (Travis, McBride, and Solomon 2005). That parent's self-perception will change—in a way, losing a partner might end up improving his or her confidence and self-efficacy. After a while, this becomes the new normal for the entire family. When the offender is finally released, successful reentry can be a problem because the family the now ex-convict left behind is really not the family he or she is coming home to. I imagine this would be especially true for men, who perhaps saw themselves as "the Man" at home before they went to prison and are coming back to find that not to be the case anymore. There's also no way to truly know what the remaining parent and family members—or possibly a new partner—have told any children about the crime committed, why their parent is in prison, what prison is like, and so on (Travis, McBride, and Solomon 2005). The point is, an offender will not return to the exact same family he or she left behind.

What does any of that have to do with reentry? With all the difficulties the newly released have adjusting to life after prison—which could even include trying to relearn how to prepare food—familiarity will help reentry go more smoothly. A family that has become unfamiliar can hinder reentry. A family resistant to further change, to a return to the way things were before, will be a source of stress and upset for many offenders and could propel them into future bad behavior.

Not only has the family changed during the period of incarceration, but obviously the offender wasn't just sitting quietly by him- or herself all that time. The offender will have changed as well. In theory, this change should be for the better. That's what prison is supposed to do, right? Give criminals an opportunity to get their heads on straight, recognize the error of their ways, and all that.

As discussed previously, prison does not necessarily have that effect. Life for a prison inmate can be incredibly stressful. Violence, both physical and sexual, perpetrated by other inmates and by the staff, is a very real problem. We know that victimization can change people. Even being exposed to the threat of violence can change someone. So not only is the released ex-offender returning to a family that he or she doesn't recognize anymore, but the family is welcoming home someone that they might not recognize anymore either, someone who is dealing with the psychological trauma of exposure to violence.

Now, a lot of what we've been talking about so far with the family and reentry has focused, indirectly, on male offenders. Men do make up the majority of offenders, after all. But it would be foolish to assume that women reentering society undergo the exact same types of problems as men—that their experiences of being taken away from the people in their lives and dealing with the ex-convict identity and label are no different from those of male offenders. How do you think the lives of women reentering society differ from the lives of their male counterparts? What problems do you think women in this position encounter?

The Positive Role of Family Bonds

Much of what I have argued so far has pointed to how the family dynamic can shift while one member is incarcerated, which can in turn erect a barrier to successful reentry, because the newly released no longer feels at home. Research also points to how the family can proactively help prevent the newly released from recidivating. For example, Berg and Huebner (2011) show that family ties have no direct relationship to recidivism and say that employment is the crucial factor. But family ties do become important with regard to employment. Good family relationships can help offenders find employment: family members can pass along information about potential jobs, and offenders may be motivated to find work to keep them happy. Berg and Huebner also argue that offenders who do find work may experience a significant improvement in their family relationships because their employment may shift how other family members perceive them. Berg and Huebner noted one respondent who said employment signaled to their family that he was no longer a "druggie."

Given everything we've talked about in this book, is the data outlined by Berg and Huebner (2011) consistent for both men and women? Following on this line of inquiry, Cobbina, Huebner, and Berg (2012) examined the role of gender as well as the quality of offenders' familial relationships. First, they found a significant gender difference in the role of family relationships in reducing recidivism overall. Their findings show that family relationships, especially with parents and intimate partners, matter much more for women than for men. For men, the quality of these relationships did reduce the likelihood that they would offend again, but mostly in cases where the offender didn't have much of a criminal history. In keeping with Berg and Huebner's (2011) study showing that family relationships could fall apart because of the offender's behavior, Cobbina, Huebner, and Berg show that an extensive criminal background can reduce family relationship quality, which can then increase the likelihood of recidivism. However, the relationship between criminal propensity, poor family relationships, and recidivism only really exists for men: the findings suggest that female offenders can maintain good relationships with their parents regardless of their criminal backgrounds. In other words, families seem to be a stronger protection against recidivism for women than for men. If that is indeed the case, maybe the prior finding on the importance of employment pertains more to male offenders.

Is Meaningful Employment Possible?

I'd like to draw your attention to a very important study that addresses the importance of employment in reducing recidivism on a much broader scale. Until now, we've been talking about employment reducing recidivism as if jobs—especially meaningful jobs—are always available. What happens during times of economic recession or depression? Alternatively, what happens when the economy is thriving? If employment is such a crucial factor in recidivism, does this mean that the recidivism rate ebbs and flows with the economy?

Mears, Wang, and Bales (2014) address this very question, and though they focus on race, not gender, I think their study is still very useful to our discussion. They found a significant race difference in the relationship between unemployment and recidivism. For black offenders, returning to areas with a high level of black unemployment increased the likelihood of future violent behavior; for white offenders, returning to areas with high white unemployment increased the likelihood that they would commit some sort of property crime in the future.

In considering whether the relationship between employment and recidivism may be more important for male rather than female ex-offenders, the findings by Mears, Wang, and Bales (2014) highlight the importance of something we'll be talking about in our final chapter: intersectionality. When talking about gender differences, we need to remember that not all men and not all women experience the world in the same way. In this case, we hypothesize that employment may be a more crucial factor for reducing recidivism for men, but we can't assume that every male has the same likelihood of finding work; his chances will depend in large part on the neighborhood he lives in and/or on his racial or ethnic background. This means that any blanket generalization that increasing employment opportunities will reduce recidivism has to come with a big asterisk that acknowledges the systemic racism that still exists in our society.

I really like how Mears, Wang, and Bales (2014) frame their findings in terms of general strain theory (Agnew 1992; Kaufman et al. 2008), because it's easy to utilize the same theoretical perspective and shift the discussion to gender. In terms of race, strain theory argues that blacks commit more crime than whites because they are exposed to many, many more stressors in their lives; they have a greater chance of being victimized, an infinitely greater chance of experiencing some form of racial discrimination, and a greater chance of living in debilitating poverty than even the poorest whites (Kaufman et al. 2008). The difference in the types of offenses blacks and whites are more likely to commit after release also speaks to the importance of intersectionality. Mears, Wang, and Bales argue that whites are more likely to commit property crime because it is generally accepted that they will be successful in life; when they run into postrelease barriers, they use property crime as a way to keep up the illusion of their success. Blacks, on the other hand, are more likely to resort to violence because of the tremendous stress and frustration associated with being both poor and nonwhite.

As discussed earlier, gender differences in the types of stressors men and women experience (Broidy and Agnew 1997) generate unique motivations for criminal behavior. This is where employment comes into play. Traditionally, men have been socialized to view their career as a key component of their identity. For men unable to find meaningful work that allows them to demonstrate their masculinity, crime becomes an attractive option (we discussed this earlier when we talked about the code-of-the-street hypothesis [Anderson 1999]). The connection between employment, recidivism, and gender is clear now. It stands to reason that employment will matter more in future offending for men than for women because many men still have an ingrained idea that their career is their life; if they can't find anything worthwhile post release, then returning to their old ways seems logical.

So how does employment help men and women across racial groups successfully reenter society? Continuing general strain theory's logic and drawing on the conclusions of Kaufman et al. (2008) and Broidy and Agnew (1997), it stands to reason that there are likely some significant differences in how black women and white women, and black men and white men, experience life after release. If we broaden this to include all people of color (which we should), no doubt the differences will be substantial.

Women and Reentry

Andrea Leverentz (2014), in her book on issues facing women in the reentry and desistance processes, says that we should think about desistance not as a single point in time but rather as a longer process wherein past criminal behaviors gradually fade away and the offender settles into a more pro-social life. In her study of women reentering society, she notes that many of the women she interviewed struggled with desisting from their antisocial behaviors and that desistance took a lot of work. Desistance entails more than just stopping criminal behavior; it is about changing your identity and learning to embody the pro-social behaviors you're learning.

Leverentz (2014) highlights the issue of self-confidence and self-efficacy. For the women in Leverentz's study, reentering society meant dealing with things they might not have encountered before, like living alone or trying to find legitimate full-time employment. This isn't to say that male ex-offenders don't struggle in this area as well—but for females, depending on their background, this could be completely new and become a source of frustration in their lives. As Leverentz found, living alone, while liberating, was also isolating and increased the likelihood of boredom—and boredom carried with it the risk of a return to bad habits. To try to stave off boredom, these women had to find legitimate work or educational opportunities to keep busy—this speaks to the involvement component of social control that Hirschi (1969) wrote about. The more time they spent occupied with legitimate endeavors, the less time they had to get into trouble. But, as we all know, finding a job or starting college can be very intimidating. That intimidation can cause further frustration and lead to a relapse into bad habits.

Gender Differences in Sentencing Revisited

Earlier we talked about several gender differences in how sentencing works, specifically with regard to stereotypes that benefit women. Judges will sometimes give lighter punishments to female defendants because of the idea that removing them from their families is unfair to both the children and the mother (Doerner and Demuth 2010). We could argue that the opposite is also true then—that they view fathers as inconsequential to their children's lives. This has seriously negative outcomes for the male offender, once he's served his sentence and paid his debt to society.

Interestingly, while we think of mothers as more important than fathers, many people will quickly claim that a single mother is incapable of raising kids alone—because dad isn't around to provide that fatherly guidance that many kids (supposedly) need. So we're setting up moms to fail, if you think about it. We can't fathom a situation in which we will separate them from their children unless absolutely necessary, so we claim to value that mother-child bond; then we turn around and blame single mothers for the woes of the world, accusing them of being wholly unable to raise their children to be decent, respectful people. That's blatantly hypocritical.

So there is a difference in terms of risk of being sentenced and for how long, which means an overall difference in the likelihood of kids experiencing some major disruption in their family life, and a significant difference (presumably) in how they are going to bond with their parents, the type of relationship they will have, and how they will develop into adulthood.

Gender difference in sentencing is important because—I realize that, at this point, this is going to sound like the most obvious thing in the world—the severity of the sentence an offender receives may actually increase the likelihood that he or she will recidivate. In other words, not only does using prison as a punishment rather than employing some alternative treatment increase the chances that a person will commit another crime after release (Mears, Cochran, and Bales 2012), but the longer a person is in prison, the more likely he or she is to recidivate, right? Sounds to me like this is evidence that the prison component of the criminal justice system is an obvious candidate for complete overhaul. Unfortunately, because of the prison-industrial complex—in many places, prisons are effectively businesses—scrapping this system and starting from scratch to find something more effective is much easier said than done.

Recidivism Versus Reentry

Throughout this chapter, we've been talking about the recidivism rate as if it were the only real measure of whether the system has successfully reformed a person (or an offender has reformed him- or herself despite the system). Much of the discussion on this subject takes that approach: you either recidivate, or you don't. However, some people released from prison do not recidivate and are thus never rearrested, but nor do they successfully reenter society. Think about the things we said were either barriers to reentry or risk factors for recidivism: relationships with family members, friends who are still involved in criminal activities, lack of satisfying or fulfilling job opportunities, and so on (Gendreau, Little, and Goggin 1996; Benda 2005; Travis, McBride, and Solomon 2005).While examining why people reoffend after release is important, it is just as important to approach the issue of life after incarceration from the opposite perspective: How do people successfully reenter society? What are their lives like? Do they just not experience any of the challenges discussed in the research on recidivism, or is something more complex going on?

Visher and Travis (2003) approach this question in terms of the life course of the offender, the state policies dictating the conditions of their release, and their postrelease opportunities. Utilizing this approach, they identify a number of major factors identified by research on reentry that can help offenders successfully reintegrate into society. As they are taking a longitudinal approach, they first examine the conditions in offenders' lives prior to going to prison: physical and mental health, substance use and abuse, and work history all play an important part in determining how well an offender will reenter society. Next, the offenders' experiences in prison determine how well they'll be able to reintegrate. The length of their sentence can disrupt their relationships on the outside, which can inhibit reentry (Mears, Cochran, and Bales 2012). Whether the prison offers programming to give offenders skills to better their chances on the outside also plays a major part (Visher and Travis 2003). Providing offenders an opportunity to make something of themselves and develop a meaningful identity will reduce the chances that they'll fall back into old habits, but obviously this idea hasn't really caught on in general. Why do you think that is? (By the way, the type of identity being described here—self-respect derived from some meaningful work skill—really applies more to male than female offenders.)

In terms of life after release, Visher and Travis (2003) don't approach it as a sort of now-you're-in-prison, now-you're-not proposal. It's not like flipping a light switch. In keeping with the research we've seen on recidivism, they argue that what happens to offenders immediately after release is as important as what happens to them over the long term. They face all sorts of challenges: finding a place to live, finding a job, finding transportation, making that initial first contact with family, children, friends, and their old neighborhood. These often difficult and frustrating situations can cause them to act out and engage in antisocial behavior that will land them back in prison. For many, the negative stereotypes associated with being an "ex-con" pose enough of a barrier to block successful reentry, no matter how motivated the offender is to prove his or her worth to family, friends, and community. As Bruce's story shows, there are many things that we take for granted in our everyday lives on the outside that people lose when they go to prison, and suddenly having the ability to do them again can be thrilling—or quite intimidating (Heinlein 2013).

Let's talk about the importance of the neighborhood the offender is returning to. We've hinted at the idea that people going back to criminogenic life circumstances, including communities where crime was already a problem, are at greater risk of recidivating. At the same time, we know that some neighborhoods do have the capacity to reduce criminal activity, and so maybe offenders released into neighborhoods with this quality are more successful in moving away from crime. Drawing on the concept of collective efficacy (Sampson, Raudenbush, and Earls 1997), a term describing how close-knit and trusting a neighborhood is, Visher and Travis (2003) argue that offenders released into neighborhoods with higher levels of collective efficacy may be more likely to reintegrate into society because they have a greater support system to help them handle immediate postrelease problems (employment, transportation, etc.). It's not hard to imagine how a neighborhood with a higher level of collective efficacy can help offenders deal with any number of postrelease issues, for men and women, above and beyond those problems identified by Visher and Travis.

Visher and Travis (2003) also find that one of the biggest factors in determining how well an offender reintegrates into society is how willing society itself is to receive him or her. Over the past thirty years or so, the government—at multiple levels—has enacted policies that are increasingly punitive to ex-offenders, even after they've paid their debt to society. For example, in many states, ex-convicts are denied access to public housing, which means that they won't be able to return to their families, effectively denying them that mechanism to help them reenter society. This is another example of how we can be so hypocritical with our policies. We pretend to be so sorry for kids who grow up without their fathers but then drive a wedge between dads and their kids. We trumpet the importance of mothers but then jump at every single chance to vilify single mothers.

In the end, the best way to successfully help people reenter society after they've been incarcerated is to help them deal with whatever lingering health problems they have and develop gender-specific programs to help men and women cope with the multitude of challenges they face upon returning to society (Spjeldnes and Goodkind 2009). While all offenders will face the problems identified by Visher and Travis (2003), for the most part, we know that there is a clear gender difference in who will have more problems navigating different dimensions (Spjeldnes and Goodkind 2009). Many male and female ex-offenders will have to reconnect with their children, but obviously in different ways; many will have to find employment, but the meaning of that job will vary (Spjeldnes and Goodkind 2009). Implementing policies that focus on problems unique not only to gender but to race and age will go a long way toward helping individuals successfully reenter society.

10

The Intersection of Gender, Race, and Class: Everything Matters

As we have seen thus far, the experiences of crime and criminal justice can vary wildly for men and women based on socially constructed gender roles. The most popular criminological theories don't always work the same way for women and men. The types of crime people engage in or are victims of differ for women and men; the way we're treated by the system as either offenders or agents of the system differs by gender. I hope that by this point you're all aware of that fact.

Now, while we have focused primarily on how gender helps shape criminal behavior and treatment of offenders by the criminal justice system, any book that focuses on one element of the social structure would be incomplete without a recognition that other sociodemographic characteristics shape the experiences of people in that structural category. Therefore, in terms of talking about the relationship between gender, crime, and the criminal justice system, it is vital to discuss how gender itself might vary across race, ethnicity, and socioeconomic status. In other words, does everyone experience gender the same way? Does masculinity—and its relationship to crime—work the same way for men of different races or ethnicities? Ages? Social classes? What differences might exist in the ways that women have experienced crime? Do white and nonwhite women experience crime the same way? Does age matter? What about social class? We can even broaden this to include generational and regional differences within gender, not to mention the role that sexuality can play. Clearly, the relationship between gender and crime can differ among men and among women in many ways.

What Is Intersectionality and Why Is It So Important?

Intersectionality, which refers to the overlap between elements of the social structure, is considered one of the feminist movement's biggest contributions to the social sciences (Davis 2008). In short, the concept is that if we're going to truly understand the consequences of gender, we must also acknowledge how gendered experiences differ by race, social class, age, and so on. There are some (more or less) universal experiences associated with masculinity and femininity, but it also makes sense that the experience of "being" a woman or a man is different for, say, rich people and people in poverty or for white people and people of color.

There is a basic sociological question that many professors like to ask our intro students when we cover social structure: Between gender, race/ethnicity, and social class, which is the most important in determining quality of life? Obviously there is no correct answer—not in my opinion, at least—but it's a good thought experiment because it forces us all to consider the privilege and oppression associated with the dominant groups in our society. What must it be like to be a part of one dominant group and one oppressed group? How does the power imbalance work? And what happens to you if you're in multiple oppressed groups? We can use Marilyn Frye's (1983) birdcage analogy to better understand this. Frye likened systems of oppression to a birdcage. Viewing each type of oppression, or bar, individually, nothing seems to stop the bird from flying free; however, when linked together, they greatly limit the bird's opportunity—its freedom.

Now, in thinking about intersectionality in terms of criminal behavior and the criminal justice system, we need to consider (1) general differences in the realities of the people's lives across different groups, (2) specific ways that the theories we've discussed might differ across various groups while also including the role of gender, and (3) specific ways that the system itself might work differently for different groups of people within gender, in terms of both the offenders caught up in the system and the people who are in charge of it. By trying to pull apart the effects of race, class, age, and the multitude of other factors that constitute the birdcage, we can come closer to understanding the reality of crime and criminal justice in the United States today.

Social Stratification in the United States

Before we talk about the relationship between intersectionality and crime and criminal justice, I want to review the concept of social stratification in the United States. When we're talking about stratification, we're referring to the distribution of resources throughout society, with the understanding that it is unequal, which gives certain groups more power than others. When we're talking about resources, the most obvious example is money. Just in terms of gender, there is a well-documented difference between men and women in terms of pay, with men making more money than women both on average and for doing the same work.

Another way to think about power is in terms of knowledge. French social theorist Michel Foucault (1980) saw power and knowledge as so closely related that he couldn't really conceptualize them as different, instead referring to them as powerknowledge. So how can we determine how this type of power differs between men and women? First, we can think about it in terms of access to education. Obviously, we know that access to education was extremely limited for women up until the very recent past, with generations of women denied the opportunity to pursue an advanced education or, when they did, were pushed toward what were considered gender-appropriate degrees (the lame joke at the time was—and this shows you how much humor has evolved—that a girl in college was just going for her "Mrs." degree). Of course, access to education for girls and women has improved dramatically in recent history. According to a Pew Research Center analysis of Census Bureau data, in 2012, 71 percent of women who graduated high school immediately enrolled in college, while only 61 percent of male high school graduates did the same (Lopez and Gonzalez-Barrera 2014). Comparing these rates to the percentage of high school graduates immediately enrolling in college in 1994, the Pew report also shows that the percentage of women increased among blacks, Hispanics, Asians, and whites, while the number of men remained more or less stagnant among these same populations, with the exception of Hispanic males, who went from 52 percent in 1994 to 62 percent in 2012 (Lopez and Gonzalez-Barrera 2014), putting them even with the proportion of young white men enrolling in college immediately after high school.

Access to education is one way to approach gender differences in access to power, but just because people have the opportunity to go to college in no way means that they will. So another way we can think about the stratification of power is in terms of school performance. After all, we've all heard the myths about the inability of women to perform well in math and science, and that while more young women are getting into college, they're doing worse than the men (spoiler: they're doing better). Conger and Long (2010), in a study of students enrolled in universities in Florida and Texas, found that male students performed worse than their female peers from the beginning of their college careers. They argue that these men entered college at a cognitive disadvantage because they weren't as well prepared in high school as the women. This means that the difference in power—in knowledge—manifests itself much earlier than college. In fact, there is ample evidence to suggest that girls outperform boys in terms of scholastic achievement and high school completion and have done so for some time (Buchmann, DiPrete, and McDaniel 2008).

So, more women than men are going to college, and they're doing better overall once they're there. Remember what I said about gender differences in the types of majors young people were pushed toward based on gender norms? Do you think maybe women are doing better than men in college because they're

majoring in "easier" fields? In an extensive overview of the literature, Gerber and Cheung (2008) show that since the 1970s,
women have made significant advancements into many majors
that had been male dominated, with the exception of computer
science, physics, and engineering. So it looks like that theory is
out the window. It's interesting that the pay gap favors men, but
the gender dynamic is reversed when it comes to academic performance and completion. What do you think about that? Since
we now live in a society in which more female college graduates
have performed better than their male peers, what do you think
will happen in the long run?

Now, we have limited this discussion so far to access to
resources and power solely in gender terms, but we know there
are other differences to consider within gender. We know that
schools that serve impoverished areas are typically performing
below our standards and expectations, which can lead to an
increase in the dropout rate. Because the student body at impoverished schools tends to consist largely of minority students, there
results a massive systemic imbalance in education, both in terms
of access and performance.

With that said, the question to explore now is this: Are there
race or class differences in how boys and girls approach school, or
do the larger gender issues, coupled with the effect of poverty on
the school's ability to deliver on its promise, tell the whole story?

As important a factor as gender has been and continues to be,
when we're talking about things in terms of intersectionality we
can't say that one element of the social structure matters any more
than another. Lee and Bean (2004, 2012) argue that race relationships in the United States have moved away from a simple
white/nonwhite dichotomy to a more complex black/nonblack or
black/nonblack/other system, where the single most important
racial category in American society today is black. In fact, Lee
and Bean (2012) argue that whiteness as a racial category may be
expanding to include some people of Asian or Hispanic descent,
which could return society back to the simple white/black racial
dichotomy that has been the hallmark of race relations in the
United States.

It's also important to point out the stratification of resources by race. Numerically, more whites live in poverty than any other racial or ethnic group in the United States, but relative to the rest of the population, blacks and Hispanics experience a disproportionate amount of poverty, with 24 percent of Hispanics and 26 percent of blacks living in poverty compared to 10 percent of whites (National Center for Law and Economic Justice n.d.). Furthermore, the poorest whites are still typically substantially better off than the poorest blacks or Hispanics. More than twice as many Hispanics live in deep poverty than whites, and more than three times as many blacks live in deep poverty than whites. Deep poverty affects those living halfway or further below the poverty line; the poverty line for a family of four in 2015 was $24,250, so a family in deep poverty would have an income of $12,125.

Pulling these together, we get a clearer picture of the different lives people lead in the United States based solely on race and gender and how those elements of social structure shape their opportunities. Drawing on conflict theory and critical criminology, you hopefully have a much better understanding of why things are the way they are in society. Remember, this perspective on crime and crime control focuses on the criminal justice system as a tool of oppression used by those in authority to perpetuate their advantage while simultaneously keeping the proverbial boot on the throats of those struggling to pull themselves up. Historically, laws have been written and enforced by powerful white men. There are some indications this is changing, as more women gain access to education. This doesn't necessarily mean that things will get better in terms of the fairness of the law, since we're looking at a world where white people still have the greatest share of the pie. This is part of the complexity of intersectionality, because we always have to consider differences within groups. As more women in general gain access to education, there's still going to be racism. Fordham (1993) showed how black women in the academy face resistance from white women because of their "loudness." In other words, racism is not limited to white men, and though both groups of women have experienced sexism, there is still a tendency for white women to dehumanize black women, even in an academic setting. As more women become more educated and more powerful in American society, perhaps this will change sooner rather than later.

Gender, Race, and Crime

Race and class are the most commonly mentioned social structures associated with crime. Thus, examining specific race and class differences presents the most obvious way to talk about intersectionality in terms of gender and crime. What could the possible intersection of gender and race look like? This topic has only recently come to the forefront in criminological research, as until recently many criminologists avoided meaningful discussions of race and instead reduced this issue to "simplistic arguments about culture versus social structure" (Sampson and Wilson 1995, 38).

This has had a long-term detrimental effect on criminological research, because not only have we allowed ourselves to reduce the relationship between race and crime to these simplistic ideas, but we have also done a less than stellar job of talking about race overall. In fact, one could say that the vast majority of criminological research focusing on race has specifically looked at crime committed either by blacks—or compared black and white behaviors specifically, leaving out cultural experiences and structural factors related to crime associated with any other racial or ethnic group—or by persons who are bi- or multiracial. Obviously, people who are both nonwhite and nonblack are also perpetrators and victims of crime, but much of the research, at least until recently, focused on the white-black dichotomy. This dichotomy is apparent in much of our national discussion on violence. The race of the perpetrator and of the victim plays a significant part in how we frame our conversations. (See Box 10.1 for more on this.)

It's understandable that this obsession with race has persisted for so long, especially if Lee and Bean's (2004, 2012) insight is correct that race relations in the United States have shifted toward blackness as the ultimate defining racial factor—we seem determined as a society to continue othering blackness and pushing

**Box 10.1   Race and Gender: The Coverage of
Michael Brown and Dylann Roof**

Two major events dominated the news in 2014 and 2015, contributing in their own ways to what some have called the next wave of the civil rights movement. On August 9, 2014, Michael Brown, eighteen, was shot and killed by Officer Darren Wilson, a member of the police department in Ferguson, Missouri. Though police violence toward black individuals has been common throughout US history, the murder of Michael Brown struck a chord with people across the country, launching what has since become the #BlackLivesMatter movement. Protests took place from coast to coast, and for possibly the first time in American history, they were broadcast to the entire world, unfiltered. That lack of filter is important, because many major news outlets across the country seemed to go into overdrive to depict Michael Brown not as a victim but as someone whose death was no real loss. For example, the *New York Times* depicted Brown as a violent substance user who had recently turned to writing sometimes vulgar rap lyrics. This framing of Brown tells the audience that it's OK not to care that he died, because he wasn't that great of a person to begin with. Similar narratives were written in the weeks and months to follow, as police brutality became one of the most discussed social problems in the country. Tamir Rice, twelve, shot and killed for carrying a toy gun, was described as "menacing." Eric Garner, strangled to death in New York City for selling loose cigarettes, was blamed for his death because he became upset when confronted by the police. (Garner, it turned out, had filed a suit against the New York Police Department years earlier, after being sexually assaulted by an officer during a stop.)

Flash forward to June 17, 2015, when twenty-one-year-old Dylann Roof murdered nine people during a prayer meeting at the Emanuel African Methodist Episcopal Church in Charleston, South Carolina. Roof, a devout white supremacist, spent an hour with his victims, sitting in on their meeting before telling them, "I have to do it. You rape our women and you're taking over our country." He told the police later that he almost didn't go through with it because they'd been so nice to him, but his larger desire to start a race war won out. In the news, Roof has been labeled as a loner, a troubled kid, mentally ill, and easily misled by the magic of the Internet. Despite Roof's obvious motive—racial hatred—many politicians and journalists speculated openly about what could have led this young man astray. This is especially sad, given South Carolina's place in American history: it was the first state to secede from the Union during the Civil War, and the first real battle of the war took place at Fort Sumter. Yet many presumably intelligent people chose to overlook all of this and question why this poor white soul was pushed to the brink. After he was arrested and complained about being hungry, the arresting officers drove him to Burger King and bought him a meal. Their job is, after all, to protect and serve.

To those of us on the outside looking in, without knowing anything about the personal beliefs of the officers involved in either incident, it certainly seems obvious that race was an extremely important factor in how these two men were treated. Michael Brown, dead black man and alleged cigar thief, was "no angel" and deserved to die; Roof, white mass-murderer, was taken alive and bought a value meal. It may not have been the officers acting on their own beliefs, but again, as an outsider, it certainly looks like there was some institutional bias at work here.

We can expand this to the riots and protests that happen across the United States with some regularity. Protests linked with the #BlackLivesMatter movement, especially those in Ferguson, Missouri, and Baltimore, Maryland, which saw clashes with the police, arson, and looting, are damned—the protesters, themselves mostly black, are labeled as "thugs." However, when rioting occurs following major sports events, especially those that happen on college campuses, the coverage essentially boils down to "Oh, those crazy college kids," even though the property damage is comparable. In short, though gender is important, we cannot view criminal and deviant behavior in terms of singular elements of the social structure. Instead, we must think about how different elements of the social structure intersect to shape our viewpoints for better or worse.

continues

Box 10.1 continued

Think about it like this: in the two major cases mentioned above, ask yourself how the coverage of the stories, hence popular opinion, would change if the race of the people involved were reversed—if a black separatist murdered nine white people in a church and a black police officer murdered an eighteen-year-old white man under suspect circumstances. You can do this exercise in other major cases too, of course. Eric Frein ambushed two Pennsylvania State Police officers, killing one and then hiding out in the woods for forty-eight days, leading nearly 1,000 police officers on a wild goose chase through the wilderness. Frein was captured alive in the end (and, like Dylann Roof, said he did what he did in hopes of starting a revolution, though not necessarily one based on race). Do you think the pursuit of Frein would have been different if he were black?

---

black people into a position where they are unwelcome in their own country. We don't need to rehash the entirety of black history here, but we know that untold horrors have been inflicted on countless blacks during US history. Even today, as of this writing, a second civil rights movement appears to have begun. That said, we absolutely should not confuse race and poverty as the same thing; being black does not in any way suggest automatic poverty. In any event, I don't want you coming out of this thinking there has been no research that invokes both gender and race. Let's spend some time highlighting some different areas of research within this idea of gender, race, and crime.

Gender, Race, and Drug Use

First I'd like to focus on the intersection of gender and race with drug use. Overall, our attitude toward drug use has shifted over the past century, moving away from viewing drug addiction as a moral failure toward recognizing it as a disease. Not everyone has bought into this ideological shift, but these things don't happen overnight. Public perception of drug dealing has also begun to change, at least as of this writing, with a public push to legalize marijuana and release nonviolent drug offenders (including dealers) from prison.

But as we know too well, there is a major difference between public perception and outcry and the reality of a situation. What are the realities for drug addicts and dealers in the United States today? What motivates someone into becoming a pusher, a user, or both? What causes these behaviors, and how do they intersect with race and gender?

First, let's talk about things from the drug-dealing perspective. Here, we can see gender as a driving force behind the behavior for some—if not most—drug dealers. For instance, Bourgois (1996, 2003) spent time living in Spanish Harlem, observing crack dealers in a study that is remarkably similar to Anderson's (1999) work on Philadelphia (see Chapter 3). Bourgois finds men trapped by their own conception of masculinity, unable to maintain legitimate work because it doesn't allow them to portray themselves as men in the cultural terms they aspire to; drug dealing becomes an obvious career path because it allows them to perform their gender. We covered this concept quite a bit in Chapter 3, so I don't want to delve much further into it than this, other than to say that the code of the street (Anderson 1999) doesn't apply only to poor blacks; nor is it unique to American culture, as Brookman et al. (2011) find evidence of street-code types of motivations for violent behavior in their study of the narratives of convicted violent offenders in the United Kingdom.

In any event, the street-code mentality coupled with this very narrow sense of what constitutes acceptable masculine work tends to drive a lot of the discussion around drug dealing. But we should know better than to think about all drug dealers as identical—some must be dealing for other reasons, right? Are they all doing it to feel masculine? Shook, Vaughn, and Salas-Wright (2013) looked at drug dealing among adolescents and found three distinct types of dealers: dabblers, delinquents, and externalizers. Dabblers use

alcohol and tobacco, aren't likely to be violent or otherwise delinquent, have experimented with other drugs, and have only sold
drugs once or twice before. Delinquents have a relatively lower
alcohol and tobacco use, are more likely to be violent or delinquent, and have extremely low levels of other drug use. These
kids sell drugs more frequently than the dabblers. Finally, externalizers have the highest usage rate of all types of drugs, are very
violent and delinquent, and sell drugs at a moderate rate. Of these
three groups, males, as well as blacks and Hispanics, were most
likely to fall into the delinquent grouping, while whites were most
likely to be grouped into the externalizer category. This means
that the race difference identified here isn't that whites are innocent and nonwhites are criminal; rather, all races are selling drugs
and engaging in other criminal activities and differ in their drug
usage (at least, in this study, anyway). I also want to point out the
gender difference here. Young men were most likely to fall into
the delinquent category (almost 80 percent of the kids in this category were male), but across all three categories males made up
the majority of the group. Across the board, the young women in
this study comprised the minority of dealers. Externalizers had
the highest proportion of young women, comprising roughly one-
third of the group.

In a way, gender may also operate as a mechanism to make
drug dealing easier. For instance, Ludwick, Murphy, and Sales
(2015) interviewed over two hundred female drug dealers in the
San Francisco area about the challenge of breaking into a traditionally male economy. The women surveyed saw their gender as
a means to get away with their dealing, because, as women, no
one would suspect them. On the flip side, they also knew that
within this underground economy, they could be seen as vulnerable, which required them to intentionally violate gender norms in
order to protect themselves. So, while masculinity may be seen as
a restrictive force that pushes some men into drug dealing, femininity may be more fluid and freeing, at least in the drug market.
This could explain other gender differences in dealing as well,
such as Senjo's (2005) finding that, at least among meth dealers,
men approached dealing more like a business and were more will-

ing to engage in violence, whereas women were less likely to have been arrested, more likely to have an education (including graduate degrees, in some instances), and more willing to try drug treatment to address their concurrent addiction. If we think of masculinity as very rigid, it makes perfect sense that the men in Senjo's study refused treatment.

The intersection of race and gender can come about in other ways related to drug use, too, of course. For example, Mason et al. (2014) examined race and gender as moderating effects in the relationship between drug use and peer attitudes toward drug use among adolescents. Remember, the term *moderating effect* indicates that an effect is stronger for a group. Mason et al. found that white kids are much more susceptible to the attitudes of their friends than black or Hispanic kids, meaning that if their friends have positive attitudes toward drugs, white kids are more likely to fall in line with the crowd. Girls were also more susceptible than boys to their friends' attitudes toward drugs. Overall, Mason et al. found that white girls were more influenced by their friends than any other group. So, a simple question follows: What about being white, female, and an adolescent makes this subset of kids so much more easily influenced by their friends? Remember, we're only talking about friends' ability to influence us and about not actual group differences in drug use: white teenage girls aren't the biggest substance abusers in society.

What about friendship groups as teenagers enter early adulthood? McCabe et al. (2007) examined race and gender differences in drug use among a sample of college students. They found that male students were more likely to report drug use than female students. White students and Hispanic students were also more likely than black or Asian students to report drug use currently or prior to coming to college. A college's athletic division could also have an effect on student substance use; Milroy et al. (2014) found that student-athletes at Division III schools were more likely to drink to get drunk or to relieve stress (among other reasons) than student-athletes at Division I or Division II schools.

Miriam Boeri's (2013) *Women on Ice* is one of the most interesting studies of drug use. Boeri interviewed suburban women about their methamphetamine use. This is a completely different take on drug use and drug dealing compared to the typical approach to the subject; suburban women are maybe the last people anyone would expect to be serious meth users and dealers (maybe babies would be a less likely cohort). The stories of the women Boeri interviewed are absolutely heartbreaking. They tell tales of extreme sexual abuse and domestic violence—sometimes starting when they were children—coupled with major family disruption (sudden, unexpected death of a caregiver, leading to a sudden transformation of family life for the worse), which led to their meth addiction. These factors also launched many of these women on downward spirals of poverty, sex work, further victimization, and other criminal behavior. Their meth use gave them energy to deal with their many, many problems while also allowing them emotional relief from that stress. Poverty is an interesting aspect here, as many people believe the suburbs are entirely middle class. That is not the truth of the matter. Many of the women in Boeri's study lived in exurban areas on the outskirts of the suburbs, in very shoddy, poorly maintained, and sometimes very violent trailer parks, or in their cars; one woman even talked about a brief period as a teenager when she lived in the woods. Poverty in the suburbs is practically invisible, cutting many of these women off from social services that could help them. Also note that the majority of the women in this study were white, and the few nonwhite women Boeri interviewed got into methamphetamine use through the white women in their social networks.

Importantly, Boeri's (2013) study draws on location-based stereotypes. Maybe you reacted to hearing about this study like I did: imagining the presence of a drug as insidious as methamphetamine in the suburbs is like imagining the Detroit Lions in the Super Bowl—impossible. In reality, the lives of the women Boeri interviewed were incredibly bleak, despite their suburban residence. This harkens back to our conversation earlier about urban bias in the study of violence, leading to a virtual ignorance of rural violence. The stereotypes associated with the places we live can lead to a considerable prejudice in how we think of the people who live there and how we treat them when serious problems arise. With the urban-rural dichotomy, we saw rural victims of violence largely ignored by research and by the public, when in reality their isolation increased the negative effects associated with their victimization. Our general idea of the suburbs as a middle- or upper-middle-class paradise, the picture of the American dream, means that we will likely view any suggestion of drug use or sex work happening there with skepticism. We've been taught that the real problems lay in the inner cities and that the people in distress are the urban poor. Our geographic biases lead to a severe mistreatment and misrepresentation of people who are suffering. So, if we've got a skewed view of people living in rural and suburban areas and the types of crimes they experience as victims, offenders, or both, do you think our perception of people living in urban areas could be wrong, too?

Gender, Race, and the Spectrum of Violent Behavior

As I have mentioned numerous times throughout this book, talking about violence in terms of social structure has been difficult historically because so many people have used race as an indicator of poverty. This is extremely problematic, because it biases us to think of nonwhites, especially blacks and Hispanics, as the only groups to experience poverty and as the only groups responsible for violence. This is patently false. Because so much research tends to group together race and poverty in ways that make it exceptionally difficult to pull them apart, we have to be extra careful not to fall into the same trap that previous generations of criminologists did with this—we can't use race as a stand-in for poverty. They are two completely different things. So maybe the best thing to do is to look at violence committed by one of the least studied groups in the social sciences: white people.

In terms of contemporary research on violence perpetrated by whites, there isn't really a lot to go on. Again, this is because the research has been biased toward studying violence committed by blacks and Hispanics living in disadvantaged urban neighborhoods. Bias also exists in terms of other forms of violence. Simi

(2010) argues that terrorism research has made a critical mistake in neglecting to study white supremacist organizations as terrorist groups. Simi argues that our perception of white supremacist groups is fundamentally flawed and has caused most researchers to view them as a nonthreat.

Even though there just hasn't been much interest in researching whites, that doesn't mean research on them is completely nonexistent and unrelated to anything else out there. For example, Lee and Shihadeh (2009) talk about white violence in terms of what they refer to as "argument-based violence" in the American South. Drawing on a history of violence in southern culture, their conception of argument-based violence is not at all dissimilar from Anderson's (1999) code of the street. In fact, we could argue that the old system of southern honor has direct links to the street-code logic we see today (Butterfield 1995). Lee and Shihadeh (2009) discuss this type of violence in terms of spatial concentration—meaning that the more white people condensed into certain areas in the south, the more likely it is that there will be violence—but for our purposes, I just want to draw your attention to this concept. They also acknowledge that the culture of southern honor that condoned violent behavior in the past has clearly faded quite substantially over the past 150 years, though it has not been eradicated entirely. Similarly, McVeigh and Cunningham (2012) examine the relationship between Ku Klux Klan activism in the 1960s and an increase in homicide in later decades. They argue that such extreme right-wing organizations, though unable to gain a significant foothold in the national conversation and not taken seriously, nonetheless majorly disrupt the communities where they exist, potentially destroying communal bonds and sowing the seeds of mistrust toward the police for decades to come. This increases social disorganization and violence in these areas.

Presumably, the types of violence perpetrated by white people are committed largely by white men. Organizations like the Klan or concepts like southern pride, historically, haven't centered on women. Does this mean that white women haven't been responsible for any acts of violence or any crimes at all? Definitely not. An extreme example is Aileen Wuornos, a serial killer who murdered seven men in Florida, who she claimed had raped her during the course of her work as a prostitute. Wuornos suffered almost unthinkable abuse as a child, was impregnated at fourteen by a friend of her grandfather, and was thrown out of her house at fifteen. She ultimately received multiple death sentences and was executed in 2002. Wuornos was obviously an exception to the norm; women don't typically engage in serious violence. Nor are serial killers common either. I present Wuornos only as an example that, yes, women can be violent too.

Let's turn our attention away from white violence, as I do not want to neglect the intersection of race and gender among other groups. We need to continue discussing the consequences of overlapping disadvantages. Remember when we talked about the research on violence committed by blacks in Chapter 5? There, we talked about the idea that a lot of violent behavior stems from systemic racism, which created extreme poverty and segregation. Now I want to talk about how we can merge this idea with the intersection of race and gender. Simpson (1991) examined violence committed by women in terms of race and the role of racial and gender discrimination. Simpson shows that among adolescents, young black women were much more likely than young white women to have committed some sort of assault. She also argues that, at least at the time she was writing, black women represented a greater proportion of female offenders than black men did of male offenders. Simpson attempts to use a number of theoretical perspectives to explain this difference with some success — she correctly notes that differences in power (discussed in multiple forms) can explain part of this difference — but ultimately concludes that we needed to revise our current theoretical processes. Today, I would argue that institutionalized sexism in a society still very much engaged in systemic racist practices clearly explains the difference she sees. It seems to me that the most likely theoretical explanation merges these types of oppression and takes into account the stress that accompanies these experiences. Remember when we talked about gender differences in stress in Chapter 3? We can also think about stress in terms of race. Kaufman et al. (2008) argue that blacks experience unique types of strain and more strain than whites, including strain related to economic problems, education, family distress, criminal victimization, and discrimination, which increases criminality. The combination of racial and gender differences in strain (which include discrimination and family stress) makes it easier to see how the lives of many young black women are incredibly challenging— and I would argue that this overlapping discrimination has rendered many young black women almost completely invisible to the rest of society.

Another factor associated with violence, especially in the news media, is mental illness. While we often hear that common mental health disorders like depression are linked to violent behavior, how much connection is there really, and does it differ in any way across racial and ethnic lines? Yabko, Hokoda, and Ulloa (2008) looked at the role of depression as a factor in several types of violent relationships within families among a population of Latino youths, finding that depression mediated the relationship between poor family relationship dynamics and peer victimization across the board for boys, but only between father's controlling behaviors and peer victimization for girls. Hoskin (2013) demonstrated that experiencing prejudice in school is a type of strain that can lead to criminal coping. Peck (2013) found that experiencing strain correlated with an increase in depressive symptoms, but depression did not completely explain the relationship between strain and offending—in other words, experiencing strain increased both the likelihood of depression and the likelihood of offending. However, the types of strain Peck examined in this study do not speak to racial differences in strain and how those stressors might have a unique effect on depression. She correctly indicates that family disruption and both individual and neighborhood poverty could contribute to it. I would argue those are also racially unique types of stress, along the lines of Kaufman et al. (2008). In reality, our understanding of the connection between depression and offending remains quite limited. There appear to be no long-term causal relationships between the two, though in the short term, the relationship between depression and criminal offending is strong (Siennick 2007).

This is just a small sampling of the much larger body of research on the relationship between gender, race, and crime—it is certainly not an undiscovered country. While there has been a lot of research on race and gender differences in crime, there has not been much on criminality within racial and ethnic groups, specifically violence committed by whites. This is a glaring hole in the research.

Gender, Class, and Crime—Bad Rich People!

As is the case with many criminology textbooks, the majority of the content we've covered here has been about the upsetting types of crime that dominate the news and keep us up at night: violence, drugs, and so on. Not invited to the party is white-collar crime or corporate crime, which includes crimes committed by higher-class people in the course of their jobs, usually in the name of maximizing profit. Though fascinating as any murder mystery, these types of crimes lose public interest quickly because the details tend to get complicated and boring. People can understand the threat of the mugger, rapist, or murderer lurking in the shadows, the terrorist waiting to strike, or the pedophile hanging around outside a school, and they will react with the anger and disgust we've come to expect. Because of the complexity, people tend not to get worked up to that level of rage when it comes to corporate or white-collar crime. Furthermore, there may also be some resistance to taking white-collar crime as seriously as other types of crime because we can think of these types of crimes as another example of overconformity. After all, this is America, where people are supposed to be doing everything they can to make as much money as possible, right? The coupling of the complexity of the crimes with the air of conformity is unfortunate, because there is ample evidence that these types of crimes—and the fallout from them—are the most harmful, as we will see when we discuss the Enron case momentarily.

So, what about the relationship between corporate crime and gender? Kathleen Daly (1989) showed that more men than women engaged in this particular type of crime (which is consistent with what we know about all types of crime). At the time, Daly argued that men and women committed white-collar crimes for different reasons, owing to gender differences in workplace status: men were more likely to be working in groups, using their workplace authority to their advantage to gain more power within their company. This difference is reflected in the motivations to engage in this type of criminal behavior; of the people convicted of some white-collar crime in Daly's sample, women were more likely than men to say that they did it for some financial need (for themselves or their families). In fact, when looking at the socioeconomic backgrounds of the women and men in her sample, Daly questioned whether we can truly call the women "white collar," as most were black, most did not graduate from college, and most were clerical workers. In other words, maybe we can think about corporate or white-collar crime as happening for very different reasons and in very different ways, depending on who's involved.

Now, Daly conducted her research in the early 1980s; a lot has changed since then in terms of women's employment, hasn't it? According to the US Department of Labor, the number of women in the labor force has more than doubled since 1970, although, because of population growth, that amounts to only a 9 percent increase in their share of the labor force (the number of men in the labor force has also increased since 1970, but their share of the labor force has decreased by 9 percent) ("Civilian Labor Force by Sex" n.d.). That said, do Daly's findings stand up today?

Klenowski, Copes, and Mullins (2011) examined the role of gender in constructing neutralizations of behavior among white-collar criminals and found that gender was very much a crucial factor in how their sample of convicted offenders framed their stories. The male white-collar offenders justified their behavior in terms of the image of the successful Western businessman: they had to commit the crime to compete because failure was not an option (real men don't fail, in this vision of masculinity). Much as Daly (1989) had found, female white-collar offenders' justifications tended to fall in line more with the idea of women as caregivers than anything else—almost none of the male respondents used this type of justification. What about entry into white-collar crime? Steffens-meier, Schwartz, and Roche (2013) looked at the role of gender across eighty-three corporate fraud cases, finding that women make up a very small percentage of corporate offenders (less than 10 percent). There were no instances of a group of women within a company conspiring to commit a crime, while the majority of crimes were committed by groups of men. Women didn't receive as much money as men did, and their involvement was much more reactive—in most cases they got involved because of a close relationship with someone else committing the crime, or because they were in a position of power within the company and their corruption was necessary for the fraud to succeed. In a way, the research on gender in corporate and white-collar crime mirrors that on gender and street crime: men are more likely to be involved; women who get involved are relegated to inferior positions. Ultimately, this shouldn't come as a major surprise, as women currently account for only 4.6 percent of Fortune 500 CEOs ("Women CEOs of the S&P 500" n.d.). There just aren't a lot of opportunities for women to commit these types of crimes, especially on the scale of Bernie Madoff or Enron.

Perhaps nowhere is the role of "traditional" masculinity more on display than in the Enron case. At the height of its power in mid-2000, Enron stock traded at over $90 a share, plummeting to less than $1 a share by November 2001. Why did this happen? Simple: the culture of hypermasculinity cultivated by Enron's president and chief operating officer, Jeffrey Skilling. In their account of Enron's downfall, later made into a documentary in 2005, McLean and Elkind (2003) portray Skilling as a hypercompetitive would-be Superman, transforming himself from a soft, nerdy executive into one of the cool kids, the king of the nerds and the smartest guy in the room. McLean and Elkind show a company where top-level executives were taking part in extreme sports, where strippers were being brought back to the office, where the idea of competition was worshipped so intensely that Skilling created a performance review system that would find 15 percent of employees lacking and give them two weeks to either find another job within the company or be fired. This is hyper-conformity to both masculinity and American capitalism.

On the outside, Enron was a model company—making money hand over fist in new and ingenious ways. The problem was, Enron was using an unusual accounting technique that basically based profits on what it thought was going to happen instead of what actually did happen. That's sort of like predicting that this book will sell 10 million copies and making payments to all parties accordingly. Or telling your parents that your GPA is going to be a 4.0 this semester, so they should reward you now. In both cases, neither has happened yet, and yet Enron inhabited this fantasy land, which allowed it to project an image of undeniable success. And why wouldn't it, given the culture Skilling had created? If you're going to be the best at something, even when you're faking it, you're still going to predict incredible success. Because businessmen are supposed to be successful, right?

In reality, Enron wasn't making money. It spent a fortune on a power plant in India that failed miserably. It concocted a plan to turn Internet bandwidth into a tradable commodity and failed. It was at least partially responsible for the California energy crisis in 2000–2001 (which resulted in Arnold Schwarzenegger, most famous for his role as Mr. Freeze in *Batman and Robin*, being elected governor of California—and then had Schwarzenegger supporters calling for a constitutional amendment that would allow "the Governator" to run for president). Like rats fleeing a sinking ship, Enron executives cashed in their stock for tens of millions of dollars and rode off into the sunset—or so they thought. In 2006, trials began against Skilling and Enron founder Kenneth Lay. Both were found guilty, and Skilling—one of sixteen Enron employees convicted—is currently serving time in prison. Lay's conviction was swept under the rug when he died suddenly of a heart attack prior to beginning his sentence. All this resulted from a commitment to hypermasculinity. (For more on the relationship between socioeconomic class, hypermasculinity, and crime, including the details behind Lay's conviction, see Box 10.2.)

Enron is often used as an example of corporate crime because of the depth of the company's commitment to making money at whatever cost; however, it certainly isn't the norm for this sort of criminal behavior. Most white-collar or corporate crime is much

Box 10.2   Class and Gender: Money Talks

It seems like two types of crimes attract mainstream national attention: those where the details are so bizarre or unusual that we can't help but watch, rubbernecking from afar via TV or social media, and those that involve celebrities or the fabulously wealthy, no matter how minor (either in terms of the seriousness of the crime or the star power of the celebrity).

Plenty of cases illustrate the power of social class in the criminal justice system and demonstrate, at least anecdotally, that people from more privileged socioeconomic backgrounds typically receive better treatment, no matter the crime. Relating the power of social class to gender in terms of how these aspects of social structure can sway the criminal justice system is difficult. Perhaps this has to do with the combined power of both dominant statuses; perhaps it also has to do with the fact that cases in which class and gender do come into play also involve race, and race becomes the dominant factor.

That said, one man's traditional masculinity and socioeconomic status factored into the things that he did. Vince McMahon, longtime owner of World Wrestling Entertainment, is one of the wealthiest and most influential sports entertainment moguls in the United States today. In 1993–1994, he was prosecuted for distributing steroids to his performers. In today's culture, we think of steroids as performance-enhancing drugs that give athletes a competitive edge in their sport, but in professional wrestling, I assume you're aware (sorry, "It's Still Real to Me" guy), the outcomes are predetermined, so what does taking a performance-enhancing drug gain? In this case, the type of steroids used—anabolic steroids—enhanced appearance rather than performance, bulking the wrestlers up so that audiences would buy more readily into them as real-life superheroes. The prosecution's star witness was Hulk Hogan, the very picture of late-twentieth-century American hypermasculinity. As for the conclusion of the trial, I'll paraphrase the classic Hulk Hogan line: Whatcha gonna do when Hulk Hogan changes his story on you? The Hulkster, as he is wont to do,

continues

Box 10.2 continued

---

testified that McMahon never instructed him to take or distribute steroids and that he made the choice to do so himself. Taking his vitamins, indeed. The point here is that the combination of wealth, the media, and extreme adherence to a very limited idea of gender created a situation in which men allegedly engaged in criminal activities to perpetuate this stereotype.

Part of the challenge with talking about the overlap between gender and social class is that the types of crimes unique to the wealthy are very difficult for the average person to understand. They're extremely complicated. For instance, the rapid rise and collapse of Enron in 2000–2001 involved speculative accounting practices, manipulation of the availability of electricity by shutting down power plants or physically transferring power across the grid, and ownership of a massive power plant in India that quickly turned into a ghost town. Once Enron declared bankruptcy and its chairman, Kenneth Lay, was found guilty of fraud—which could have carried a sentence of at least twenty years—Lay was permitted not only to remain free prior to sentencing but also to travel. And so ended the story of Kenneth Lay, who died at a ski resort in Colorado of a heart attack. Following his death, the charges against him were vacated. I can't say that his treatment stemmed entirely from his social class background and the social capital he had built up in his life (he was very close to both President George H. W. Bush and President George W. Bush), but it isn't unfair to ask if that's why he was allowed to go on a ski trip out of state months before he was supposed to begin serving his time.

---

less devious, just as not everyone engaging in some type of violence does so at the level of, say, Jeffrey Dahmer.

I want to briefly go back to the ideas of drug dealing and sex work, because our social class biases and everything we see on the news can convince us that only the poor and the desperate sell drugs or their bodies. This is definitely not true. Sudhir Venkatesh's 2013 pseudo-memoir and qualitative exploration of New York City's underground economy, *Floating City*, provides a good example. Venkatesh infiltrates the city's underground sex and drug economy, interacting with both the very poor and the very rich. He spends considerable time following a drug dealer named Shine, who is looking to expand his business into the white, upper-class market. In a scene straight from a movie, Venkatesh describes when Shine meets a contact, the madam for a high-end escort business, in a sort of "this is the beginning of a beautiful friendship" kind of way. He also spends some time talking to a number of johns—the men who buy the services of prostitutes—who are also definitely not poor. In short, Venkatesh encounters people from all walks of life who engage in these sorts of illicit activities—drug use and sex work are not confined strictly to people living in poverty.

This brings us to one of the most interesting aspects of the relationship between social class and criminal behavior. Even though so much research has focused on the relationship between poverty and crime, and we know that white-collar or corporate crime exists, people don't always blame upper-class people for committing a crime the same way they do the poor. When poor people commit a crime, we seem to blame them for their poverty when we condemn their behavior. When rich people commit a crime, if we even care, we seem to chalk their actions up to greed, but that greed also must have helped them become successful, and in the United States, we're supposed to admire that kind of material success, aren't we?

How does social class background shape criminality? In other words, do the motivations for committing a crime differ across class lines, or is all criminal behavior just a matter of greed? The fact of the matter is, our social class background has a tremendous influence on self-perception, our chances of success, our relationship with power, and our sense of place in the world. All of these things play into whether we will commit any crime, regardless of which theoretical perspective you use to frame that behavior.

Since both lower- and upper-class people commit crimes, we want to find out if their actual behavior differs by class. Wright et al. (1999) came to some very powerful conclusions about the way that class status shapes our actions. For people of lower socioeconomic status, Wright et al. (1999) argue that criminal behavior could correlate with decreased educational and occupational opportunities and aspirations, aggression, alienation, and, yes, financial strain, all resulting specifically from poverty. For people from more advantaged backgrounds, social class position conveys the authority to challenge conventional values and take risks, often generating an inflated sense of power, which in turn could lead to criminal behavior. In other words, you could argue that poor people commit crimes because they feel powerless and invisible, while rich people commit crimes because they feel powerful and invincible.

Intersectionality and Victimization

As we discussed in our conversations on relationship violence and sexual violence, overconformity to gender roles, specifically an overcommitment to "traditional" masculine values and conduct, serves as a motivating factor for these types of behavior. Men socialized to view women as inferior, as sexual objects, or as less than human are more likely to commit some type of physical or sexual violence against them. We also saw that intimate partner violence knows no racial or social class difference—women from all walks of life are at risk of victimization in their lifetimes.

    I want to talk now about a different type of victimization that is still very much gendered and can also be related to sexuality: hate-crime victimization, specifically against members of the LGBT community. Interestingly, a lot of research on this subject from the intersectional perspective looks at victimization not in terms of risk or prevalence but with regard to how social structure influences victims' perception of and reaction to their victimization. For example, Meyer (2010) found that victims' perception of the severity of their victimization depended on their racial and class backgrounds, with middle-class white victims more likely than poor and working-class people of color to view their victimization as "severe." Throughout his study, Meyer cites instance after instance of minority hate-crime victims hearing from those around them that they are lucky because they could've been hurt much more severely, whereas people around white middle-class victims reinforced the severity of their victimization, and in some cases legitimized it by offering to put them in touch with services that could assist them (e.g., counseling). Minority victims were not typically offered this type of support from the people in their lives, though Meyer does note that the friends and family members of these victims did provide emotional support.

Meyer (2012) builds on this previous research by evaluating how LGBT hate-crime victims perceive their victimization with regard to their racial background and identity and their quality of life moving forward. Not surprisingly, this is much more complex than we might initially think. This is another interesting way to think about intersectionality, as Meyer notes that past studies of violence against the LGBT community have tended to paint these individuals as homogenous, lacking any kind of in-group diversity. Obviously, this is not the case. Meyer found that the Latino/a and black respondents in his study were much more likely to feel that they had been victimized because their sexual identity "betrayed" or otherwise cast a negative light on their racial community, while white victims did not view race as a motivating factor in their victimization at all. Consequently, Meyer found significant race and gender differences in how LGBT victims of hate crime responded to their victimization. Because of the challenge to their racial identity, LGBT victims of color often coped with their victimization in ways that asserted their positive racial identity and place within their community. For example, Meyer highlights two middle-aged lesbian women: Jetta, who is black, and Martha, who is white. Both Jetta and Martha experienced violence in public, while with their partners. Both believed they were victimized (and their partners were not) because of their more masculine appearance. Following their victimization, both expressed some desire to be able to do what they want. The difference is that because Jetta also believed that her victimizer saw her as having "betrayed" the black community, she felt a much stronger need to assert her autonomy than Martha—Jetta asserted that she was free to do as she chose, had done nothing wrong, and was a valuable member of the black community. Because of white privilege—the

idea that white people are provided more opportunities and typically given the benefit of the doubt, compared to people who are
not white—Martha faced no such challenge to her place within
the white community.

Meyer also reveals racial differences in how gay men responded
to their victimization. Like the women in his study, black and Hispanic gay men viewed their victimization as stemming from some
belief that they had betrayed their racial community, which, again,
white men did not experience. Here, though, the supposed betrayal
fell in line with the stereotype of gay men being somehow physically and emotionally weaker than straight men—so by being gay in
public, these men had betrayed their racial community by effectively
being weak in public. Because of this, the nonwhite respondents
Meyer interviewed placed serious emphasis on their strength, especially their emotional strength, sometimes going so far as to suggest
that they were substantially stronger than the people who had
inflicted violence on them. Conversely, white men were more flip-
pant about this supposed weakness, and because they did not experience any sort of threat to their racial identity, they could shrug it
off as no big deal. Finally, Meyer also found gender differences in
the evaluation of the seriousness of violence. Lesbian victims,
regardless of race, rated physical violence as a greater threat to them
than verbal violence, whereas gay men were more likely to rate verbal assaults as their biggest concern and downplay the threat of
physical violence. Why do you think that is?

Moving away from sexuality and sexual identity in thinking
about intersectionality and violence, I want to turn your attention
briefly to another overlooked element of intersectionality: where
we live. We've talked about the importance of neighborhoods and
communities at various points throughout this book, in terms of
things like social disorganization and collective efficacy, or the
relationship between neighborhood poverty and gang violence.
Try to think about how differences in where we live can affect our
lives. Obviously, growing up in a rich neighborhood gives you
advantages and opportunities not likely available to people growing up in poor neighborhoods, which in turn influences your perspective on the world around you.

Let's go back to something we briefly touched on in Chapter 5: the differences between urban, suburban, and rural life. When we talk about urban areas, we all know that they include a massive amount of diversity in terms of race, class, religion, and so on. When we think about rural communities, however, we tend to fall back on old stereotypes: the people living there are all backward, hillbillies, stupid, and so on. And if we're going to be fair and honest, the stereotype of the inbred white redneck out in the country is just as harmful as that of the drug-dealing black or Hispanic "gangbanger" in the inner city. So what's going on?

One branch of intersectional research on the urban/rural dichotomy focuses on intimate partner violence in rural communities. Sandberg (2013) notes that there has been a bias toward exclusively studying violence in urban communities. This is problematic, she says, because it ignores unique geographic or spatial factors potentially related to intimate partner violence, and it assumes that the experiences of people living in urban centers is generalizable to the rest of the population. This means that the experience of someone who is a victim of violence in, say, Houston, Texas, the third-largest city in the United States, is the same as that of another victim who lives in Fairfield, Texas, population approximately 3,000. Sandberg (2013) also argues that this lack of research on intimate partner violence in rural communities has happened because of the relationship between power and place: urban centers are stronger socioeconomically (despite also being home to some of the poorest of the poor), and the word "center" itself implies power and importance, while rural communities, depicted as on the edge or the periphery, are less powerful and therefore less important and not worth our time. This bias toward urban violence and the centering of urban life has done a disservice to victims of violence living in rural areas. The question then, is, what makes intimate partner violence different or distinct in rural areas? Does it happen for different reasons? Are the lives of the victims different? What do you think?

One factor to consider here is isolation. Victims of intimate partner violence become isolated as a consequence of their victimization, and their abusers may seek to physically cut them off

Gender, Crime, and Justice

from the rest of their social world. Rural victims of intimate partner violence experience an even greater magnitude of isolation,
because of the nature of their communities—there are fewer
opportunities to seek help and less chance that a neighbor will
overhear or witness something (Sandberg 2013). That said,
research suggests that rural communities are much more closely
knit socially than urban communities. In other words, it's not
uncommon to find small, rural areas where everyone seems to
know everyone else, and everyone is in everyone else's business.
However, this intimacy may not provide protection for victims of
intimate partner violence but instead put added pressure on them
to avoid the stigma of victimization (Sandberg 2013). Beyond the
social isolation of rural life, victims of intimate partner violence
also must contend with the physical characteristics of their communities, which can be barriers to their freedom—almost literally.
Disadvantaged rural communities may lack public transportation
and infrastructure and may be subject to harsher weather conditions than urban areas, all of which can trap a victim of intimate
partner violence (Sandberg 2013). In sum, at least in terms of intimate partner violence, it appears that victims in rural communities
face challenges to their freedom and their health and well-being
that victims in urban areas may not. If nothing else cements the
seriousness of this to you, consider this: according to data from
the National Crime Victimization Survey, divorced or separated
women living in rural areas are at greater risk of rape or sexual
assault than divorced or separated women living in urban areas
(Rennison, DeKeseredy, and Dragiewicz 2012). Rural women
separated from their spouses are at significantly greater risk of
intimate partner rape or sexual assault than women living in urban
or suburban areas (Rennison, DeKeseredy, and Dragiewicz 2012).
Note that the experiences of rural victims of intimate partner violence discussed here don't necessarily indicate that the overall
rate of intimate partner violence is higher in rural areas; Edwards
(2014), in a review of the existing research, argues that the rate of
intimate partner violence across rural, suburban, and urban communities is roughly the same, with a key difference being the risk
rural women face for the types of violence just discussed.

In talking about differences in intimate partner violence by geographic area, let's ask another question: Are the causes of this type of violence different in rural areas? In Chapter 6, we talked about intimate partner violence as a learned behavior that stems from a desire to exert power and control over the victim. Even rape and sexual assault are attempts to exert power and control rather than to achieve some sort of sexual gratification. We can safely assume that this is also the case in rural areas. (An enterprising undergraduate could do a senior thesis on determining whether this is true.) Edwards (2014) says that the existing research points to more serious and chronic intimate partner violence in rural communities, which she suggests could relate to a higher rate of unemployment and substance abuse. What else might be going on here? What do you think about the attitude toward intimate partner violence in these areas, compared to others? Can how we think, feel, and react to intimate partner violence and sexual violence depend on where we live?

Intersectionality over Time

Though the idea of intersectionality is relatively new, the reality it describes has always existed. It's sort of like how everything wasn't floating around until Isaac Newton "discovered" gravity. Our experiences have always varied greatly based on gender, race, age, social class status, and sexual orientation. We can try to frame this again in terms of opportunities and stress, but the biggest experiential difference among individuals of different backgrounds has to do with oppression, which sometimes overlaps with privilege, putting us in sometimes uncomfortable, confusing, or bizarre situations.

One of the biggest reasons for this, in American society, is our obsession with race and our long history of racism. Many people point to two historical events as the "obvious" end of racism in the United States—President Abraham Lincoln's emancipating the slaves and the election of President Barack Obama. But let's not kid ourselves, the United States is still very racist. It is also a very oppressive society in general, despite massive victories won in the name of racial equality, women's rights, and the beginning of expanded rights for the LGBT community (the repeal of "Don't Ask, Don't Tell" in the military and the Supreme Court's recognition of same-sex couples' right to marry are two recent examples).

In discussing oppression in terms of either individual discrimination or something more systemic or structural, people always tend to think of race first. But that isn't the only way that the system has been oppressive. When we look back at American history, the very idea that "all men are created equal" points to the hypocrisy this nation was founded on—equality didn't extend beyond white, male property owners. Oppression on a national scale was the name of the game, and when the government tells you that it's OK to treat people poorly and enacts laws allowing them to be treated poorly, guess how most people are going to respond? So when we look back at the struggles of the women's suffrage movement in the late nineteenth and early twentieth centuries, the battles fought by the civil rights movement in the 1960s, and the incredible ways in which the #BlackLivesMatter movement has utilized social media to bypass traditional media outlets to spread information and organize, and we wonder why this is still happening, the answer is pretty simple: it's engrained in us. It's a part of who we are. We've been told for much of our lives that it's acceptable to mistreat, abuse, hurt, and kill people who aren't like us, not because they're different but because they're a threat to the status quo. We see, over the past few centuries, a simultaneous erosion of this authority and its transformation into something else—women gaining the right to vote but still crushed by public perception of beauty and chattel slavery legally ending, replaced by a system of mass incarceration that is arguably slavery by another name. The more things change, the more they stay the same.

References

ABC News. 2006. "Teen Girls' Stories of Sex Trafficking in the U.S." ABC News. http://abcnews.go.com/Primetime/story?id=1596778&page=1 (accessed February 2, 2016).

Adams, Kenneth. 1992. "Adjusting to Prison Life." *Crime and Justice* 16: 275–359.

"Addressing Anti-transgender Violence: Exploring Realities, Challenges and Solutions for Policymakers and Community Advocates." N.d. Human Rights Campaign. http://hrc-assets.s3-website-us-east-1.amazonaws.com// files/assets/resources/HRC-AntiTransgenderViolence-0519.pdf (accessed April 26, 2016).

Adler, Freda. 1975. *Sisters in Crime: The Rise of the New Female Criminals.* New York: McGraw-Hill.

Agnew, Robert. 1992. "Foundation for a General Strain Theory of Crime and Delinquency." *Criminology* 30: 47–88.

———. 2001. "Building on the Foundation of General Strain Theory: Specifying the Types of Strain Most Likely to Lead to Crime and Delinquency." *Journal of Research in Crime and Delinquency* 38: 319–361.

———. 2002. "Experienced, Vicarious, and Anticipated Strain: An Exploratory Study on Physical Victimization and Delinquency." *Justice Quarterly* 19: 603–632.

Alexander, Michelle. 2012. *The New Jim Crow: Mass Incarceration in the Age of Colorblindness.* New York: New Press, 2012.

Anderson, Elijah. 1999. *Code of the Street: Decency, Violence, and the Moral Life of the Inner City.* New York: Norton.

Archbold, Carol A., and Kimberly D. Hassell. 2009. "Paying a Marriage Tax: An Examination of the Barriers to the Promotion of Female Police Officers." *Policing: An International Journal of Police Strategies and Management* 32: 56–74.

Armstrong, Edward G. 1981. "The Sociology of Prostitution." *Sociological Spectrum* 1: 91–102.

Armstrong, Elizabeth A., Laura Hamilton, and Brian Sweeney. 2006. "Sexual Assault on Campus: A Multilevel, Integrative Approach to Party Rape." *Social Problems* 53: 483–499.

Asbury, Herbert. 1927 [2008]. *The Gangs of New York: An Informal History of the Underworld.* New York: Vintage Books.

Asscher, Jessica J., Claudia E. Van der Put, and Geert Jan J. M. Stams. 2015. "Gender Differences in the Impact of Abuse and Neglect Victimization on Adolescent Offending Behavior." *Journal of Family Violence* 30: 215–225.

Baker, Katie J. M. 2016. "Here Is the Powerful Letter the Stanford Victim Read Aloud to Her Attacker." Buzzfeed. https://www.buzzfeed.com /katiejmbaker/heres-the-powerful-letter-the-stanford-victim-read-to-her-ra?utm_term=.ma2NBN24n#.pw9KxKkM8 (accessed December 28, 2016).

Baker, Robert. 2016. "Dalton Man Admits Role in Sex Assaults." *Wyoming County Press Examiner.* http://wcexaminer.com/news/dalton-man-admits -role-in-sex-assaults-1.2052293 (accessed November 15, 2016).

Bartusch, Dawn Jeglum, and Ross L. Matsueda. 1996. "Gender, Reflected Appraisals, and Labeling: A Cross-Group Test of an Interactionist Theory of Delinquency." *Social Forces* 75: 145–176.

Bateman, Oliver. 2014. "The Year I Discriminated Against Everyone." Good Men Project. http://goodmenproject.com/featured-content/year -discriminated-everyone (accessed January 29, 2016).

Beck, Allen J., David Cantor, John Hartge, and Tim Smith. 2012. *Sexual Victimization in Juvenile Facilities Reported by Youth, 2012.* Washington, DC: Bureau of Justice Statistics.

Beck, Allen J., Ramona R. Rantala, and Jessica Rexroat. 2014. *Sexual Victimization Reported by Adult Correctional Authorities, 2009–11.* Washington, DC: Bureau of Justice Statistics.

Belknap, Joanne, Dora-Lee Larson, Margaret L. Abrams, Christine Garcia, and Kelly Anderson-Block. 2012. "Types of Intimate Partner Homicides Committed by Women: Self-Defense, Proxy/Retaliation, and Sexual Proprietariness." *Homicide Studies* 16: 359–379.

Bell, Kerryn. 2009. "Gender and Gangs: A Quantitative Comparison." *Crime and Delinquency* 55: 363–387.

Benda, Brent B. 2005. "Gender Differences in Life-Course Theory of Recidivism: A Survival Analysis." *International Journal of Offender Therapy and Comparative Criminology* 49: 325–342.

Berg, Mark T., and Beth M. Huebner. 2011. "Reentry and the Ties That Bind: An Examination of Social Ties, Employment, and Recidivism." *Justice Quarterly* 28: 382–410.

Bertrand, Marie Andrée. 1969. "Self-Image and Delinquency: A Contribution to the Study of Female Criminality and Women's Image." *Acta Criminologica: Études sur la Conduite Antisociale* 2: 71–144.

Bierie, David M. 2012. "Prison Violence, Gender, and Perceptions: Testing a Missing Link in Discretion Research." *American Journal of Criminal Justice* 37: 209–228.

Bimbi, David S. 2007. "Male Prostitution: Pathology, Paradigms, and Progress in Research." *Journal of Homosexuality* 53: 7–35.

Bjerregaard, Beth, and Carolyn Smith. 1993. "Gender Differences in Gang Participation, Delinquency, and Substance Use." *Journal of Quantitative Criminology* 9: 329–355.

Boeri, Miriam. 2013. *Women on Ice: Methamphetamine Use Among Suburban Women*. New Brunswick, NJ: Rutgers University Press.

Booth, Jeb A., Amy Farrell, and Sean P. Varano. 2008. "Social Control, Serious Delinquency, and Risky Behavior: A Gendered Analysis." *Crime and Delinquency* 54: 422–456.

Bourgois, Philippe. 1996. "In Search of Masculinity: Violence, Respect and Sexuality Among Puerto Rican Crack Dealers in East Harlem." *British Journal of Criminology* 36: 412–427.

———. 2003. *In Search of Respect: Selling Crack in El Barrio*. Cambridge: Cambridge University Press.

Bourke, Michael L., and Andres E. Hernandez. 2009. "The 'Butner Study' Redux: A Report of the Incidence of Hands-On Child Victimization by Child Pornography Offenders." *Journal of Family Violence* 24: 183–191.

Braithwaite, John. 1989. *Crime, Shame and Reintegration*. Cambridge: Cambridge University Press.

———. 2002. *Restorative Justice and Responsive Regulation*. Oxford: Oxford University Press.

Branson, Susan. 2008. *Dangerous to Know: Women, Crime, and Notoriety in the Early Republic*. Philadelphia: University of Pennsylvania Press.

Broidy, Lisa, and Robert Agnew. 1997. "Gender and Crime: A General Strain Theory Perspective." *Journal of Research in Crime and Delinquency* 34: 275–306.

Brookman, Fiona, Trevor Bennett, Andy Hochstetler, and Heith Copes. 2011. "The 'Code of the Street' and the Generation of Street Violence in the UK." *European Journal of Criminology* 8: 17–31.

Brotherton, David C. 2008. "Beyond Social Reproduction: Bringing Resistance Back in Gang Theory." *Theoretical Criminology* 12: 55–77.

Brunson, Rod K., and Ronald Weitzer. 2009. "Police Relations with Black and White Youths in Different Urban Neighborhoods." *Urban Affairs Review* 44: 858–885.

Buchmann, Claudia, Thomas A. DiPrete, and Anne McDaniel. 2008. "Gender Inequalities in Education." *Annual Review of Sociology* 34: 319–337.

Buntin, John. 2010. *LA Noir: The Struggle for the Soul of America's Most Seductive City*. New York: Broadway Books.

Burgess, Robert L., and Ronald L. Akers. 1966. "A Differential Association-Reinforcement Theory of Criminal Behavior." *Social Problems* 14: 128–147.

Burt, Callie Harbin, Ronald L. Simons, and Leslie G. Simons. 2006. "A Longitudinal Test of the Effects of Parenting and the Stability of Self-Control: Negative Evidence for the General Theory of Crime." *Criminology* 44: 353–396.

Butterfield, Fox. 1995. *All God's Children: The Bosket Family and the Tradition of American Violence*. New York: Knopf.

Campbell, Anne. 1993. *Men, Women, and Aggression*. New York: Basic Books.

Campbell, Colin. 2000. "Shopaholics, Spendaholics, and the Question of Gender." In *I Shop, Therefore I Am: Compulsive Buying and the Search for Self*, edited by A. L. Benson, 57–75. Lanham, MD: Rowman and Littlefield.

Carlson, Bonnie E., Katherine Maciol, and Joanne Schneider. 2006. "Sibling Incest: Reports from Forty-One Survivors." *Journal of Child Sexual Abuse* 15: 19–34.

Carpenter, Belinda. 1998. "The Prostitute and the Client: Challenging the Dualisms." *Women's Studies International Forum* 21: 387–399.

Carson, Dena C., Dana Peterson, and Finn-Aage Esbensen. 2013. "Youth Gang Desistance: An Examination of the Effect of Different Operational Definitions of Desistance on the Motivations, Methods, and Consequences Associated with Leaving the Gang." *Criminal Justice Review* 38: 510–534.

Carson, E. Anne. 2015. *Prisoners in 2014*. Washington, DC: Department of Justice, Bureau of Justice Statistics.

Cashmore, Judith, and Rita Shackel. 2014. "Gender Differences in the Context and Consequences of Child Sexual Abuse." *Current Issues in Criminal Justice* 24: 75–104.

Catalano, Shannan. 2012. "Stalking Victims in the United States—Revised." Department of Justice, Bureau of Justice Statistics. https://www.bjs.gov/content/pub/pdf/svus_rev.pdf.

Cates, Jim A., and Jeffrey Markley. 1992. "Demographic, Clinical, and Personality Variables Associated with Male Prostitutes by Choice." *Adolescence* 27: 695–707.

Cavezza, Cristina, and Troy E. McEwan. 2014. "Cyberstalking Versus Off-Line Stalking in a Forensic Sample." *Psychology, Crime and Law* 20: 955–970.

Chesney-Lind, Meda. 1989. "Girls' Crime and Woman's Place: Toward a Feminist Model of Female Delinquency." *Crime and Delinquency* 35: 5–29.

Chesney-Lind, Meda, and Lisa Pasko. 2004. *The Female Offender: Girls, Women, and Crime*. 2nd ed. Thousand Oaks, CA: Sage.

Children's Bureau. 2014. *Child Maltreatment 2014*. US Department of Health and Human Services. http://www.acf.hhs.gov/sites/default/files/cb/cm2014.pdf (accessed April 28, 2016).

Cillessen, Antonius H. N., and Amanda J. Rose. 2005. "Understanding Popularity in the Peer System." *Current Directions in Psychological Science* 14: 102–105.

"Civilian Labor Force by Sex, 1970–2012." N.d. US Department of Labor. http://www.dol.gov/wb/stats/Civilian_labor_force_sex_70_12_txt.htm.

Cobbina, Jennifer E., Beth M. Huebner, and Mark T. Berg. 2012. "Men, Women, and Postrelease Offending: An Examination of the Nature of the Link Between Relational Ties and Recidivism." *Crime and Delinquency* 58: 331–361.

Cohen, Geoffrey L., and Mitchell J. Prinstein. 2006. "Peer Contagion of Aggression and Health Risk Behavior Among Adolescent Males: An

Experimental Investigation of Effects on Public Conduct and Private Attitudes." *Child Development* 77: 967–983.

Cohn, D'Vera, Jeffrey S. Passel, Wendy Wang, and Gretchen Livingston. 2011. "Barely Half of U.S. Adults Are Married—A Record Low." Pew Research Center. December 4. http://www.pewsocialtrends.org/2011/12/14/barely-half-of-u-s-adults-are-married-a-record-low/.

Coker, Donna. 2006. "Restorative Justice, Navajo Peacemaking and Domestic Violence." *Theoretical Criminology* 10: 67–85.

Conger, Dylan, and Mark C. Long. 2010. "Why Are Men Falling Behind? Gender Gaps in College Performance and Persistence." *Annals of the American Academy of Political and Social Science* 627: 184–214.

"Crime in the United States." 2014. FBI. https://www.fbi.gov/about-us/cjis/ucr/crime-in-the-u.s/2014/crime-in-the-u.s.-2014 (accessed April 26, 2016).

Crosnoe, Robert. 2002. "Academic and Health-Related Trajectories in Adolescence: The Intersection of Gender and Athletics." *Journal of Health and Social Behavior* 43: 317–335.

Crowder, Adrienne, and Rob Hawkings. 1995. *Opening the Door: A Treatment Model for Therapy with Male Survivors of Sexual Abuse*. New York: Brunner/Mazel.

Daly, Kathleen. 1989. "Gender and Varieties of White☐Collar Crime." *Criminology* 27: 769–794.

Daly, Kathleen, and Meda Chesney-Lind. 1988. "Feminism and Criminology." *Justice Quarterly* 5: 497–538.

Davis, Kathy. 2008. "Intersectionality as Buzzword: A Sociology of Science Perspective on What Makes a Feminist Theory Successful." *Feminist Theory* 9: 67–85.

Davis, Kelly Cue, Jeanette Norris, William H. George, Joel Martell, and Julia R. Heiman. 2006. "Rape-Myth Congruent Beliefs in Women Resulting from Exposure to Violent Pornography: Effects of Alcohol and Sexual Arousal." *Journal of Interpersonal Violence* 21: 1208–1223.

Davis, Nanette J., ed. 1993. *Prostitution: An International Handbook on Trends, Problems, and Policies*. London: Greenwood Press.

De Bruyn, Eddy H., Antonius H. N. Cillessen, and Inge B. Wissink. 2010. "Associations of Peer Acceptance and Perceived Popularity with Bullying and Victimization in Early Adolescence." *Journal of Early Adolescence* 30: 546–566.

De Li, Spencer, and Doris Layton Mackenzie. 2003. "The Gendered Effects of Adult Social Bonds on the Criminal Activities of Probationers." *Criminal Justice Review* 28: 278–298.

Decker, Scott H., David C. Pyrooz, and Richard K. Moule Jr. 2014. "Disengagement from Gangs as Role Transitions." *Journal of Research on Adolescence* 24: 268–283.

DeLisi, Matt, Kevin M. Beaver, Michael G. Vaughn, Chad R. Trulson, Anna E. Kosloski, Alan J. Drury, and John Paul Wright. 2010. "Personality, Gender, and Self-Control Theory Revisited: Results from a Sample of Institutionalized Juvenile Delinquents." *Applied Psychology in Criminal Justice* 6: 31–46.

Demuth, Stephen. 2003. "Racial and Ethnic Differences in Pretrial Release Decisions and Outcomes: A Comparison of Hispanic, Black, and White Felony Arrestees." *Criminology* 41: 873–908.

Demuth, Stephen, and Darrell Steffensmeier. 2004. "The Impact of Gender and Race-Ethnicity in the Pretrial Release Process." *Social Problems* 51: 222–242.

Dhaliwal, Gurmeet K., Larry Gauzas, Daniel H. Antonowicz, and Robert R. Ross. 1996. "Adult Male Survivors of Childhood Sexual Abuse: Prevalence, Sexual Abuse Characteristics, and Long-Term Effects." *Clinical Psychology Review* 16: 619–639.

Doerner, Jill K., and Stephen Demuth. 2010. "The Independent and Joint Effects of Race/Ethnicity, Gender, and Age on Sentencing Outcomes in US Federal Courts." *Justice Quarterly* 27: 1–27.

Dorahy, Martin J., and Ken Clearwater. 2012. "Shame and Guilt in Men Exposed to Childhood Sexual Abuse: A Qualitative Investigation." *Journal of Child Sexual Abuse* 21: 155–175.

Duffy, Rónán. 2016. "'Pro-Rape' Group Cancel Meetings Because They're Worried About Their Own Safety." *TheJournal.ie*. http://www.thejournal.ie/return-of-kings-cancelled-meeting-2583818-Feb2016 (accessed February 5, 2016).

Durkheim, Emile. 1897 [1979]. *Suicide: A Study in Sociology*. New York: Free Press.

Durkin, Keith F., and Clifton D. Bryant. 1999. "Propagandizing Pederasty: A Thematic Analysis of the On-Line Exculpatory Accounts of Unrepentant Pedophiles." *Deviant Behavior* 20: 103–127.

Durose, Matthew R., Alexia D. Cooper, and Howard N. Snyder. 2014. *Recidivism of Prisoners Released in 30 States in 2005: Patterns from 2005 to 2010*. Washington, DC: Department of Justice, Bureau of Justice Statistics.

Dutton, Donald G. 2012. "The Case Against the Role of Gender in Intimate Partner Violence." *Aggression and Violent Behavior* 17: 99–104.

Edwards, Katie M. 2014. "Intimate Partner Violence and the Rural-Urban-Suburban Divide: Myth or Reality? A Critical Review of the Literature." *Trauma, Violence, and Abuse* 16: 359–373.

Egley, Arlen, Jr., James C. Howell, and Meena Harris. 2014. "Highlights of the 2012 National Gang Youth Survey." Office of Juvenile Justice and Delinquency Prevention. http://www.ojjdp.gov/pubs/248025.pdf (accessed February 17, 2015).

Elder, Glen H., Jr. 1994. "Time, Human Agency, and Social Change: Perspectives on the Life Course." *Social Psychology Quarterly* 57: 4–15.

"Elizabeth Cady Stanton: The Destructive Male." 1868. History Place: Great Speeches Collection. http://www.historyplace.com/speeches/stanton.htm (accessed February 5, 2016).

English, T. J. 2005. *Paddy Whacked: The Untold Story of the Irish American Gangster*. New York: Harper Collins.

Erikson, Kai T. 1962. "On the Sociology of Deviance." *Social Problems* 9: 307–314.

Esbensen, Finn-Aage, and Dena C. Carson. 2012. "Who Are the Gangsters? An Examination of the Age, Race/Ethnicity, Sex, and Immigration Status of Self-Reported Gang Members in a Seven-City Study of American Youth." *Journal of Contemporary Criminal Justice* 28: 465–481.

Esbensen, Finn-Aage, Elizabeth Piper Deschenes, and L. Thomas Winfree Jr. 1999. "Differences Between Gang Girls and Gang Boys: Results From a Multisite Survey." *Youth and Society* 31: 27–53.

Fagan, Abigail A., M. Lee Van Horn, J. David Hawkins, and Michael W. Arthur. 2007. "Gender Similarities and Differences in the Association Between Risk and Protective Factors and Self-Reported Serious Delinquency." *Prevention Science* 8: 115–124.

Farrington, David P. 1986. "Age and Crime." *Crime and Justice* 7: 189–250.

Faugier, Jean, and Steven Cranfield. 1995. "Reaching Male Clients of Female Prostitutes: The Challenge for HIV Prevention." *AIDS Care* 7, no. 1 (1995): 21–32.

Felson, Richard B., and Dana L. Haynie. 2002. "Pubertal Development, Social Factors, and Delinquency Among Adolescent Boys." *Criminology* 40: 967–988.

Felson, Richard B., and Steven F. Messner. 1998. "Disentangling the Effects of Gender and Intimacy on Victim Precipitation in Homicide." *Criminology* 36: 405–424.

Finkelhor, David. 1980. "Sex Among Siblings: A Survey on Prevalence, Variety, and Effects." *Archives of Sexual Behavior* 9: 171–194.

———. 1982. "Child Abuse: A Sociological Perspective." *Child Abuse and Neglect* 6: 95–102.

Finn, Jerry. 2004. "A Survey of Online Harassment at a University Campus." *Journal of Interpersonal Violence* 19: 468–483.

Flores, Edward. 2014. *God's Gangs: Barrio Ministry, Masculinity, and Gang Recovery.* New York: New York University Press.

Fordham, Signithia. 1993. "'Those Loud Black Girls': (Black) Women, Silence, and Gender 'Passing' in the Academy." *Anthropology and Education Quarterly* 24: 3–32.

Foubert, John D., Matthew W. Brosi, and R. Sean Bannon. 2011. "Pornography Viewing Among Fraternity Men: Effects on Bystander Intervention, Rape Myth Acceptance and Behavioral Intent to Commit Sexual Assault." *Sexual Addiction and Compulsivity* 18: 212–231.

Foucault, Michel. 1980. *Power/Knowledge: Selected Interviews and Writings.* New York: Pantheon.

Frankland, Andrew, and Jac Brown. 2014. "Coercive Control in Same-Sex Intimate Partner Violence." *Journal of Family Violence* 29: 15–22.

Franklin, Cortney A. 2007. "Male Peer Support and the Police Culture: Understanding the Resistance and Opposition of Women in Policing." *Women and Criminal Justice* 16: 1–25.

"Frequently Asked Questions About the Change in the UCR Definition of Rape." 2014. FBI. https://ucr.fbi.gov/recent-program-updates/new-rape-definition-frequently-asked-questions.

Freund, Matthew, Nancy Lee, and Terri Leonard. 1991. "Sexual Behavior of Clients with Street Prostitutes in Camden, NJ." *Journal of Sex Research* 28: 579–591.

Frye, Marilyn. 1983. *The Politics of Reality: Essays in Feminist Theory.* Freedom, CA: Crossing Press.

Gabbidon, Shaun L., George E. Higgins, and Hillary Potter. 2011. "Race, Gender, and the Perception of Recently Experiencing Unfair Treatment by the Police: Exploratory Results from an All-Black Sample." *Criminal Justice Review* 36: 5–21.

Gächter, Martin, David A. Savage, and Benno Torgler. 2011. "Gender Variations of Physiological and Psychological Strain Amongst Police Officers." *Gender Issues* 28: 66–93.

Gardner, Margo, Jodie Roth, and Jeanne Brooks-Gunn. 2009. "Sports Participation and Juvenile Delinquency: The Role of the Peer Context Among Adolescent Boys and Girls with Varied Histories of Problem Behavior." *Developmental Psychology* 45: 341–353.

Gendreau, Paul, Tracy Little, and Claire Goggin. 1996. "A Meta-Analysis of the Predictors of Adult Offender Recidivism: What Works!" *Criminology* 34: 575–608.

Gerber, Theodore P., and Sin Yi Cheung. 2008. "Horizontal Stratification in Postsecondary Education: Forms, Explanations, and Implications." *Annual Review of Sociology* 34: 299–318.

Gilfoyle, Timothy J. 1992. *City of Eros: New York City, Prostitution, and the Commercialism of Sex.* W. W. Norton.

Giordano, Peggy C., Stephen A. Cernkovich, and Jennifer L. Rudolph. 2002. "Gender, Crime, and Desistance: Toward a Theory of Cognitive Transformation." *American Journal of Sociology* 107: 990–1064.

Giordano, Peggy C., Ryan D. Schroeder, and Stephen A. Cernkovich. 2007. "Emotions and Crime over the Life Course: A Neo-Meadian Perspective on Criminal Continuity and Change." *American Journal of Sociology* 112: 1603–1661.

Goffman, Alice. 2014. *On the Run: Fugitive Life in an American City.* Chicago: University of Chicago Press.

Gordon, Jill A., Blythe Proulx, and Patricia H. Grant. 2013. "Trepidation Among the 'Keepers': Gendered Perceptions of Fear and Risk of Victimization Among Corrections Officers." *American Journal of Criminal Justice* 38: 245–265.

Gossett, Jennifer Lynn, and Joyce E. Williams. 1998. "Perceived Discrimination Among Women in Law Enforcement." *Women and Criminal Justice* 10: 53–73.

Gottfredson, Michael, and Travis Hirschi. 1986. "The True Value of Lambda Would Appear to Be Zero: An Essay on Career Criminals, Criminal Careers, Selective Incapacitation, Cohort Studies, and Related Topics." *Criminology* 24: 213–234.

———.1990. *A General Theory of Crime.* Stanford, CA: Stanford University Press.

Greenberg, David F. 1977. "Delinquency and the Age Structure of Society." *Contemporary Crises* 1: 189–223.

Hagan, John, and Holly Foster. 2001. "Youth Violence and the End of Adolescence." *American Sociological Review* 66: 874–899.

Halim, Shaheen, and Beverly L. Stiles. 2001. "Differential Support for Police Use of Force, the Death Penalty, and Perceived Harshness of the

Courts: Effects of Race, Gender, and Region." *Criminal Justice and Behavior* 28: 3–23.

Hansen, Laura L. 2005. "Girl 'Crew' Members Doing Gender, Boy 'Crew' Members Doing Violence: An Ethnographic and Network Analysis of Maria Hinojosa's New York Gangs." *Western Criminology Review* 6: 134–144.

Harcourt, Christine, and Basil Donovan. 2005. "The Many Faces of Sex Work." *Sexually Transmitted Infections* 81: 201–206.

Haynie, Dana L. 2003. "Contexts of Risk? Explaining the Link Between Girls' Pubertal Development and Their Delinquency Involvement." *Social Forces* 82: 355–397.

Haynie, Dana L., Peggy C. Giordano, Wendy D. Manning, and Monica A. Longmore. 2005. "Adolescent Romantic Relationships and Delinquency Involvement." *Criminology* 43: 177–210.

Haynie, Dana L., Richard J. Petts, David Maimon, and Alex R. Piquero. 2009. "Exposure to Violence in Adolescence and Precocious Role Exits." *Journal of Youth and Adolescence* 38: 269–286.

Heidensohn, Frances M. 1968. "The Deviance of Women: A Critique and an Enquiry." *British Journal of Sociology* 19: 160–176.

Heimer, Karen, and Stacy De Coster. 1999. "The Gendering of Violent Delinquency." *Criminology* 37: 277–318.

Heinlein, Sabine. 2013. "Dinner with Bruce." *Contexts*. https://contexts.org /articles/dinner-with-bruce (accessed February 11, 2016).

Henning, Kris, Angela R. Jones, and Robert Holdford. 2005. "'I Didn't Do It, but if I Did I Had a Good Reason': Minimization, Denial, and Attributions of Blame Among Male and Female Domestic Violence Offenders." *Journal of Family Violence* 20: 131–139.

Hirschfield, Paul J. 2008. "Preparing for Prison? The Criminalization of School Discipline in the USA." *Theoretical Criminology* 12: 79–101.

Hirschi, Travis. 1969. *Causes of Delinquency*. Berkeley: University of California Press.

Hirschi, Travis, and Michael Gottfredson. 1983. "Age and the Explanation of Crime." *American Journal of Sociology* 89: 552–584.

Holzman, Harold R., and Sharon Pines. 1982. "Buying Sex: The Phenomenology of Being a John." *Deviant Behavior* 4: 89–116.

Hoskin, Anthony W. 2013. "Experiencing Prejudice and Violence Among Latinos: A General Strain Theory Approach." *Western Criminology Review* 14: 25–38.

Houston, Eric, and David J. McKirnan. 2007. "Intimate Partner Abuse Among Gay and Bisexual Men: Risk Correlates and Health Outcomes." *Journal of Urban Health* 84: 681–690.

Hsu, L. K. George. 1989. "The Gender Gap in Eating Disorders: Why Are the Eating Disorders More Common Among Women?" *Clinical Psychology Review* 9: 393–407.

Huesmann, L. Rowell, Leonard D. Eron, Monroe M. Lefkowitz, and Leopold O. Walder. 1984. "Stability of Aggression over Time and Generations." *Developmental Psychology* 20: 1120–1134.

Hume, Tim, Lisa Cohen, and Mira Sorvino. 2013. "The Women Who Sold Their Daughters into Sex Slavery." CNN. http://www.cnn.com

/interactive/2013/12/world/cambodia-child-sex-trade (accessed February 2, 2016).

"Idaho." N.d. National Human Trafficking Resource Center. http://traffickingresourcecenter.org/state/idaho (accessed February 3, 2016).

Ikner, Michael A., Janice Ahmad, and Alejandro del Carmen. 2005. "Vehicle Cues and Racial Profiling: Police Officers' Perceptions of Vehicles and Drivers." *Southwest Journal of Criminal Justice* 2: 82–100.

Ivie, Don, and Brett Garland. 2011. "Stress and Burnout in Policing: Does Military Experience Matter?" *Policing: An International Journal of Police Strategies and Management* 34: 49–66.

Jiang, Shanhe, and L. Thomas Winfree. 2006. "Social Support, Gender, and Inmate Adjustment to Prison Life: Insights from a National Sample." *Prison Journal* 86: 32–55.

Joe, Karen A., and Meda Chesney-Lind. 1995. "'Just Every Mother's Angel': An Analysis of Gender and Ethnic Variations in Youth Gang Membership." *Gender and Society* 9: 408–431.

Jordan, Jan. 1997. "User Pays: Why Men Buy Sex." *Australian and New Zealand Journal of Criminology* 30: 55–71.

Kaufman, Joanne M., Cesar J. Rebellon, Sherod Thaxton, and Robert Agnew. 2008. "A General Strain Theory of Racial Differences in Criminal Offending." *Australian and New Zealand Journal of Criminology* 41: 421–437.

Keady, Cameron. 2015. "Chicago Police Throw Daddy-Daughter Dance, Personally Escort Girls Without Fathers." *Huffington Post*. http://www.huffingtonpost.com/2015/05/26/chicago-police-father-daughter-dance_n_7443506.html (accessed April 29, 2016).

Klein, Malcolm W., and Cheryl L. Maxson. 2006. *Street Gang Patterns and Policies*. New York: Oxford University Press.

Klenowski, Paul M., Heith Copes, and Christopher W. Mullins. 2011. "Gender, Identity, and Accounts: How White Collar Offenders Do Gender When Making Sense of Their Crimes." *Justice Quarterly* 28: 46–69.

Koehler, Sezin. 2013. "From the Mouths of Rapists: The Lyrics of Robin Thicke's Blurred Lines." *The Society Pages*. https://thesocietypages.org/socimages/2013/12/30/from-the-mouths-of-rapists-the-lyrics-of-robin-thickes-blurred-lines (accessed April 28, 2016).

Kreager, Derek A. 2004. "Strangers in the Halls: Isolation and Delinquency in School Networks." *Social Forces* 83: 351–390.

———. 2007a. "Unnecessary Roughness? School Sports, Peer Networks, and Male Adolescent Violence." *American Sociological Review* 72: 705–724.

———. 2007b. "When It's Good to Be 'Bad': Violence and Adolescent Peer Acceptance." *Criminology* 45: 893–923.

Krienert, Jessie L., and Jeffrey A. Walsh. 2011. "Sibling Sexual Abuse: An Empirical Analysis of Offender, Victim, and Event Characteristics in National Incident-Based Reporting System (NIBRS) Data, 2000–2007." *Journal of Child Sexual Abuse* 20: 353–372.

Kruttschnitt, Candace. 1996. "Contributions of Quantitative Methods to the Study of Gender and Crime, or Bootstrapping Our Way into the Theoretical Thicket." *Journal of Quantitative Criminology* 12: 135–161.

Kuhl, Danielle C., David F. Warner, and Tara D. Warner. 2015. "Intimate Partner Violence Risk Among Victims of Youth Violence: Are Early Unions Bad, Beneficial, or Benign?" *Criminology* 53: 427–456.

Kuhl, Danielle C., David F. Warner, and Andrew Wilczak. 2012. "Adolescent Violent Victimization and Precocious Union Formation." *Criminology* 50:1089–1127.

LaGrange, Teresa C., and Robert A. Silverman. 1999. "Low Self-Control and Opportunity: Testing the General Theory of Crime as an Explanation for Gender Differences in Delinquency." *Criminology* 37: 41–72.

Laidler, Karen Joe, and Geoffrey Hunt. 2001. "Accomplishing Femininity Among the Girls in the Gang." *British Journal of Criminology* 41: 656–678.

Lanctôt, Nadine, Stephen A. Cernkovich, and Peggy C. Giordano. 2007. "Delinquent Behavior, Official Delinquency, and Gender: Consequences for Adulthood Functioning and Well☐Being." *Criminology* 45: 131–157.

Langan, Neal P., and Bernadette M. M. Pelissier. 2001. "Gender Differences Among Prisoners in Drug Treatment." *Journal of Substance Abuse* 13: 291–301.

Lanning, Kenneth V. 1987. *Child Molesters: A Behavioral Analysis. For Law-Enforcement Officers Investigating Cases of Child Sexual Exploitation.* Washington, DC: National Center for Missing and Exploited Children.

Latzman, Robert D., and Raymond R. Swisher. 2005. "The Interactive Relationship Among Adolescent Violence, Street Violence, and Depression." *Journal of Community Psychology* 33: 355–371.

Laub, John H., Daniel S. Nagin, and Robert J. Sampson. 1998. "Trajectories of Change in Criminal Offending: Good Marriages and the Desistance Process." *American Sociological Review:* 225–238.

Laub, John H., and Robert J. Sampson. 1993. "Turning Points in the Life Course: Why Change Matters to the Study of Crime." *Criminology* 31: 301–325.

———. 2003. *Shared Beginnings, Divergent Lives: Delinquent Boys to Age 70.* Cambridge, MA: Harvard University Press.

Lawrence, Richard, and Sue Marian. 1998. "Women Corrections Officers in Men's Prisons: Acceptance and Perceived Job Performance." *Women and Criminal Justice* 9: 63–86.

Lee, Jennifer, and Frank D. Bean. 2004. "America's Changing Color Lines: Immigration, Race/Ethnicity, and Multiracial Identification." *Annual Review of Sociology* 30: 221–242.

———. 2012. "A Postracial Society or a Diversity Paradox?" *Du Bois Review: Social Science Research on Race* 9: 419–437.

Lee, Matthew R., and Edward S. Shihadeh. 2009. "The Spatial Concentration of Southern Whites and Argument-Based Lethal Violence." *Social Forces* 87: 1671–1694.

Lever, Janet, and Deanne Dolnick. 2000. "Clients and Call Girls: Seeking Sex and Intimacy." In *Sex for Sale: Prostitution, Pornography, and the Sex Industry,* edited by R. Weitzer, 85–100. New York: Routledge.

Leverentz, Andrea M. 2014. *The Ex-prisoner's Dilemma: How Women Negotiate Competing Narratives of Reentry and Desistance*. New Brunswick, NJ: Rutgers University Press.

Lockhart, Lettie L., Barbara W. White, Vicki Causby, and Alicia Isaac. 1994. "Letting Out the Secret: Violence in Lesbian Relationships." *Journal of Interpersonal Violence* 9: 469–492.

Lombroso, Cesare, and Guglielmo Ferrero. 1893 [2004]. *Criminal Woman, the Prostitute, and the Normal Woman*. Translated and with a new introduction by Nicole Hahn Rafter and Mary Gibson. Durham, NC: Duke University Press.

Lopez, Mark Hugo, and Ana Gonzalez-Barrera. 2014 "Women's College Enrollment Gains Leave Men Behind." Pew Research Center. http://www.pewresearch.org/fact-tank/2014/03/06/womens-college-enrollment-gains-leave-men-behind.

Ludwick, Micheline D., Sheigla Murphy, and Paloma Sales. 2015. "Savvy Sellers: Dealing Drugs, Doing Gender, and Doing Difference." *Substance Use and Misuse* 50: 708–720.

Malamuth, Neil L., Tamara Addison, and Mary Koss. 2000. "Pornography and Sexual Aggression: Are There Reliable Effects and Can We Understand Them?" *Annual Review of Sex Research* 11: 26–91.

Maloney, Michael T., and Robert E. McCormick. 1993. "An Examination of the Role That Intercollegiate Athletic Participation Plays in Academic Achievement: Athletes' Feats in the Classroom." *Journal of Human Resources* 28: 555–70.

"Maria." N.d. Coalition to Abolish Slavery and Trafficking. http://www.castla.org/maria (accessed February 2, 2016).

Martz, Denise M., Kevin B. Handley, and Richard M. Eisler. 1995. "The Relationship Between Feminine Gender Role Stress, Body Image, and Eating Disorders." *Psychology of Women Quarterly* 19: 493–508.

Mason, Michael J., Jeremy Mennis, Julie Linker, Cristina Bares, and Nikola Zaharakis. 2014. "Peer Attitudes Effects on Adolescent Substance Use: The Moderating Role of Race and Gender." *Prevention Science* 15: 56–64.

Matsueda, Ross L., and Karen Heimer. 1997. "A Symbolic Interactionist Theory of Role-Transitions, Role-Commitments, and Delinquency." In *Developmental Theories of Crime and Delinquency*, edited by Terence P. Thornberry, 163–213. New Brunswick, NJ: Transaction.

Mayer, Adele. 1985. *Sexual Abuse: Causes, Consequences and Treatment of Incestuous and Pedophilic Acts*. Holmes Beach, FL: Learning Publications.

Mayeux, Lara, Marlene J. Sandstrom, and Antonius H. N. Cillessen. 2008. "Is Being Popular a Risky Proposition?" *Journal of Research on Adolescence* 18: 49–74.

Mazerolle, Paul, Robert Brame, Ray Paternoster, Alex Piquero, and Charles Dean. 2000. "Onset Age, Persistence, and Offending Versatility: Comparisons Across Gender." *Criminology* 38: 1143–1172.

McCabe, Sean Esteban, Michele Morales, James A. Cranford, Jorge Delva, Melnee D. McPherson, and Carol J. Boyd. 2007. "Race/Ethnicity and Gender Differences in Drug Use and Abuse Among College Students." *Journal of Ethnicity in Substance Abuse* 6: 75–95.

McCarty, William P., Jihong "Solomon" Zhao, and Brett E. Garland. 2007. "Occupational Stress and Burnout Between Male and Female Police Officers: Are There Any Gender Differences?" *Policing: An International Journal of Police Strategies and Management* 30: 672–691.

McClellan, Dorothy Spektorov. 1994. "Disparity in the Discipline of Male and Female Inmates in Texas Prisons." *Women and Criminal Justice* 5: 71–97.

McClellan, Dorothy S., David Farabee, and Ben M. Crouch. 1997. "Early Victimization, Drug Use, and Criminality: A Comparison of Male and Female Prisoners." *Criminal Justice and Behavior* 24: 455–476.

McCormack, Simon. 2015. "Arrest Made in Deadly Beating of Transgender Woman Islan Nettles." *Huffington Post*. March 3. http://www.huffingtonpost.com/2015/03/03/arrest-islan-nettles_n_6794680.html.

McKeganey, Neil. 1994. "Why Do Men Buy Sex and What Are Their Assessments of the HIV-Related Risks When They Do?" *AIDS Care* 6: 289–301.

McLaughlin, Eliott C., Sara Sidner, and Michael Martinez. 2016. "Oklahoma City Cop Convicted of Rape Sentenced to 263 Years in Prison." http://www.cnn.com/2016/01/21/us/oklahoma-city-officer-daniel-holtzclaw-rape-sentencing.

McLean, Bethany, and Peter Elkind. 2003. *The Smartest Guys in the Room: The Amazing Rise and Scandalous Fall of Enron.* New York: Portfolio.

McVeigh, Rory, and David Cunningham. 2012. "Enduring Consequences of Right-Wing Extremism: Klan Mobilization and Homicides in Southern Counties." *Social Forces* 90: 843–862.

Mears, Daniel P., Joshua C. Cochran, and William D. Bales. 2012. "Gender Differences in the Effects of Prison on Recidivism." *Journal of Criminal Justice* 40: 370–378.

Mears, Daniel P., Xia Wang, and William D. Bales. 2014. "Does a Rising Tide Lift All Boats? Labor Market Changes and Their Effects on the Recidivism of Released Prisoners." *Justice Quarterly* 31: 822–851.

Melde, Chris, and Finn-Aage Esbensen. 2011. "Gang Membership as a Turning Point in the Life Course." *Criminology* 49: 513–552.

———. 2014. "The Relative Impact of Gang Status Transitions: Identifying the Mechanisms of Change in Delinquency." *Journal of Research in Crime and Delinquency* 51: 349–376.

Melde, Chris, Terrance J. Taylor, and Finn-Aage Esbensen. 2009. "'I Got Your Back': An Examination of the Protective Function of Gang Membership in Adolescence." *Criminology* 47: 565–594.

Merton, Robert K. 1938. "Social Structure and Anomie." *American Sociological Review* 3: 672–682.

———. 1957. *Social Theory and Social Structure.* New York: Free Press.

Messerschmidt, James. 1993. *Masculinities and Crime: Critique and Reconceptualization of Theory.* Lanham, MD: Rowman and Littlefield.

Messinger, Adam M. 2014. "Marking 35 Years of Research on Same-Sex Intimate Partner Violence: Lessons and New Directions." In *Handbook of LGBT Communities, Crime, and Justice,* edited by D. Peterson and V. R. Panfil, 65–85. New York: Springer.

Meyer, Doug. 2010. "Evaluating the Severity of Hate-Motivated Violence: Intersectional Differences Among LGBT Hate Crime Victims." *Sociology* 44: 980–995.

———.2012. "An Intersectional Analysis of Lesbian, Gay, Bisexual, and Transgender (LGBT) People's Evaluations of Anti-queer Violence." *Gender and Society* 26: 849–873.

Miller, Jody. 2008. *Getting Played: African American Girls, Urban Inequality, and Gendered Violence.* New York: New York University Press.

Miller, Michael. 2016. "All-American Swimmer Found Guilty of Sexually Assaulting Unconscious Woman on Stanford Campus." *Washington Post.* https://www.washingtonpost.com/news/morning mix/wp/2016/03/31 /all-american-swimmer-found-guilty-of-sexually-assaulting-unconscious -woman-on-stanford-campus/?utm_term=.e1eabda6e52e (accessed December 28, 2016).

Milroy, Jeffrey J., Muhsin M. Orsini, David L. Wyrick, Melodie Fearnow-Kenney, Samantha E. Kelley, and Jane Burley. 2014. "A National Study of the Reasons for Use and Non-use of Alcohol Among College Student-Athletes by Sex, Race, and NCAA Division." *Journal of Alcohol and Drug Education* 58: 67–87.

Mirowsky, John, and Catherine A. Ross. 1995. "Sex Differences in Distress: Real or Artifact?" *American Sociological Review* 60: 449–468.

Moffitt, Terrie E. 1993. "Adolescence-Limited and Life-Course-Persistent Antisocial Behavior: A Developmental Taxonomy." *Psychological Review* 100: 674–701.

Moffitt, Terrie E., and Avshalom Caspi. 2001. "Childhood Predictors Differentiate Life-Course- Persistent and Adolescence-Limited Antisocial Pathways Among Males and Females." *Development and Psychopathology* 13: 355–375.

Monto, Martin A. 1999. "Focusing on the Clients of Street Prostitutes: A Creative Approach to Reducing Violence Against Women." Washington, DC: National Institute of Justice.

———. 2004. "Female Prostitution, Customers, and Violence." *Violence Against Women* 10: 160–188.

Muise, Aleixo M., Debra G. Stein, and Gordon Arbess. 2003. "Eating Disorders in Adolescent Boys: A Review of the Adolescent and Young Adult Literature." *Journal of Adolescent Health* 33: 427–435.

Mullings, Janet L., Deborah J. Hartley, and James W. Marquart. 2004. "Exploring the Relationship Between Alcohol Use, Childhood Maltreatment, and Treatment Needs Among Female Prisoners." *Substance Use and Misuse* 39: 277–305.

Murray, Christine E., and A. Keith Mobley. 2009. "Empirical Research About Same-Sex Intimate Partner Violence: A Methodological Review." *Journal of Homosexuality* 56: 361–386.

Na, Chongmin, and Raymond Paternoster. 2012. "Can Self-Control Change Substantially over Time? Rethinking the Relationship Between Self- and Social Control." *Criminology* 50: 427–462.

National Center for Law and Economic Justice (NCLEJ). N.d. "The Poverty Rate Has Not Improved Since 2013." NCLEJ. http://nclej

.org/wp-content/uploads/2015/11/2014PovertyStats.pdf (accessed May 2, 2016).

"National Youth Gang Survey Analysis." N.d. National Gang Center. https://www.nationalgangcenter.gov/survey-analysis/demographics (accessed September 13, 2015).

Nieves, Alicia. 2015. "Man Accused of Child Rape, Said Victim Sent 'Mixed Signals.'" WNEP. http://wnep.com/2015/05/19/man-accused-of-child-rape-said-victim-sent-mixed-signals (accessed June 23, 2015).

Nofziger, Stacey, and L. Susan Williams. 2005. "Perceptions of Police and Safety in a Small Town." *Police Quarterly* 8: 248–270.

"North Dakota." N.d. National Human Trafficking Resource Center. http://traffickingresourcecenter.org/state/north-dakota (accessed February 3, 2016).

O'Leary, Patrick J., and James Barber. 2008. "Gender Differences in Silencing Following Childhood Sexual Abuse." *Journal of Child Sexual Abuse* 17: 133–143.

O'Neal, Eryn Nicole, Scott H. Decker, Richard K. Moule Jr., and David C. Pyrooz. 2016. "Girls, Gangs, and Getting Out: Gender Differences and Similarities in Leaving the Gang." *Youth Violence and Juvenile Justice* 14: 43–60.

Odgers, Candice L., Terrie E. Moffitt, Jonathan M. Broadbent, Nigel Dickson, Robert J. Hancox, Honalee Harrington, Richie Poulton, Malcolm R. Sears, W. Murray Thomson, and Avshalom Caspi. 2008. "Female and Male Antisocial Trajectories: From Childhood Origins to Adult Outcomes." *Development and Psychopathology* 20: 673–716.

Office for Victims of Crime. 2012. "Transgender Rates of Violence." FORGE. http://forge-forward.org/wp-content/docs/FAQ-10-2012-rates-of-violence.pdf (accessed July 10, 2015).

Paoline, Eugene A., and William Terrill. 2005. "Women Police Officers and the Use of Coercion." *Women and Criminal Justice* 15: 97–119.

Park, Robert E. 1926. "The Urban Community as a Spatial Pattern and a Moral Order." *The Urban Community*, edited by E. W. Burgess, 3–18. Chicago: University of Chicago Press.

Park, Robert E., and Ernest W. Burgess. 1924. *Introduction to the Science of Sociology*. 2nd ed. Chicago: University of Chicago Press.

Peake, Anne. 1989. "Issues of Under-reporting: The Sexual Abuse of Boys." *Educational and Child Psychology* 6: 42–50.

Peck, Jennifer H. 2013. "Examining Race and Ethnicity in the Context of General Strain Theory, Depression, and Delinquency." *Deviant Behavior* 34: 706–726.

"Pennsylvania." N.d. National Human Trafficking Resource Center. http://traffickingresourcecenter.org/state/pennsylvania (accessed February 2, 2016).

Peterson, Dana. 2012. "Girlfriends, Gun-Holders, and Ghetto-Rats? Moving Beyond Narrow Views of Girls in Gangs." In *Delinquent Girls: Contexts, Relationships, and Adaptation*, edited by S. Miller, L. D. Leve, and P. K. Kreig, 71–84. New York: Springer.

Polivy, Janet, and C. Peter Herman. 2002. "Causes of Eating Disorders." *Annual Review of Psychology* 53: 187–213.

Price, Peter. 2009. "When Is a Police Officer an Officer of the Law? The Status of Police Officers in Schools." *Journal of Criminal Law and Criminology* 99, no. 2 (2009): 541–570.

"Prisoners and Prisoner Reentry." N.d. Department of Justice. https://www.justice.gov/archive/fbci/progmenu_reentry.html (accessed March 1, 2017).

Quayle, Ethel, and Max Taylor. 2002. "Child Pornography and the Internet: Perpetuating a Cycle of Abuse." *Deviant Behavior* 23: 331–361.

Quinney, Richard. 1977. *Class State and Crime: On the Theory and Practice of Criminal Justice*. New York: McKay.

———.1980. *Providence: The Reconstruction of Social and Moral Order*. London: Longman Publishing Group.

Rabe-Hemp, Cara E., and Amie M. Schuck. 2007. "Violence Against Police Officers: Are Female Officers at Greater Risk?" *Police Quarterly* 10: 411–428.

Rennison, Callie Marie, Walter S. DeKeseredy, and Molly Dragiewicz. 2012. "Urban, Suburban, and Rural Variations in Separation/Divorce Rape/Sexual Assault: Results from the National Crime Victimization Survey." *Feminist Criminology* 7: 282–297.

Rhodes, Anne E., Michael H. Boyle, Lil Tonmyr, Christine Wekerle, Deborah Goodman, Bruce Leslie, Polina Mironova, Jennifer Bethell, and Ian Manion. 2011. "Sex Differences in Childhood Sexual Abuse and Suicide☐Related Behaviors." *Suicide and Life-Threatening Behavior* 41: 235–254.

Rios, Victor M. 2011. *Punished: Policing the Lives of Black and Latino Boys*. New York: New York University Press.

Romano, Elisa, and Rayleen V. De Luca. 2001. "Male Sexual Abuse: A Review of Effects, Abuse Characteristics, and Links with Later Psychological Functioning." *Aggression and Violent Behavior* 6: 55–78.

Rouner, Jef. 2015. "The Apparently Immoral Shoulders of My 5-Year-Old Daughter." *Houston Press*. http://www.houstonpress.com/arts/the-apparently-immoral-shoulders-of-my-five-year-old-daughter-7372634 (accessed July 7, 2015).

Sadler, Anne G., Brenda M. Booth, Brian L. Cook, and Bradley N. Doebbeling. 2003. "Factors Associated with Women's Risk of Rape in the Military Environment." *American Journal of Industrial Medicine* 43: 262–273.

Sampson, Robert J., and John H. Laub. 1992. "Crime and Deviance in the Life Course." *Annual Review of Sociology* 18: 63–84.

———. 1993. *Crime in the Making: Pathways and Turning Points Through Life*. Cambridge, MA: Harvard University Press.

———. 1997. "A Life-Course Theory of Cumulative Disadvantage and the Stability of Delinquency." *Developmental Theories of Crime and Delinquency* 7: 133–161.

Sampson, Robert J., John H. Laub, and Christopher Wimer. 2006. "Does Marriage Reduce Crime? A Counterfactual Approach to Within—Individual Casual Effects." *Criminology* 44: 465–508.

Sampson, Robert J., Stephen W. Raudenbush, and Felton Earls. 1997. "Neighborhoods and Violent Crime: A Multilevel Study of Collective Efficacy." *Science* 277: 918–924.

Sampson, Robert J., and William Julius Wilson. 1995. "Toward a Theory of Race, Crime, and Urban Inequality." In *Crime and Inequality*, edited by J. Hagan and R. D. Peterson, 37–54. Stanford, CA: Stanford University Press.

Sandberg, Linn. 2013. "Backward, Dumb, and Violent Hillbillies? Rural Geographies and Intersectional Studies on Intimate Partner Violence." *Affilia* 28: 350–365.

Sanford, J. B. 1911. "Argument Against Women's Suffrage, 1911." San Francisco Public Library. http://sfpl.org/pdf/libraries/main/sfhistory /suffrageagainst.pdf (accessed February 4, 2016).

Sanger, William W. 1897 [1937]. *The History of Prostitution*. New York: Eugenics Publishing Company.

Scheb, John M., William Lyons, and Kristin A. Wagers. 2009. "Race, Gender, and Age Discrepancies in Police Motor Vehicle Stops in Knoxville, Tennessee: Evidence of Racially Biased Policing?" *Police Practice and Research: An International Journal* 10: 75–87.

Schneider, Rachel Zimmer. 2014. *Battered Women Doing Time: Injustice in the Criminal Justice System*. Boulder, CO: FirstForum Press.

Scott, John, Victor Minichiello, Rodrigo Marino, Glenn P. Harvey, Maggie Jamieson, and Jan Browne. 2005. "Understanding the New Context of the Male Sex Work Industry." *Journal of Interpersonal Violence* 20: 320–342.

Scully, Diana, and Joseph Marolla. 1984. "Convicted Rapists' Vocabulary of Motive: Excuses and Justifications." *Social Problems* 31, no. 5: 530–544.

Senjo, Scott R. 2005. "Trafficking in Meth: An Analysis of the Differences Between Male and Female Dealers." *Journal of Drug Education* 35: 59–77.

Sexual Assault Prevention and Response Office. 2014. *Department of Defense Annual Report on Sexual Assault in the Military*. Washington, DC: Department of Defense.

Shaw, Clifford, and Henry McKay. 1942. *Juvenile Delinquency and Urban Areas*. Chicago: University of Chicago Press.

———. 1969. *Juvenile Delinquency and Urban Areas*. Rev. ed. Chicago: University of Chicago Press.

Sheehan, Connor M., Richard G. Rogers, George W. Williams, and Jason D. Boardman. 2013. "Gender Differences in the Presence of Drugs in Violent Deaths." *Addiction* 108: 547–555.

Shook, Jeffrey J., Michael G. Vaughn, and Christopher P. Salas-Wright. 2013. "Exploring the Variation in Drug Selling Among Adolescents in the United States." *Journal of Criminal Justice* 41: 365–374.

Short, Mary B., Lora Black, Angela H. Smith, Chad T. Wetterneck, and Daryl E. Wells. 2012. "A Review of Internet Pornography Use Research: Methodology and Content from the Past 10 years." *Cyberpsychology, Behavior, and Social Networking* 15: 13–23.

Siennick, Sonja E. 2007. "The Timing and Mechanisms of the Offending-Depression Link." *Criminology* 45: 583–615.

Simi, Pete. 2010. "Why Study White Supremacist Terror? A Research Note." *Deviant Behavior* 31: 251–273.

Simpson, Sally. 1991. "Caste, Class, and Violent Crime: Explaining the Difference in Female Offending." *Criminology* 29: 115–135.

Smith, Michael R., Matthew Makarios, and Geoffrey P. Alpert. 2006. "Differential Suspicion: Theory Specification and Gender Effects in the Traffic Stop Context." *Justice Quarterly* 23: 271–295.

Sorensen, Jon R., Mark D. Cunningham, Mark P. Vigen, and S. O. Woods. 2011. "Serious Assaults on Prison Staff: A Descriptive Analysis." *Journal of Criminal Justice* 39: 143–150.

"South Dakota." N.d. National Human Trafficking Resource Center. http://traffickingresourcecenter.org/state/south-dakota (accessed February 3, 2016).

Spataro, Josie, Simon A. Moss, and David L. Wells. 2001. "Child Sexual Abuse: A Reality for Both Sexes." *Australian Psychologist* 36: 177–183.

Spjeldnes, Solveig, and Sara Goodkind. 2009. "Gender Differences and Offender Reentry: A Review of the Literature." *Journal of Offender Rehabilitation* 48: 314–335.

Staff, Jeremy, and Derek A. Kreager. 2008. "Too Cool for School? Violence, Peer Status and High School Dropout." *Social Forces* 87: 445–471.

Steffensmeier, Darrell J., Jennifer Schwartz, and Michael Roche. 2013. "Gender and Twenty-First-Century Corporate Crime: Female Involvement and the Gender Gap in Enron-Era Corporate Frauds." *American Sociological Review* 78: 448–476.

Steffensmeier, Darrell, Jeffery Ulmer, and John Kramer. 1998. "The Interaction of Race, Gender, and Age in Criminal Sentencing: The Punishment Cost of Being Young, Black, and Male." *Criminology* 36: 763–798.

Stewart, Eric A., Christopher J. Schreck, and Ronald L. Simons. 2006. "'I Ain't Gonna Let No One Disrespect Me': Does the Code of the Street Reduce or Increase Violent Victimization Among African American Adolescents?" *Journal of Research in Crime and Delinquency* 43: 427–458.

Stolzenberg, Lisa, and Stewart J. D'Alessio. 2004. "Sex Differences in the Likelihood of Arrest." *Journal of Criminal Justice* 32: 443–454.

Strawhun, Jenna, Natasha Adams, and Matthew T. Huss. 2013. "The Assessment of Cyberstalking: An Expanded Examination Including Social Networking, Attachment, Jealousy, and Anger in Relation to Violence and Abuse." *Violence and Victims* 28: 715–730.

Stubbs, Julie. 2007. "Beyond Apology? Domestic Violence and Critical Questions for Restorative Justice." *Criminology and Criminal Justice* 7: 169–187.

"'Superpredators' Arrive." 1996. *Newsweek*. http://www.newsweek.com /superpredators-arrive-176848 (accessed February 17, 2015).

Sutherland, Edwin. 1947. *Principles of Criminology*. Philadelphia: Lippincott.

Sykes, Gresham M., and David Matza. 1957. "Techniques of Neutralization: A Theory of Delinquency." *American Sociological Review* 22: 664–670.

Taylor, Matthew J., John T. Nanney, Desiree Z. Welch, and Rachel A. Wamser-Nanney. 2016. "The Impact of Sports Participation on Female Gang Involvement and Delinquency." *Journal of Sport Behavior* 39: 317–343.

Taylor, Terrance J., Kelly B. Turner, Finn-Aage Esbensen, and L. Thomas Winfree. 2001. "Coppin' an Attitude: Attitudinal Differences Among Juveniles Toward Police." *Journal of Criminal Justice* 29: 295–305.

Tjaden, Patricia, and Nancy Thoennes. 1998. "Prevalence, Incidence, and Consequences of Violence Against Women: Findings from the National Violence Against Women Survey. Research in Brief." National Institute of Justice. https://archive.org/stream/ERIC_ED434980/ERIC_ED 434980_djvu.txt

————. 2000. *Extent, Nature, and Consequences of Intimate Partner Violence: Findings from the National Violence Against Women Survey.* Vol. 181867. Washington, DC: National Institute of Justice.

————. 2006. *Extent, Nature, and Consequences of Rape Victimization: Findings from the National Violence Against Women Survey.* Washington, DC: Department of Justice, Office of Justice Programs, National Institute of Justice.

Travis, Jeremy, Elizabeth Cincotta McBride, and Amy L. Solomon. 2005. "Families Left Behind: The Hidden Costs of Incarceration and Reentry." Urban Institute. http://www.urban.org/research/publication/families -left-behind.

Turell, Susan C. 2000. "A Descriptive Analysis of Same-Sex Relationship Violence for a Diverse Sample." *Journal of Family Violence* 15: 281–293.

UCR (Federal Bureau of Investigation Uniform Crime Reporting Statistics). Various years. US Department of Justice. ucr.fbi.gov.

Varriale, Jennifer A. 2008. "Female Gang Members and Desistance: Pregnancy a Possible Exit Strategy?" *Journal of Gang Research* 15: 35–64.

Vega, Manuel, and Ira J. Silverman. 1982. "Female Police Officers as Viewed by Their Male Counterparts." *Police Studies: The International Review of Police Development* 5 (1982): 31.

Venkatesh, Sudhir Alladi. 1997. "The Social Organization of Street Gang Activity in an Urban Ghetto." *American Journal of Sociology* 103: 82–111.

————. 1998. "Gender and Outlaw Capitalism: A Historical Account of the Black Sisters United 'Girl Gang.'" *Signs* 23: 683–709.

————. 2008. *Gang Leader for a Day: A Rogue Sociologist Takes to the Streets.* New York: Penguin.

————. 2013. *Floating City: A Rogue Sociologist Lost and Found in New York's Underground Economy.* New York: Penguin.

Visher, Christy A. 1983. "Gender, Police Arrest Decisions, and Notions of Chivalry." *Criminology* 21: 5–28.

Visher, Christy A., and Jeremy Travis. 2003. "Transitions from Prison to Community: Understanding Individual Pathways." *Annual Review of Sociology* 29: 89–113.

Wade, Terrance J., John Cairney, and David J. Pevalin. 2002. "Emergence of Gender Differences in Depression During Adolescence: National Panel Results from Three Countries." *Journal of the American Academy of Child and Adolescent Psychiatry* 41: 190–198.

Warr, Mark. 1998. "Life-Course Transitions and Desistance from Crime." *Criminology* 36: 183–216.

Webb, Liane, Jackie Craissati, and Sarah Keen. 2007. "Characteristics of Internet Child Pornography Offenders: A Comparison with Child Molesters." *Sexual Abuse: A Journal of Research and Treatment* 19: 449–465.

Weisheit, Ralph A., David N. Falcone, and L. Edward Wells. 2005. *Crime and Policing in Rural and Small-Town America.* Long Grove, IL: Waveland Press.

Weisheit, Ralph A., and L. Edward Wells. 2004. *Youth Gangs in Rural America.* Washington, DC: National Institute of Justice.

Weitzer, Ronald. 2000. "Deficiencies in the Sociology of Sex Work." *Sociology of Crime, Law, and Deviance* 2: 259–279.

———. 2005. "New Directions in Research on Prostitution." *Crime, Law and Social Change* 43: 211–235.

———. 2007. "Prostitution: Facts and Fictions." *Contexts* 6: 28–33.

———. 2009. "Sociology of Sex Work." *Annual Review of Sociology* 35: 213–234.

Wertsch, Teresa Lynn. 1998. "Walking the Thin Blue Line: Policewomen and Tokenism Today." *Women and Criminal Justice* 9: 23–61.

"What We Investigate: Gangs." N.d. FBI. https://www.fbi.gov/about-us/investigate/vc_majorthefts/gangs (accessed February 17, 2015).

Williamson, Celia, and Terry Cluse-Tolar. 2002. "Pimp-Controlled Prostitution Still an Integral Part of Street Life." *Violence Against Women* 8: 1074–1092.

Williamson, Celia, and Gail Folaron. 2003. "Understanding the Experiences of Street Level Prostitutes." *Qualitative Social Work* 2: 271–287.

Wodda, Aimee, and Vanessa R. Panfil. 2015. "'Don't Talk to Me About Deception': The Necessary Erosion of the Trans* Panic Defense." *Albany Law Review* 78: 927–971.

Wolak, Janis, David Finkelhor, and Kimberly Mitchell. 2011. "Child Pornography Possessors: Trends in Offender and Case Characteristics." *Sexual Abuse: A Journal of Research and Treatment* 23: 22–42.

"Women CEOs of the S&P 500." N.d. Catalyst. http://www.catalyst.org/knowledge/women-ceos-sp-500 (accessed September 8, 2015).

Wright, Bradley R. Entner, Avshalom Caspi, Terrie E. Moffitt, Richard A. Miech, and Phil A. Silva. 1999. "Reconsidering the Relationship Between SES and Delinquency: Causation but Not Correlation." *Criminology* 37: 175–194.

"Wyoming." N.d. National Human Trafficking Resource Center. http://traffickingresourcecenter.org/state/wyoming (accessed February 3, 2016).

Yabko, Brandon A., Audrey Hokoda, and Emilio C. Ulloa. 2008. "Depression as a Mediator Between Family Factors and Peer-Bullying Victimization in Latino Adolescents." *Violence and Victims* 23: 727–742.

Zimmer, Lynn. 1987. "How Women Reshape the Prison Guard Role." *Gender and Society* 1: 415–431.

Index

femininity: framing white-collar crime, 248–249; girl gangs, 118–119; opposition to women's suffrage, 21–22; sex and gender, 7; as social construction, 31; transgender and, 44
feminism: causes of first- and second-wave feminism, 27, 29; changing the view of domestic violence, 144; crime and early feminism, 26–36; defining SWERFs and TERFs, 43–44; gender- and sexuality-based hate crimes, 44–46; increasing knowledge of gender and crime, 11; liberation hypothesis, 29–30; modern feminism, 36–40; as outgrowth of Marxism, 25; postmodern feminism, 40–42; postwar motivations, 22–23; revealing deviant behavior in women, 39–40; scientific explanations for crime, 26–27; shifting the focus of, 38–39; as social construction, 31
Ferguson, Missouri, 236
Fifteenth Amendment rights, 28–29
first-wave feminism, 27
Floating City (Venkatesh), 168, 253
Foucault, Michel, 231
fraternity members, pornography use among, 177

Gang Leader for a Day (Venkatesh), 112–113
gang membership and activity: community service, 112–113; desistance, 123–127; gang migration, 121–122; girl gangs, 114–119; history of gangs in the US, 106–108; individual and social benefits of, 113–114; as a life transition, 122–123; moving from the city to the suburbs, 13–14; role of neighborhood in, 66; rural gangs, 120–122; sports and violence in high school, 91–92; street crime, 109; violence and, 108–110. *See also* juvenile delinquency
gang rape, 42
Gang Resistance Education and Training (GREAT) program, 109
Garner, Eric, 236
Gates, Bill, 58
gay panic, 87–88
gender: defining transgender, 43–44; as factor in self-control and social control, 51–52; gender-based

violence, 15; general strain theory, 63–64; importance of family bonds after reentry, 220–221; intersection of race, crime, and, 235–238; intersection of race, drug use, and, 238–243; intersection of race, violence, and, 243–247; sex and, 7–8; as social construction, 31; social learning theories and, 54–55; as spectrum of traits, 48; theory of crime and, 54
gender differences: among police officers, 196–198; bias in the criminal justice and prison systems, 186–187, 200–202; child abuse and molestation, 136–137; child pornography consumers, 179–180; corporate crime, 249; discipline and treatment of prison inmates, 205–206; dress codes in school, 78–79; drug use and, 120; gang membership, 108–110; girl gangs, 114–119; girls' views on violence among peers, 90; juvenile crime, 77–78, 85–86; male prostitution, 165; male victims of rape in the military, 164; measures of desistance, 72–73; men as rape victims, 157, 164; motivations for crime, 26; perceptions of the police, 195–196; police offers' job performance, 198–199; police profiling, 194–195; police profiling juveniles, 194; puberty and the onset of criminal behavior, 83–84; in rape victims, 149–150; recidivism rate, 211–212; reexamining conditions for criminality, 30–31; religion, gangs, and, 125–126; school performance, 232–233; sports and violence in high school, 91–92; stalking and cyberstalking behaviors, 141–143; teachers' treatment of students, 189; women and reentry, 223–224; women committing domestic violence, 147
gender dysphoria, 87
gender fluidity, 86–88
gender roles: Child Savers Movement forcing girls into, 33; in college campus rape, 160–161; early gangs, 106–107; family reinforcing, 33–34; as inhibitor for recidivism, 214; relationship violence, 131. *See also* femininity; masculinity

Thicke, Robin, 133–134
third-wave feminism, 40–42
timing of lives, 67–68, 81, 83–84, 99–101
tokenism: police officers, 197
total institutions, 163–164
toxic masculinity, 76
trans panic, 87–88
trans-exclusionary radical feminists
 (TERFs), 43–44
transgender and transsexual individuals,
 43–44, 86–88
transphobia, 87–88
Turner, Brock, 3–4

University of Chicago: urban sociology,
 64–65
University of North Carolina, 56
urban crime: code-of-the-street
 hypothesis, 60–61; diversity, 257;
 organized crime, 14; proxies for social
 class, 42; risk of rape in rural versus
 urban areas, 258; suburban and rural
 crime and, 13–15; urban sociology
 examining, 64–65. *See also* gang
 membership and activity
urban sociology, 64–66

victim blaming: child molestation, 139,
 153–154; family violence, 144–145;
 rape, 148; as social class issue, 253;
 trivializing Michael Brown's death,
 236
victim precipitation theory, 144–145
victims and victimization: bullying in
 schools, 93–94; child abuse and
 molestation, 136–141, 153–154; code-
 of-the-street as protection from
 violence, 61; consequences of teens'
 exposure to violence, 100–101; gender
 dictating girls' delinquency, 34–35;
 gender victimology of relationship
 violence, 131; general strain theory,
 63; intersectionality and, 254–259;
 male and female victims of sexual
 violence, 41
Victory Outreach, 126–127
violence: code-of-the-street as protection
 from, 61; committed by the elderly,

103–104; experiences of victims and
 offenders, 19–20; exposure to violent
 pornography, 176–177; gender-based,
 15; intersection of race, gender, and,
 243–247; overlap with drug crime,
 119–120; relationship between sports
 and, 56–57, 90–92; response to police
 violence, 195–196; in sex work, 165–
 177; sexuality and, 36–37; social
 isolation triggering, 89–90; stalking
 and cyberstalking, 142–143; teens'
 exposure to, 100–101; against the
 trans community, 44, 87–88. *See also*
 gang membership and activity

War on Crime, 217
War on Drugs, 217
Wells, Damon, 153
white supremacists, 236–237, 244
white violence, 243–245
white-collar crime, 58–59, 247–248
Wilson, Darren, 236
Wilson, Paris, 46
The Wire (television program), 13
women: centrality to criminal theory
 discourse, 31–34
Women on Ice (Boeri), 241–242
women's suffrage movement, 21–22, 27–
 29
work ethic: strain theory and criminal
 behavior, 58
work force: human trafficking for
 domestic labor, 180–181; jobs for ex-
 gang members, 125–127; male
 prostitutes, 171; Marxism growing out
 of capitalism, 24; masculinity and
 drug dealing, 239–240; possibilities
 upon reentry, 221–223; prostitution as
 a paying job, 167–168; role of family
 in reentry, 220; tokenism among
 police forces, 197; traditional gender
 roles, 22; warding off recidivism, 214.
 See also sex work
World Wrestling Entertainment,
 251–252
Wuornos, Aileen, 244–245

zones of transition, 64

About the Book

Exactly what role does gender play in crime, and in the criminal justice system? Addressing this two-part question from the perspective of the offender, the victim, the community, and the overall justice system, Andrew Wilczak provides an accessible introduction to the full range of issues involved.

Notably, this comprehensive text:

- features an inclusive focus on both men and women
- encompasses theory, as well as realities on the ground
- draws on popular culture
- challenges students to ask difficult questions
- ties concepts to students' own lives
- incorporates an intersectional approach

Designed to simultaneously engage and instruct, the book is ideally suited for classroom use.

Andrew Wilczak is assistant professor of criminology and sociology at Wilkes University.